COMPLETE LIBERTY

COMPLETE LIBERTY

The Demise of the State and the Rise of Voluntary America

L

by

Wes Bertrand

Large Print Edition published 2012 by Skyler J. Collins.
Visit: www.skylerjcollins.com

Cover image by StockFreeImages.com

ISBN-13: 978-1479314744
ISBN-10: 1479314749

CONTENTS

V

VI

VII

VIII

IX

X

PREFACE

There's not a single aspect of your life that's not affected, either directly or indirectly, by politics. So, the purpose of this book is to provide you with a clear understanding of modern politics and the proper response to it—complete liberty. My first book on the general subject, *The Psychology of Liberty*, was a wide-ranging philosophical treatise and was considerably longer than this one. In contrast, you'll find that *Complete Liberty* has a non-scholarly, conversational style. It's designed for that special person in your life you want to persuade, which includes yourself. This person, for some good reason or another, isn't interested in perusing long volumes on the fine details of libertarianism or vast tomes about the workings of free market economics. While those types of books certainly have their merits, here I aim to cut to the chase.

We'll discover what's so special about the liberty that we humans have been missing all these years. "All these years" basically means since the time we began uttering words alongside our unfortunate Neanderthal cousins. Indeed, we've never experienced complete liberty as a species. Rather, we've continually experienced some form of oppression by groups of individuals who are interested in running our lives, making it seem as if no one has the right to live for one's own sake. In modern times, these groups of people take the form of the State.

As noted in the first chapter, totalitarian governments aren't what specifically concern us here. Be they monarchies or dictatorships, they're *way* too easy to criticize. Without at least semi-free speech, press, due process, and trial by jury, all bets are off. Seriously. Run for your life. Save yourself and your loved ones.

Instead of dealing with the insanities of outright autocracy, we're going to examine the inherent problems of the traditionally esteemed democratic Republic, a government of, by, and for the People. This is the stuff of high school U.S. history and government classes—stars and stripes, hand-over-your-heart, national anthem, apple pie goodness. We'll explore the major, irreconcilable flaws in this political system (although apple pie will remain beyond reproach).

Of course, when the People aren't aware of more enlightened political, economic, and ethical ideas, *any* type of government they sanction remains a big problem. Without a principled understanding of how to peacefully live alongside others, we simply can't overcome the permanent difficulties of politics. The essential problem is this: The State—government in all its facets—coercively controls aspects of the economy, which means aspects of people's lives and property. This is the furthest from a good thing.

Nearly all intellectuals today, such as professors, talk show hosts, political pundits, and reporters, approve of the State's involuntary nature. Why? There are many reasons, but mainly because those who claim the right to use coercive power, as well as those who support them, have not morally integrated the benefits of completely respectful human interaction. Sure, they may engage in respectful *social* interaction on many levels and in many contexts, but respectful *political* interaction is like an unknown foreign language to them. Anyone speak Neanderthalian?

Legislation, log-rolling, pork barrels, earmarks, politicians, lobbyists, regulators, taxes, law-enforcement and judges. All go hand in hand, or more aptly, fist in hand. These iron fists are adept at ruining our lives, our self-respect, and our respect for others—all while severely crippling our economy. If you find that hard to believe, well, it's my intention to firmly convince you of it in the ensuing pages.

I also intend to convince you of the excellent alternative of complete liberty. Imagine a world in which your own choices and voluntary associations with other people in the marketplace of goods, services, and ideas are treated with dignity. Imagine a world without "politics." That's what I'm talking about.

The ideas in this book are not new; most have been around for centuries. I've endeavored to steer clear of accusations or arguments that can't be validated with sound evidence and logic. I've also constructed an extensive bibliography that includes a variety of reputable sources and articles on the Web as well as from many books; Wikipedia was one of those Web sources (tip of the hat to Jimmy Wales and all those Wikipedians). You are free to compare notes as a result, via all the provided Web links, which may be of great interest to the more voracious, scholarly, or skeptical readers.

In addition to understanding what complete liberty is all about, we'll investigate how in the world we can ever achieve it. After all, these ideas must compete not only with present politics and institutions, but also with our vibrant culture filled with many enjoyable activities to occupy our precious time. Yet, a distracted society soon becomes an unaware and complacent one. Without mastery of these ideas, we face a future of many more lost opportunities and much less fun. That's for certain. A big picture book of the former U.S.S.R. or even of the Great Depression illustrates just how bad it can get for humans—or rather, how bad they can make it for themselves, courtesy of the State.

What's happening on the political front in America today might lead us back to such dismal times, especially if we don't pay close attention to a variety of nasty political magic tricks. So, let's inspect the things being pulled out of the statist hat, and proceed to get our money back from this bad world of illusion. We all deserve better—much, much better.

I

WHY POLITICS IS SO CONFUSING

Politics In Mid-Stream

Here's the bottom line, the condition of our political patient we call America: It's in the intensive care unit, suffering from all sorts of cuts and contusions, and quite a bit of internal bleeding. It's been attacked by an onslaught of injustice and immorality. Simply put, we don't live in a free country. America is not the land of the free. It never really was. I know, I know, that's not what we've been constantly told.

Understanding how freedom manifests itself is part of the waking-up process, politically. If you believe in the idea of human freedom, but aren't sure how it should manifest itself, then you've opened the right book.

I'm sure all of us have noticed the pundits on TV and radio who promote their latest cutting-edge analysis of the leading political stories. Rarely, if ever, do we hear an analyst, expert, or commentator call into question the true essence of that process we call, with varying degrees of cynicism and eye-rolling, "politics."

It's an endless unspoken debate on political news channels: Should we have 25%, 30%, or 35% freedom? The best way of describing such a process is "politics in midstream." This is a more specific version of what novelist/philosopher Ayn Rand called "philosophizing in mid-stream," in which she criticized most intellectuals' penchant for ignoring the fundamental premises contained in their arguments. "Check your premises," Rand advised, though she herself forgot to check a few at times, particularly regarding government. Such is the misleading nature of unexamined assumptions.

The consequences of operating in intellectual midstream might not seem as severe as its physical counterpart. Imagine if, instead of testing a river's waters to see how swift and deep the current is, you just stepped in and hoped for the best. Well, in regard to politics, it's not just your own life at stake. The fate of a whole country hangs in the balance. That's why it's vital to stay on shore awhile and figure things out, instead of taking political ideas and their effects for granted and trying to reason correctly from there. When we are swept downstream, logic and evidence tend to remain on the shore.

So, before we step into that big river, let's assess some things. What is the process of politics really about? Well, here's what no politician or judge will explicitly tell you: Essentially, politics is the process by which people discretely (or not so discretely) attempt to convince you that your individual life is not as important as the nation, society, community, or "others." The better their convincing is, the worse politics gets. This of course has repercussions for how we treat each other—how we treat family members, friends, neighbors, co-workers, employees, employers, and especially politicians, judges, police officers, bureaucrats and other less influential strangers.

"Would you rather have 25%, 30%, or 35% freedom?" basically means "How much of yourself do you want to recognize?" And these are probably conservative estimates. If you actually defend your right to life, to your decisions, and to what you own, law enforcers and their judicial accomplices who seek to deny you these rights will want to bestow 0% freedom upon you. Nonetheless, feel free to assign the particular percentages to the political group that you think fits best. It turns out that no matter how they're assigned, the results end up being the same. Lost liberties and lost opportunities.

How did it come to this, or rather, why has it been like this for untold centuries? Well, that's a really long story that's been told quite well in many other books, and now in our highly connected age of the Internet (see bibliography). Fortunately, there's no "required reading" to comprehend the pages that follow—just a critical mindset for finding, and accepting, the truth.

It's safe to say that most people in America understand the utter folly of advocating either a dictatorship or full-blown Communism (which is essentially dictatorial in nature). The poor economic results and inherent evils of these systems of government have been confirmed repeatedly in both theory and bloody practice. It's no surprise that most people who experience such wretchedness strive to escape it. Unfortunately, after a regime of fear is firmly instituted, fleeing often proves difficult, as well as dangerous to friends and family members left behind. They frequently suffer the consequences of political misbehavior.

Totalitarian regimes skillfully create ruthless, loyal police and secret police agencies that foster a populace of snitches. Most informants hope that their thuggish rulers will favor those who provide them with the most provocative and useful information about who is being disobedient. The disobedient can be alleged to be anyone; anyone can be fingered as "subversive." So allegations run rampant and, soon, those who dare express their contrary political opinions do so in whispers—for even the walls have ears.

The Timeless Allure Of Communism

We certainly don't want to end up in that sort of societal predicament. Nonetheless, quite a few in America promote the essence of the politics of Socialism, or "Social Democracy." Many of them are guided by the economic ideals of Karl Marx and Friedrich Engels, who were passionate proponents of social justice and class equality. Unfortunately, the means by which they wanted to achieve such goals were not reason-based, and therefore not in accordance with the ideas of life, liberty, and the pursuit of happiness. Jeffersonian they were not.

In order for us to begin to grasp the meaning of complete liberty, it's wise to first explore the fundamental forces that continue to oppose it. Here is what Engels wrote about *The Communist Manifesto* in the Preface to the 1888 English edition:

> The Manifesto being our joint production, I consider myself bound to state that the fundamental proposition which forms the nucleus belongs to Marx. That proposition is: That in every historical epoch, the prevailing mode of economic production and exchange, and the social organization necessarily following from it, form the basis upon which it is built up, and from that

which alone can be explained the political and intellectual history of that epoch; that consequently the whole history of mankind (since the dissolution of primitive tribal society, holding land in common ownership) has been a history of class struggles, contests between exploiting and exploited, ruling and oppressed classes; That the history of these class struggles forms a series of evolutions in which, nowadays, a stage has been reached where the exploited and oppressed class—the proletariat—cannot attain its emancipation from the sway of the exploiting and ruling class—the bourgeoisie—without, at the same time, and once and for all, emancipating society at large from all exploitation, oppression, class distinction, and class struggles.

Obviously, Engels was also passionate about writing long sentences (a particularly German phenomenon). However, let's distill the essentials of what he meant. He and Marx correctly stated that many groups of individuals have been exploited and have struggled—such as, in their words, the "freeman and slave, patrician and plebian, lord and serf, guildmaster and journeyman, in a word, oppressor and oppressed."

Engels apparently believed that such conflict didn't exist in primitive tribal societies with communal ownership. Not so true. In fact, as we'll cover in a later chapter, the less understanding and delineation of property rights people have, the more potential for conflict there is. Property rights are necessary to prevent conflict. Without knowing who owns what, reaching agreement and being productive proves extremely difficult, and disputes are instead settled by the club, sword, or gun. The more powerful people and adept groups of course win in such nasty disputes. In modern civilizations, lack of property rights leads to a particularly terrible form of oppression: The State becomes King of the Mountain.

The Communist Manifesto continually contrasts the "working class," aka the proletariat, with the "exploiting and ruling class," aka the bourgeoisie. Indeed, Communist arguments depend on making such class distinctions. Without them, they could gain little traction in the minds of those concerned with social equality and economic justice.

But the distinction they should've made is between the free market and the force of the State, which reveals the difference between a free market and a controlled market. In a controlled market, the politically connected in industry and in various professions conspire (no matter their motives) with those wielding the powers of the State to reduce the choices and opportunities of not only the working class, but also the "consumer class," which means *everyone in society.*

Unlike the truly oppressed, who are kept in bondage by force, people who work in a market economy (even one that's only semi-free) do so mostly by their own volition; they're in their places of work, doing their work, by choice. Individuals choose to work for certain wages and in certain conditions, and they're free to leave and find—or better yet, *make*—work elsewhere, that is, if the State allows them. If the statist system prevents choices for workers, that's certainly not the fault of the market.

Granted, in the early and mid-1800's the marketplace offered fewer employment choices than today. There's little doubt that this environment had an influence on the ideas of Marx and Engels. The working conditions in many urban areas weren't what one would call nice by today's standards. Yet, the conditions in rural areas were typically nothing to write home about either (assuming one had something to write with), especially given the lack of medical care. Similar to the developing world today, getting sick often meant a death sentence. People frequently moved to cities to improve their lots in life, to increase their living standards and opportunities (even though mass deaths due to unsanitary conditions sometimes occurred).

Nonetheless, Marx and Engels made many false assumptions, assumptions that led them down an extremely thorny political path. One of their worst assumptions was that people who are employed are fundamentally different than those who employ them, that is, owners of businesses, managers of companies, and even entrepreneurs. They seemed to think that members of the latter "class" just jump into positions of influence, ready-made; supposedly, they are automatic owners of property and thus controllers of the economic fate of non-owners, the so-called proletariat. Again, perhaps Marx and Engels mistook the controlled economies of the State for a free market, although plenty of thinkers at the time knew better.

People who've brought themselves from rags to riches, purchased a piece of property, or just upped their income, know that it requires some long-term thinking and business savvy—the tried-and-true "perseverance, inspiration, and perspiration." A little good fortune can help too, along with a society of complete liberty (more on that later).

Another false assumption revealed more of Marx's and Engels' ignorance of economics. They believed that employers would always pay workers as little as possible; employers who kept workers surviving at mere subsistence pay could exploit and oppress them to the fullest.

Not only does this incorrectly imply that workers had no choice in their place of employment, but it also runs counter to the evidence. When one employer cuts the pay of its employees, that's an opportunity for another employer to offer a better deal to those workers. Employers compete for employees as much as workers compete with each other for the best jobs. This, again, is assuming that the State hasn't intervened in these relations. The key is to have a free market in which opportunities and choices aren't hindered.

Jobs are not a static quantity in a free market either, like one pie with only so many pieces. The free market is literally a *pie maker*, and there's no limit to the flavors offered when freedom of choice exists.

The "emancipation of the proletariat" has nothing to do with taking responsibility for one's conditions of employment and working to change them for the better. Rather, it has to do with misunderstanding the idea of "oppression" and using force (actual oppression) to achieve certain economic and societal ends. Not surprisingly, the results are nothing short of disastrous. Marx and Engels devised a special recipe for a really bad pie. Once again from *The Communist Manifesto*:

> These measures will, of course, be different in different countries. Nevertheless, in most advanced countries, the following will be pretty generally applicable.
>
> 1. Abolition of property in land and application of all rents of land to public purposes.
> 2. A heavy progressive or graduated income tax.

3. Abolition of all rights of inheritance.

4. Confiscation of the property of all emigrants and rebels.

5. Centralization of credit in the banks of the state, by means of a national bank with state capital and an exclusive monopoly.

6. Centralization of the means of communication and transport in the hands of the state.

7. Extension of factories and instruments of production owned by the state; the bringing into cultivation of waste lands, and the improvement of the soil generally in accordance with a common plan.

8. Equal obligation of all to work. Establishment of industrial armies, especially for agriculture.

9. Combination of agriculture with manufacturing industries; gradual abolition of all the distinction between town and country by a more equable distribution of the populace over the country.

10. Free education for all children in public schools. Abolition of children's factory labor in its present form. Combination of education with industrial production, etc.

You probably noticed that most items on this list are things that the U.S. Government does. Yes, America contains many aspects of Communism. Kind of makes you wonder what the Cold War was all about, doesn't it?

American politics has swallowed proposals 2, 5, and 10, hook, line, and sinker—the graduated income tax, central control and monopolization of the money supply, universal public education and child labor laws. It's also partially adopted 1 in terms of Eminent Domain, 3 in terms of the Death Tax, 4 in terms of asset forfeiture in the War on Drugs, 6 in terms of governmental ownership of highways, byways, and regulation via the FCC, FAA, TSA, NHTSA, etc., and 7 in terms of all the services that government provides and the monopoly privileges it grants businesses. I'm sure there are a few more, but you get the point.

This clearly demonstrates why it's so important to identify the rationale and methods of Communism. It still presides in the minds of those who currently wield (and those who would like to wield) political power in America, as well as all those who enable them, irrespective of their intentions.

Here are the two paragraphs that followed the above list by Marx and Engels, to sum things up for us:

> When, in the course of development, class distinctions have disappeared, and all production has been concentrated in the hands of a vast association of the whole nation, the public power will lose its political character. Political power, properly so called, is merely the organized power of one class for oppressing another. If the proletariat during its contest with the bourgeoisie is compelled, by the force of circumstances, to organize itself as a class; if, by means of a revolution, it makes itself the ruling class, and, as such, sweeps away by force the old conditions of production, then it will, along with these conditions, have swept away the conditions for the existence of class antagonisms and of classes generally, and will thereby have abolished its own supremacy as a class.
>
> In place of the old bourgeois society, with its classes and class antagonisms, we shall have an association in which the free development of each is the condition for the free development of all.

Perhaps a particular poetry exists in such twisted logic. The statement that political power "is merely the organized power of one class for oppressing another" rings true, of course. However, to speak in terms of classes gets us on the wrong track entirely, which might have been their desire. The real distinction concerns people in society who respect rights to one's person and property versus those who don't respect them, whether through misunderstanding or full clarity. The irony in the above passage is the notion that "freedom," "free development," and the end of all "antagonisms" will come when a large group of revolutionaries "sweep away by force the old conditions of production." Supposedly, once they eliminate the owners of businesses, managers of companies, and entrepreneurs, or force them into a state of being propertyless, things will become really swell.

Communism and all its watered-down variations overlook one significant detail: It's simply unjust to forcibly take property from someone who hasn't violated anyone's rights; such an action is an infringement that contradicts one's *own* right to property and self-ownership. In addition, this whole scenario begs the practical question of how an economy is supposed to function without people whose specialty is being *capitalists*. Are the workers (revolutionaries) suddenly going to acquire this skill-set without skipping a beat? More realistically, once they did get past the learning curve, who's going to take their former place as "workers," now that *they* are the "rulers"?

Apparently, Marx and Engels hadn't thought twice about the reality of jobs. A manager can't simultaneously be a machinist. A designer can't simultaneously be a traveling salesman. An engineer can't simultaneously be a deal-maker with suppliers. And a nurse can't simultaneously be a surgeon. Granted, there are quite a few Jacks-of-all-trades in the market, people who wear different hats at various times and pull it off successfully. They can be quite productive in their various lines of work. But they can only do so many things. Invariably, they must make exclusionary choices, trading one hat for another.

There's a big reason why capitalism offers us so many facets and fields of work, be they divisions of labor or areas of specialization: continual accumulation of capital and generation of higher and higher levels of productivity. Capital is the fountainhead of technology and innovation, and consequently of leisure and recreation. Without capitalism, there wouldn't be nearly as many options for creative expression in the workplace or, for that matter, possibilities for fun in the world.

The idea of class encourages people to think mainly in terms of groups. An accurate term for this is collectivism. Collectivistic thinking is both a cause and an effect of class-oriented societies. Instead of viewing each person as a worthy individual with particular capacities—skills, talents, passions, hopes, desires, and rights and opportunities—class-oriented mindsets view people as members of certain elite or downtrodden groups. On the psychological side of the latter, this has a certain payoff: One doesn't have to take responsibility for one's choices and life situation, and one can blame others such as the "bourgeoisie" for one's plight. This is the sort of self-deception that provides no fruitful individual avenues to personal growth, social mobility, and career possibilities. It's inherently self-disempowering. Plus, it encourages people to get trapped in conflicts between identified groups, and to remain frustrated by the inability to change others that are "oppressing" one's own group.

Moreover, those who consider themselves to be in the elite class typically do nothing to foster others' movement to their level, because they've attained their positions through opportunities in a controlled market of State intervention. They feel that they have much to lose if they were to promote the liberty of others, as well as their own. So, the exploitation of others for personal gain continues, as does disregarding the unjust political context in which they operate.

The way out of the class-oriented mindset is by accepting the fact that each of us is an individual with a unique identity, which thereby encourages others to shift their focus similarly. We are only being oppressed when someone is trying to prevent us from making our own choices. We are only being ruled over when someone is initiating force against us, thwarting our ability to do as we please—or not respecting the rights of others to do as they please.

So, where does this leave the ideology of Socialism? One might call it Communism-lite: half the impoverishment but the same flavor. Given the horrible nature of Communism, this isn't much of an improvement. Since Socialism contains many of the fundamental premises of Communism, it remains on that bleak continuum of statist political systems. Fascism too contains the premises of Communism. It contends that your self and property aren't strictly your own, but rather things under statist regulation and control. Full-blown Communism simply drops any pretenses at freedom and goes for full enslavement of the citizenry. All become worker bees for the mighty queen bee, the State. Even those favored few who court her as she permits aren't free. Being a slave master isn't freedom either.

American government of course can't be called either outright Socialism or Fascism, which are the two worst ways—Left wing and Right wing—of allowing some market forces to operate in order to milk citizens for all their worth. Still, America is treacherously composed of many awful aspects of each, reflecting the premises of Communism. It might best be called a semi-fascist welfare State.

This leads us to the typical views we witness in U.S. politics today. Let's inspect some of the prevailing ideologies, and see how they measure up against Communism. Most Americans, if surveyed by a set of carefully crafted political questions, could be placed by the question askers into one of the categories below. You, wise reader, are different. You're able to distance yourself from past inclinations. By reading this book on complete liberty, you've decided to take an objective look at the problems with these assorted views. Your desire and ability to remain objective will be your core strength as you continue reading, regardless of the implications for your past beliefs or the various responses of others in your midst. Of course, there's no pressure or anything. Only the future of America (and maybe the world) is to be determined. So let's proceed.

The problem with describing these political viewpoints is that, no matter how intricately each category is described, someone is bound to raise a counter argument or have a different interpretation. It's a bit like trying to decipher the exact meaning of a Biblical story. So many translations, so little time. Yet for our purposes, creating exact descriptions isn't nearly as important as identifying essentials and defining principles, which I'll make sure to do afterwards.

Conservatives are those who typically vote for the Republican Party, though some may be fed up with the differences between what Republicans profess and what they do once in office. Nonetheless, conservatism tends to arise from the traditional values of responsibility, hard work, self-reliance, social modesty and good manners.

It's often said that you become a conservative when you try to run a business and discover how much government affects your decisions and actions. Rules, regulations, and taxes are the norms in business, not the exceptions. For what it's worth, conservatives also tend to be skeptical of the motives of the environmental movement, which typically lobbies for more rules and regulations. Conservatives desire government to be smaller rather than larger and taxes and regulations to be minimal. Conservatives tend to believe that the U.S. Constitution means what it plainly states and should not be open to interpretation, especially by "activist" judges. If they had their druthers, most conservatives would rejoice in a Constitutionally limited government.

In terms of law, conservatives tend to believe that others should sometimes be forced to abide by proper community standards of behavior, usually stemming from a religious sense of morality and doing what's right (in their eyes). Naturally, they're not known to be "soft on crime" and instead favor a law-and-order society of imprisonment and punishment for criminals. Those who are declared criminals, however, aren't strictly ones who violate the rights of others (such as thieves and thugs); they can also be those who engage in consensual personal activities and voluntary exchanges that are simply not tolerated by the "moral majority." Of all the types, conservatives also tend to be the strongest advocates of gun rights, though many accept regulation of the purchase, possession, and use of various weapons.

Neoconservatives, or Neocons, might be termed "watered-down conservatives," both fiscally and socially, in that they embrace many of the same big government programs that liberals do (see below). Though some might say that they'd rather government be smaller, it's just not "practical" in this day and age. There are too many foreign interests at stake and public projects needed for creating a better world.

Neocons are probably most noted, or notorious, for being big supporters of the military/industrial complex, though they contend that such support is for "The security of our nation" and "The defense of our people." They are indeed the most hawkish in foreign policy matters, which sometimes involves bombing others in far away countries before they bomb us (the preemption doctrine), or when others get too far out of line of State and Defense Department policies and Executive opinions. They generally believe that it's America's job to be the world's policeman (Pax Americana); the U.S. government should use its power to help guide other countries along the path to Democracy, freedom, tolerance, peace and prosperity. If America withdrew its military forces from its places of influence around the globe, they believe that things would assuredly go to hell in a bobsled; chaos and political instability would supposedly ensue. Neocons generally believe that even though the spread of Communism is no longer a major threat, terrorist groups may pose an even greater challenge, which means a greater need for Neocon leadership.

Liberals, or progressives, are the next slice of political Americana. Probably because the word liberal has been used pejoratively by so many conservative pundits, writers, and talk show hosts, members of this ideology now often describe themselves as "progressives." Typically, they vote for the Democratic Party, though, like conservatives, they're not averse to criticizing the weaknesses or corruption of Democrats in office. Progressives believe that government is by and large good, but especially when they themselves are in control of it. (The same could be said of the other viewpoints, by the way.)

Because liberals believe that particular groups of people, especially "the poor," "workers," or "minority classes," are weak in comparison to corporations, big businesses, employers, majorities, etc., they believe that government is the primary way to attempt to solve any and all disparities in wealth, power, and status. Though they may advocate balanced budgets on occasion, their desire to wield the instruments of governmental power for the good of the people, particularly for "the little guy," tends to lead to major spending, regulations, and taxes.

Here are some of their mottos, both spoken and unspoken, which also apply to a greater or lesser extent to all the other viewpoints discussed here: People are weak, especially the poor and elderly, but also virtually everyone else, so the government should take care of them with "safety nets"—or what conservative Rush Limbaugh aptly calls "safety hammocks"; people can't be trusted, so the government should control them; people are greedy and selfish, so the government should force them to be moral, that is, not greedy and not selfish; people benefit from society, so they owe society—meaning that they owe the government; businesses constantly seek power and try to exploit workers and the environment, so the government should collar them and make them follow at heal.

It might be said that, compared to their political opponents, progressives aren't hypocritical when it comes to growing the size of government and using it for their particular ends. After all, Bush 43 and company (under a Republican majority Congress through 2006) have increased the size and scope of governmental spending and debt beyond the wildest hopes of many liberals. Massive expenditures in health care, education, agriculture, and of course the military, come readily to mind. We'd have to go back to the 19th century to find a U.S. President who didn't veto a single bill. James Garfield was killed his first year in office, which subsequently explained his lack of interest in the veto power. George W. Bush, on the other hand, has vetoed only one bill, halfway into his second term in office. He has, however, set a presidential record for signing statements, which are not-so-clever ways to avoid Constitutional accountability.

Independents are next. People with this view generally disagree with some things in each party platform. They are wary of ideological bias and realize that many in politics have definite axes to grind. They may consider themselves true reformers of government, sometimes similar to progressives, like those in the Green Party. Independents don't mind embracing policies of other ideologies. They tend to pick and choose between and among the other viewpoints. They typically stress the need to formulate workable governmental solutions for society's ills, as well as remedies for governmental waste, corruption, and incompetence. Nevertheless, for all their talk about reform, they tend to remain immersed in banter about the endless details of governmental policies, while leaving the essence of government intact. They may vote for candidates from different parties, but mostly for those who also classify themselves as Independent.

Moderates and centrists, like independents, also tend to avoid following strict party lines, but unlike independents, they tend to shy away from unpopular positions. They don't like anything perceived as extreme or radical. Instead of going against the grain, they go with the flow. A middle-of-the-road approach to political debate usually puts them squarely on the wide fence concerning most issues. Some may embrace a centrist or moderate viewpoint in order to fit in or appear "normal"; one doesn't have to form an unpopular opinion. Others in this group believe that government in general is good and is on the right path to dealing with society's problems; it just needs a little tweaking here and there. Of all the views presented here, moderates and centrists appear the most conforming to the status quo. They play it politically safe and tend to favor more of the same: "I'll have what they're having; vanilla, please."

Though various viewpoints within these next two ideologies are quite old, "**traditionalists**" and "**secularists**" appear to be somewhat recently delineated political divisions—mostly discussed by opinion givers who need something sensational for their daily talking points. Perhaps these two views have been popularized most by avowed cultural crusader Bill O'Reilly, self-described independent and traditionalist. The traditionalist is typically socially conservative, perhaps votes more for Republicans (and Independents) than Democrats, and looks primarily to the past and to religion for guidance in cultural matters. The secularist, on the other hand, is quite open to social change, isn't very religious, and tends to be liberal, or progressive, and usually votes for Democrats. What's common in both types, of course, is their view of government as a tool to maintain or implement their particular cultural views and moral viewpoints in society.

There's an interesting paradox about these two groups. The "religious Right" calls the "liberal Left" secularists, that is, primarily "nonbelievers" who have serious sympathies with Communism. But some liberal groups, such as the American Civil Liberties Union, are frequently the ones defending individual rights to one's own body, as well as to free speech, free press, and due process. Contrastingly, conservatives and traditionalists seek to ground freedom and the Constitution in the Judeo-Christian God. Yet they are commonly the ones who seek to impose their particular moral code on others, in violation of individual rights to one's own body, as well as to speech, press, and due process. The present legal battles over such issues as gay marriage, medical marijuana, censored speech, pornography, abortion, stem cell research, morning-after pills, teaching Intelligent Design in public schools, Commandments on court house lawns, illegal immigration, a citizen's access to justice upon arrest, etc., demonstrate the oftentimes wide-ranging nature of their debates.

Well, that concludes this brief overview of the state of our mainstream, or rather, midstream, political opinions. If the distinctions didn't come across as clearly as you would've liked, have no worries. They all share a flaw that exposes the whole flimsy house of political cards. My purpose from now on isn't to bore you with surface details of political affiliations, which you can get from any major political magazine, news program, talk show, website, or blog. Instead, it's for us to go to the heart of the matter and recognize the essential contradictions of modern politics.

A principled approach to politics is something you may have never encountered. I wasn't taught it by any teacher in school. Like most important things in life, I had to teach it to myself, through a lot of thinking, reading, and debating with others, as will probably you. It's a learning process, to be sure, regardless of your age; new ideas are equal opportunity. The key thing for us to remember in the following chapters is this: If you believe in freedom and want to have complete liberty in your lifetime, then you have to grant it to others, across the economic and social board.

This leads us to the commonality in the above political viewpoints: They all desire to impose their values of "fairness," "necessity," "rightness," and "compassion" on society with the force of the State. As a consequence, they also seek to employ coercion in the name of being altruistic. If we take altruism to mean simply being concerned with others' welfare and interests, what could possibly be worse than coercing others rather than persuading them?

After all, if people are uncaring at base, then no amount of barbarity by fellow uncaring (or caring) people in power is going to make them more caring. The opposite actually happens. The more you strip people of their property and their choices in order to "help" others, the less nice, less benevolent, and less filled with goodwill and generosity they become. They also become less honest in dealing with their oppressors, and justifiably so; so-called cheating on taxes as well as cutting regulatory corners become commonplace. Not surprisingly, these behaviors also tend to occur in people's dealings with innocent others in the marketplace. When people are constantly shoved around by government, and they accept the nature of their victimhood, their moods tend to worsen and they're inclined to become less virtuous.

Moreover, the State's version of helping others quickly becomes a euphemism for using coercive means to placate special interests, fund boondoggles, and line the pockets of politicians and their cronies—all at the expense of everyone else's wealth. As in most political issues, it's wise to follow the money trail.

So, our government's policies actually achieve the exact opposite of their stated intentions. They work to turn the personal virtues of goodwill and generosity into mere public practices reserved primarily for the non-virtuous in government. The moral of this sad story is twofold: Never coerce persons into doing things against their peaceful desires, and don't regulate or steal for the common good. Now let's see what these conclusions mean for Democracy.

II

DEMOCRACY OF THE PEOPLE, BY THE POLITICIANS, FOR WHOM AGAIN?

Choose Your Weapon: Representative Democracy Or Popular Democracy

Rather than ask the usual question about which political system is better, allow me to ask which is worse: representative Democracy or popular Democracy? On the one hand, you have political officials who enjoy astoundingly high re-election rates (percentages in the high 90's) and who aren't very accountable to the citizenry; instead, they stroll along unprincipled political paths with various special interests, all striving to control aspects of the economy, both public and private. On the other hand, you have popular ballot measures, "propositions," such as in California, in which registered voters can cast their opinions in favor, or not, of an assortment of public works issues and governmentally regulated personal freedoms. Interestingly, voters sometimes make more sensible decisions than their representatives. Sometimes they even circumvent seemingly endless bureaucracy. So much for the theory that the unrestrained masses are mostly blinded by their passions. However, regardless of which system you choose, your individual rights will tend to be disregarded, in favor of collectivism and coercion.

Consider the nature of voting in general. Imagine if, every year, a company gave you a list of issues and people that you knew nothing about and really had no direct interest in (at least before they got you involved), and then they asked you to cast your vote in favor or against each issue and person. Now imagine that this company was a legalized monopoly in its area of business and that it took your money rather than asked for it (hence getting you involved) and paid hardly any attention to its reputation and efficiency. Suddenly, you realize that this is the state of affairs today. Madness? Perhaps. But definitely the major snafu of politics.

Common And Uncommon Political Sense

In order to delve into America's system of representative Democracy, a constitutional Republic, let's have a "conversation" with one of the founding fathers of American politics, Thomas Paine. Back in his day, Thomas Paine's pamphlets of eloquent prose such as *Common Sense* motivated many people in the colonies to proceed to revolution against rule by the British crown. Paine was an outspoken advocate of liberty and, unlike most other Founders, he was also a staunch abolitionist, acknowledging publicly that slavery was terribly wrong. In addition, Paine was a critic of fundamentalist religion. Because religiosity and strict adherence to scripture were pretty popular back then, most people didn't take kindly to his writings on the subject of religious dogma and blind faith. He was pejoratively declared an atheist (though he was actually a deist) and unfortunately became somewhat of an intellectual outcast after the revolution.

Nonetheless, Thomas Paine has been considered by many historians to be one of the most important influences on political thought in early America, during the rise of the burgeoning Republic. The laity readily embraced the practicality and wisdom of his writings.

So, in the spirit of inquiry into the formation of a new nation, let's explore the philosophical side of Democracy and government from Paine's perspective—and ask some important questions. What follows is an excerpt from *Common Sense* titled "Of the origin and design of government in general, with concise remarks on the English Constitution."

> SOME writers have so confounded society with government, as to leave little or no distinction between them; whereas they are not only different, but have different origins. Society is produced by our wants, and government by our wickedness; the former promotes our happiness POSITIVELY by uniting our affections, the latter NEGATIVELY by restraining our vices. The one encourages intercourse, the other creates distinctions.

The first is a patron, the last a punisher.

Society in every state is a blessing, but Government, even in its best state, is but a necessary evil; in its worst state an intolerable one: for when we suffer, or are exposed to the same miseries BY A GOVERNMENT, which we might expect in a country WITHOUT GOVERNMENT, our calamity is heightened by reflecting that we furnish the means by which we suffer. Government, like dress, is the badge of lost innocence; the palaces of kings are built upon the ruins of the bowers of paradise. For were the impulses of conscience clear, uniform and irresistibly obeyed, man would need no other lawgiver; but that not being the case, he finds it necessary to surrender up a part of his property to furnish means for the protection of the rest; and this he is induced to do by the same prudence which in every other case advises him, out of two evils to choose the least. Wherefore, security being the true design and end of government, it unanswerably follows that whatever form thereof appears most likely to ensure it to us, with the least expense and greatest benefit, is preferable to all others.

Certainly, most of us would agree that it's best to achieve the greatest benefit to our security with the least expense. Getting more for our dollar from government seems like a very good thing. But maybe after reading this, the following questions popped into your mind: If the "necessary evil" of government arises from people's wickedness and the need to somehow restrain our vices, how can the *individuals in government* be immune from the same lack of clear, uniform, and irresistibly obeyed conscience? Further, how can we be *forced* to surrender part of our property in order to ensure its safety from thieves? Is such evil actually necessary? Do we indeed furnish the means by which we suffer —needlessly?

Let's proceed with some more of Paine's thoughts, keeping these questions in mind. After he explained why people need each other in order to survive and prosper, which is definitely true, Thomas wrote:

Thus necessity, like a gravitating power, would soon form our newly arrived emigrants into society, the reciprocal blessings of which would supercede, and render the obligations of law and government unnecessary while they remained perfectly just to each other; but as nothing but Heaven is impregnable to vice, it will unavoidably happen that in proportion as they surmount the first difficulties of emigration, which bound them together in a common cause, they will begin to relax in their duty and attachment to each other: and this remissness will point out the necessity of establishing some form of government to supply the defect of moral virtue.

Some convenient tree will afford them a State House, under the branches of which the whole Colony may assemble to deliberate on public matters. It is more than probable that their first laws will have the title only of Regulations and be enforced by no other penalty than public disesteem. In this first parliament every man by natural right will have a seat.

But as the Colony encreases, the public concerns will encrease likewise, and the distance at which the members may be separated, will render it too inconvenient for all of them to meet on every occasion as at first, when their number was small, their habitations near, and the public concerns few and trifling. This will point out the convenience of their consenting to leave the legislative part to be managed by a select number chosen from the whole body, who are supposed to have the same concerns at stake which those have who appointed them, and who will act in the same manner as the whole body would act were they present. If the colony continue encreasing, it will become necessary to augment the number of representatives, and that the interest of every part of the colony may be attended to, it will be found best to divide the whole into convenient parts, each part sending its proper number: and that the ELECTED might never form to themselves an interest separate from the ELECTORS, prudence will point out the propriety of having elections often: because as the ELECTED might by that means return and mix again with the general body of the ELECTORS in a few months, their fidelity to the public will be secured by the prudent reflection of not making a rod for themselves. And as this frequent interchange will establish a common interest with every part of the community, they will mutually and naturally support each other, and on this, (not on the unmeaning name of king,) depends the STRENGTH OF GOVERNMENT, AND THE HAPPINESS OF THE GOVERNED.

Here then is the origin and rise of government; namely, a mode rendered necessary by the inability of moral virtue to govern the world; here too is the design and end of government, viz. Freedom and security. And however our eyes may be dazzled with show, or our ears deceived by sound; however prejudice may warp our wills, or interest darken our understanding, the simple voice of nature and reason will say, 'tis right.

So, this is the general thought process about why we need representative government. Elected officials are to mimic our interests once the population increases beyond a reasonable limit (thus making meetings of everyone impossible). In addition, as Paine put it, the defect of moral virtue from people's remissness of duty and attachment to others supposedly requires a representative political system to secure everyone's interests and safety. And in order for laws to remain tied to the concerns of the people, elections should be held as frequently as possible.

All of this begins to expose the main problem inherent in such a system—namely, that those you elect are unlikely to make the same choices as yourself. And, if each individual's choice is lacking in virtue (however that's defined) how do you expect representatives to be *more* virtuous, given how removed they are from your decisions in daily life?

Notice that Paine has relied on two basic arguments for representative government, one practical, one moral. Inquiring minds *do* want to know a few things when it comes to the idea of being "managed" by others. Practically speaking, will elected officials and those they appoint have interests that coincide with the people in the community? It's nice to think that they will, but we can cite an avalanche of evidence to the contrary. Typically, the method of operation for politicians is this: Make promises; get elected; break promises and hope enough time has elapsed between the campaign and the term in office that nobody notices. In this digital age with immediate availability of new information, that's a hard one to pull off without a hitch. Usually a sizable amount of voter and non-voter apathy and resignation is needed.

Who exactly determines what's in the "public interest" anyway? Will the elected officials and those they appoint have the same concerns at stake as we ourselves do? While not likely, it depends mostly on how vocal and influential representatives' constituencies are. Sooner or later, though, as history has revealed, the game and the big prizes go to the lobbyists and those with the most political pull. The average citizen has little influence. You're usually not done any favors, and your vote is often of little or no value (regardless of whether there's an electoral college).

Since "the public" is each and every individual in a particular area, how is it possible for one person or even a group of people to represent them? In other words how can one person make choices for a group of people concerning their own personal interests? Obviously, managers of companies and even heads of households do this frequently, but there has to be some degree of agreement or at least consent about delegating one's choices to others. Since the smallest minority in the world is the individual (as Ayn Rand keenly noted), what happens when the majority or plurality of voters' opinions run counter to *your* opinions? Moreover, what's the *nature* of the decisions being made in the name of everyone's interests? Even in the earliest meetings of townsfolk who hadn't yet elected representatives, surely there was not unanimity in deciding various issues. On matters big and small, there were surely disagreements, perhaps heated ones at that.

When people are left to make decisions for their entire community, public policy becomes a veritable piñata filled with favors and tax dollars that are sweeter than candy. And like the Latin American game, the participants are blinded—in this case by irrational interests. Deciding on public policy destroys awareness of its consequences on other individuals who comprise the public. Voters' secret ballots and representatives' open (or closed) door meetings obscure understanding of the game being played: Ultimately, those who assume the right to have final say in these matters *do not own* the property in question.

This leads us to the moral part of Paine's formulation of government. What duty and attachment do people actually have to each other that begins to lapse over time and distance? When and why do they stop being fair to each other? What moral defects prevent them from running their own affairs in the midst of others? Again, how can those in government, specifically the individually elected representatives and their appointees hope to remedy any moral defects in people? How can government—consisting of persons selected from the very same populace—actually supply the defect of moral virtue? It would be ironic for Paine to expect us to accept the virtues of government (of, by, and for the people) on faith.

Paine implies that, once in larger populations, people gradually tend to become less responsible or less virtuous to each other. Well, it's certainly the case that strangers in cities tend to be more impersonal, because it's just not possible to say "Hi" to everyone you walk past. But are they less responsible and less virtuous than people in smaller communities? That depends mainly on their individual values, particularly their beliefs about how others should be treated, be they friends, relatives, business associates, etc. Having lived in large cities such as San Diego, Dallas, and Minneapolis, as well as in tiny towns such as Challis, Idaho, I'd say that Paine was indeed mistaken. Most travelers, businesspersons, and students would say the same thing. Americans in general are kind to each other.

Despite contrary "evidence" from soap operas and horror films, most people in America mean well, regardless of the population density. Because cities are primarily about commerce—and commerce involves all kinds of cooperation, collaboration, and interdependence, that is, voluntary trading of values—being virtuous and responsible to others is the key social lubricant that prevents society from grinding to a halt (and the ensuing mayhem).

It's not governmental officials, then, who can prevent vice and maintain people's virtue and responsibility. That's one of the more ridiculous notions about government, and about people's behavior. People relate to each other according to their moral codes, whether formulated implicitly or explicitly, not because others are assigned to look over their shoulders and make them behave.

If anything, the State drastically worsens people's relationships and interactions. For example, all the real-life blood baths throughout the world stem more from existing political corruption and despotism, which act as catalysts for strife, than they do from the degree of immorality and lack of enlightenment in the general populace (people's contradictory philosophical premises).

When economic conditions start to worsen, people's interpersonal ethics get put more to the test. Most people in America would never think of killing their fellow countrymen to gain any values. They would never approve of stealing sustenance from a mother in need, for instance. These things happen more in areas of strong States and impoverished economies or in tribal societies with barbarous leaders and gang rule. Americans tend to look for reasonable solutions to crises, so that a better environment can be achieved. We constantly solve problems, both simple and complex, *willingly and voluntarily*. Given similar economic conditions, most people throughout the world do too. This is clearly a testament to the human drive to respect each other, to minimize conflict, to prevent the creation of chaotic conditions.

Given these sociological and psychological dynamics, some other important questions must be asked. When members of a society can't gather in one place, what exactly do representatives do for them in terms of their security and the needs of their daily lives? What exactly are representatives in government providing us? Since we can clearly make choices and think for ourselves, do we actually need other people to do these mental tasks for us?

It's been said that Democracy basically consists of two wolves and a sheep deciding on what to have for dinner. It's also been said (by George Bernard Shaw, I believe) that those in government who rob Peter to pay Paul, can always depend on the support of Paul.

Now we're getting to the real essence of Democracy, whether representative or popular. When people get together politically, or get their representatives together, to decide on "public" issues, those who disagree aren't allowed to opt out. They are forced to participate. Ultimately, the majority or plurality rules, and the powerful and influential foster a "might makes right" mentality. The issues on the voting table concern other people's property or unclaimed property (public property) and the decision makers are paid with tax dollars rather than with profits. This is definitely not virtuous, nor is it responsible.

To infringe on another's property or to physically harm or threaten another person is *the worst political vice imaginable*. While we'll explore more of the reasons later, this is basically how individual rights are violated—through the initiation of force, which disables our ability to make choices and to act on them. Rights denote freedom of action, the liberty to respectfully do as we please in a social context. We possess rights to any actions that don't infringe on, that is, initiate force against, others and their property. We make decisions to further our lives and well-being, and others do too.

To give up one's direct say in matters of the community may be problematic in its own right. But to enable a representative group of people to make decisions that infringe on people's rights is an egregious injustice. The vices and immorality that Paine wrote of are outgrowths of the very system he and the other Founders promoted. Every election in a governmental system reflects a society in which some people, either mistakenly or deliberately, vote other people's rights away—rights to choices, actions, and ownership.

Nearly everyone who votes in a Democracy votes to diminish the liberties that a free market can bestow on them. Only the so-called public sector grants individuals this ability. During elections, any of us "law-abiding citizens" can go down and cast our ballots for anyone running for office, or we can choose a more worthy write-in candidate, such as Mickey Mouse, Donald Duck, or Bugs Bunny. Unlike these innocuous cartoon characters, elected representatives take office, appoint like-minded others, and then forward a great range of opinions that become codified in law and enforced by people willing and able to use lethal force—if threats of fines, confiscations, arrest, and imprisonment don't cause adequate conformity.

Representative government obviously overlooks the fact that people should be free to contract or not to contract with whomever they please. They should be free to make their own choices, as long as those choices don't interfere with the rights and property of others.

So, our entire political system rests on a flawed understanding of how people in large groups should behave toward each other. Whether they're members of a small group or large group, city or state, people in politics don't mind initiating force, through either physical means or fraud, which involves contracting or paying for something not agreed upon, that is, without informed consent.

What some intend Democracy to do—mainly to facilitate the communication and implementation of human desires for safety and security in a society—will thus never come to fruition. Democracy contains the seeds of its own destruction, primarily because it allows people to legally diminish each person's freedoms. The procedures of Democracy are designed to ignore their own rights-violations, of course. Never will these procedures order our representatives and the various officials who do their bidding, as well as the people who voted them into office, to cease and desist. Only a new understanding of rights and politics in the populace can accomplish that.

General Welfare, Common Good, Public Interest: The Gateway Abstractions

Now, how has America evolved, or devolved, from the time of Paine? A nice way of putting it might be that American government theoretically consists of three well-intentioned branches sprouting from one practically rotten tree.

As noted, those who don't vote in a Democracy are subjected to the same treatment as those who do. And those who voted for the representative or policy that didn't win are subjected to the same treatment as the victors. In order for anyone to contend that such a system represents justice and equal rights of individuals, he or she must twist logic beyond a pretzel into something completely unrecognizable.

Political doublespeak aids and abets such flawed reasoning: "The end justifies the means." "It's for the greater good of the people." "The general welfare must be considered." "The interest of the populace is at stake." "Equal opportunity for everyone." "A fair and level playing field must be created in this country, and in the world's markets." "We all must make sacrifices for the good of the community." "Ask what you can do for your government" (while simultaneously asking what your government can do for you). "Being a good citizen means obeying the law." "It's your civic duty, after all." "Giving back to your community is something every respectable citizen and business does."

All such phrases expose the kind of con game being played on members of a productive society. True rights concerning individuals' ability to make choices and act on them must be sacrificed to "rights" given to us by government, which means the ability to throttle people's choices and actions. Then, everyone can get a portion of the goodies from the community chest of expropriated goods. Welcome to the home of the redistribution scheme, a system of politics that forcibly extracts wealth from people in order to give less of it back in a manner different than how it was originally constituted.

I wonder what Thomas Paine would say about today's multi-trillion dollar government. For example, are the hundreds of billions of dollars spent on "national defense" actually making us more safe and secure? Think about the fact that a few pistols in the hands of the airlines' pilots of the 9/11 planes would've likely prevented the ensuing disasters. The government did not allow such simple protective measures, because it "owns" the airports and is thus in charge of airlines' security via the TSA (Transportation Security Administration) in concert with the diktats of the Department of Homeland Security. A pointed question should be asked here: Which poses a greater danger to our liberties—the threat of the State or the threat of terrorism? Being subjected to the arbitrary edicts of TSA officials, for example, undoubtedly reflects the fascist nature of the State; its members want to monitor and control your freedom to travel in order to keep you secure. But should the loss of your freedoms be the price you pay for your supposed safety? Given that Defense Department officials can't even secure their own headquarters, The Pentagon, from direct attack, might it be a bit absurd to believe that they can safeguard us, the whole of the American public? Furthermore, given that a study of the history of terrorism shows that political grievances typically stem from foreign occupation and meddling, maybe the best way to fight terrorism is to stop funding a huge government that seeks to maintain and expand its influence in foreign affairs, as well as subjugate people in all manners domestically.

As mentioned, a fairly good political rule of thumb holds that as long as the State generally permits free speech, free press, and trial by jury, there's still hope—hope of turning things around, before the place turns into a dictatorial police State, essentially a regime of fear and unspeakable cruelty (not to mention martial law). Free speech and free press obviously enable people to spread ideas and persuade others of a better way of life, as well as to criticize threats to and infringements on their liberties. Trial by jury is one of the final legal checks on statist tyranny. The Founders knew well that an innocent person stands a better chance of being tried fairly by a panel of his or her peers than by a representative of the State wielding absolute power. Absolute power reveals itself in every trial in which the presiding judge admonishes jurors to focus strictly on the facts of the case, rather than inform them of their right to judge the *morality of the law* in relation to the facts presented. Jury nullification of the law is something that undermines the State's power, of course, which explains why judges act as if it doesn't exist.

When the grand ideal of Democracy has gone terribly wrong, as all illogical ideas must, the last hope for liberty must remain with the people. Although we can vote bad people out of office, and we can try to repeal bad laws, these basic options in a Democracy don't address the main problem: A bad system will continue to generate offices for bad people as well as bad laws. Only by questioning the nature of the entire system of government—the nature of statism itself—can we begin to free ourselves from injustice and constant threats of more tyranny.

Most of us were taught in grade school to say, in zombie-like fashion, "I Pledge of Allegiance to the flag of the United States of America...." One's mind naturally attempts to finish the recitation, so ingrained are childhood memories. However, it really should be renamed the "Pledge of Allegiance to the Great Abstraction." The flag, the Republic, and the State are merely conceptual symbols that ought not obtain our allegiance unless we agree with their representatives' practices. I submit that children who are told to say the Pledge don't even know the meaning of some of its words, and they certainly don't understand what allegiance actually entails.

A study of the history of the United States reveals many things to be proud of and many things to scorn. This is because "one nation" consists of multitudes of people with multitudes of beliefs and behaviors, which are impossible to combine into something that equals our individual respect, let alone allegiance. But the Pledge is part of the collectivistic game that seeks to keep us ignorant and incapable of making important ethical distinctions, the main distinction being a voluntary America versus America's coercive government. So, it's little wonder that children are made to repeat empty phrases such as "with liberty and justice for all."

This takes us back to Thomas Paine's thoughts on the subject of representation. It would be difficult to get critically minded individuals to pledge allegiance to particular persons in their community if those persons did disrespectful or ridiculous things—especially if those persons violated the rights of individuals in their community.

Once a community reaches the size of a nation, the primary way to get people to pledge allegiance to particular representatives (that they likely will never meet) is to first have them, as children especially, pledge allegiance to a concept of goodness that those representatives are purported to reflect. Baseball, Old Glory, and our Constitutional Republic! In addition, just in case you don't buy into this confusion of terms, the people must also be convinced that it's necessary to general goodness that they be *required* to pay for the services devised and provided by the representatives. That way, no matter how much you disagree with the vote totals, as well as the ensuing policies and behaviors of the elected and appointed, you have no way of opting out of the system. It's all for the common good, you see.

How Politicians Work: Let Corruption Ring!

Have you ever wondered why incumbents are typically the ones who win elections? In an irreverent look at political life, The Daily Show with Jon Stewart described in their book *America: A Citizen's Guide to Democracy Inaction* that elections are when America decides to "change the sheets." Apparently, either the sheets aren't that dirty come election year, or it's too expensive to wash them. Expensive indeed. The enormous costs of effectively campaigning against incumbents tend to deter those not hardened by political gamesmanship and lacking sufficient funds. Incumbents have the advantage of using their political positions to do two jobs at once—"serve the people" and fund-raise/gain support for their next election.

These two jobs raise two very significant questions, questions that must be asked and answered by respectable people: How do politicians serve the people, and how do they gain supporters? It turns out that both jobs involve the same thing that corrupts politics to the core: They make use of coercive power in order to fulfill their own desires as well as the desires of various people in the citizenry.

Remember that the nature of a Democracy involves making decisions about what to do with other people's property or "government property," or unclaimed domain. Force is used with laws and regulations that ultimately translate into jail cells for the disobedient and non-conforming, and bullets for the resistant. Taxation is the means of funding this operation. Taxation is the involuntary transfer of people's wealth to government.

Now, aside from the personal gains sought by those in government, such as larger salaries, more entrenched positions, various perks, and bigger pensions, how do you suppose officials choose which political agendas to champion? After all, if everyone got a say in politics, its ludicrous nature would definitely be exposed. The State could never become big enough to provide for all the whims of every person. Such a spectacle would resemble an insatiable cannibal who, after eating everyone else, must then turn his knife and fork upon himself.

Since the dissenters and losers take a back seat in politics, which are typically the majority of the people, the driving is left to a vocal and influential minority. Corporate heads, unions of all stripes, political action committees, and so on, are the driving forces of political agendas. As long as the costs are distributed to those who are taxed throughout the entire country, state, county, city, or town, then influential minorities can obtain their desired concentration of goodies. It's all for the common good, you see.

There's a long, sordid history of people running to government to receive favors—much more than people running to government to prevent favors done for them. These favors are always administered at the expense of the people in society who seek no such favors, but are taxed anyway. Of course, from a lobbyist's point of view, what sense would it make for them to pay governmental officials in order to have the State give their money back, minus extensive administrative costs of course? That would definitely be a losing deal. So, the key is to get money from people who aren't going to benefit. It's much easier to get them to accept such a deal when they're trained to be good allegiance-pledging, tax-paying, law-abiding citizens.

Lest you start imagining that this is a grand conspiracy by the rich and powerful elites against the downtrodden, the people are far from dumb. Their own collectivistic abstractions foster conformity as well as the subtle thought of being able to get something for nothing, at the expense of others. It doesn't take much to connect the political dots here. Eventually, many more groups of people realize that they had better "get while the gettin's good," and play the game of politics with their politically minded peers. Pressure group warfare naturally ensues. The press reports. You decide.

How The Military/Industrial Complex Works: You Scratch My back, Bombs Away!

Take, for example, the situation of making weapons for the military. Since government is essentially a costly, inefficient, bloated bureaucracy, it's not very competent at building things. It's much more effective at destroying things with privately constructed weaponry. The "military-industrial complex" that President Eisenhower admonished Americans about is the quintessential case study in feeding at the collective trough of tax money. No one does it better, although groups such as the teachers' unions (NEA and AFT) and the American Association of Retired Persons (AARP) are definitely no slouches (please excuse the thousands of others I've left out).

Military contractors, essentially corporations that make weapons and equipment for governments (few, if any, questions asked), engage in what's known as political strategizing of their resources. Arguably the best way to feed at the collective trough is to get as many people as possible to have vested financial interests in maintaining contracts with the government. So, military contractors try to infiltrate all the various states in order to influence the largest number of vocal constituents in the voting public. More people working for the government, either directly or indirectly, increases the chances that elected representatives will increase or continue their funding. The potential loss of jobs gives politicians major talking points, the bread and butter of their stump speeches. If the representatives don't do the public's bidding (by public, I mean influential lobbying groups), they face the potential of being tossed out of office. Perish the thought!

In this sense, Paine was partially right: Elected representatives do pay attention to the concerns of some in their community. But they do so for reasons that have little or nothing to do with justice, virtue, and respect for property rights. Essentially, State officials legislate, execute, and adjudicate laws for the wrong reasons, and the result is that our lives, liberties, property, and pursuit of happiness are thereby greatly diminished.

Of course, many of us tend to overlook these facts, while hoping that the *next* politicians (and the judges and bureaucrats they appoint) will do our bidding this time. But no matter what you believe government is going to provide you—whether safety or security-related—it does so at a much higher price than any competitive company in the marketplace. And government programs and policies usually achieve the opposite of their goals. This is primarily because government operates outside the free market. Government essentially has nothing to offer, so long as it's funded involuntarily and uses force against rights-respecting people. Simply put, the end doesn't justify the rights-violating means. The negative economic consequences of government merely reflect this truism.

In our daily lives, trying to make ends meet and pursuing our happiness, distractions and distance can take their toll on realizing the rottenness of government. The close communities Paine envisioned that would determine social issues democratically are rarely the case. Even where present, we still face the inherent injustice of managing other people's property, as well as "government property," for the so-called common good. Voting procedures greatly distract us from honoring the essential principles of ownership and voluntary exchange.

Furthermore, evidence and logical inspection refute the widespread belief that, since humans are not "angels," then government (that is, fellow non-angels selected from society) should be relied on to foster virtue and punish vice. It turns out that *any* government, by its coercive nature, becomes much worse than the people who voted (or didn't vote) for it. Again, distractions and distance take their toll on our need to confront those who pretend to speak in our names.

The Constitution's Problems: Article I Section 8...Sadly, A Template For Disaster

Some might say that these criticisms leveled against Democracy don't pertain to their ideal—a constitutional Republic. Is such a Republic different from a representative Democracy? In form, somewhat; it depends mostly on the nature of its constitution. In terms of consequences, however, not really. The framers of the U.S. Constitution were quite aware of what could happen when legal restraints are not placed on governmental powers: A nation becomes one of unjust men and not laws.

Of course, legal restraints can take a variety of forms and need not be codified on pieces of paper. The United Kingdom, for example, has managed its political affairs for quite some time without a written constitution. Common law precedents, statutes, and parliamentary procedures take its place. Presently, in terms of people's lack of liberties, Britain isn't a whole lot different than America. The basic principles of governmental injustice remain; only the details vary.

Nevertheless, what if the framers of the U.S. Constitution knew that it would serve only as a template for an ideal Republic? The rest would be up to the people to maintain it, right? The words of Benjamin Franklin come to mind here. In 1787, when asked what they had wrought from the Constitutional Convention, a Republic or a Monarchy, Franklin was quoted as saying "A Republic, if you can keep it."

Perhaps the Framers' constitutional codification of "separation of powers" and "checks and balances" was the absolute best anybody could (or can) come up with, in order to keep a representative form of government intact. Clearly, the Framers wanted to ensure that the fruits of their labor weren't going to form another tyranny, like that of King

George III.

At this point, we can readily demonstrate that America didn't heed Franklin's words. America has been unable to keep its Republic within the confines of the Constitutional limits intended by the Framers. A case can even be made that, given that the Federalists won the debate with the Anti-Federalists over the basic construction of the Republic, the whole enterprise was doomed from the start. The Anti-Federalists, such as George Mason and Patrick Henry, were indeed correct in forecasting the eventual rise of a powerful central government, leaving the several states to tag along on its monetary and regulatory coattails—and the people to resign themselves to a new form of oppression and servitude.

Of course, even if the Anti-Federalists had succeeded in their arguments against a strong federal government, the governments of the several states (under, say, slightly modified Articles of Confederation) most likely wouldn't have prevented the actual enslavement of a sizable percentage of the American population and the terrible conditions they endured for many decades. The deaths of over 600,000 people in the Civil War, however, likely could have been avoided. Solid evidence shows that Lincoln and his followers were much more concerned about preventing secession and its detrimental impact on their despotic policies of central government (for instance, the high tariffs on imported goods bought by southerners) than they were about ending slavery.

So let's perform a thought experiment. Let's imagine what America would be like if we forced government back into its Constitutional cage, as intended by the Framers, in the spirit of the Preamble:

> We the People of the United States, in Order to form a more perfect Union, establish Justice, insure domestic Tranquility, provide for the common defence, promote the general Welfare, and secure the Blessings of Liberty to ourselves and our Posterity, do ordain and establish this Constitution for the United States of America.

Obviously, from the Constitution's inception there were some major flaws that virtually everyone today would find intolerable. The allowance of slavery was one of them; it was allowed formally under the Constitution for nearly a hundred years (until the 13th and 14th Amendments). Disenfranchisement and second-class citizenship for everyone besides white males was another flaw; amazingly, it took a Constitutional Amendment (the 19th) in 1920 to grant women the right to vote in all the states—non-white men were granted it in 1870 (with the 15th). And few realize that the income tax was not tacked on as a Constitutional Amendment (the 16th) until 1913; somehow the Republic got along fine without it for nearly a century and a half.

Over time the meaning of the Constitution and the legislation arising from it have been interpreted differently by the various courts, the Supreme Court being the most famous (or infamous) interpreter. Not surprisingly, the original intent of the Framers was oftentimes lost, like dried leaves in gusts of hot wind.

James Madison, though a Federalist, forwarded a Bill of Rights to Congress pursuant to the Constitution's ratification. He realized that acceptance of the Constitution by the majority of people throughout the states hinged on whether it included the safeguard of a Bill of Rights. Indeed, without the first ten Amendments, America may have abandoned more quickly its idea of limited government.

Nonetheless, even if we were to set aside the above-mentioned nearly universally intolerable aspects, some of which were dealt with by later Amendments, what sort of government does a Constitutionally limited one offer us?

As mentioned, the Bill of Rights with the help of the citizenry has arguably kept our country from becoming some sort of vile dictatorship. The first things that dictators get rid of are the following: free speech; free press; rights of assembly and petitioning the government; gun ownership; prohibitions on quartering of troops in the populace; warrant-required searches and seizures; just due process; evidence-based convictions; jury trials; and, fair treatment of those found guilty (not to mention those awaiting trial). This thumbnail sketch of the first eight Amendments reflects the Framers' understanding of totalitarian power.

Totalitarian regimes have no patience for anything that defies their authority or that's subversive to their control. This reminds me of a chilling documentary about the Soviet Union under the heinous Joseph Stalin. He was known to comment that all political problems arise from men—so, "No man, no problem." People who disagree with the supreme leader and his accomplices are not to be tolerated and therefore must be erased. Stalin and his henchmen erased them by the *tens of millions*.

Fortunately for us, the Framers also noted that even if the Constitution could prevent or forestall outright totalitarianism, the three branches of government (executive, legislative, and judicial) needed to be further restrained from consolidating their powers. Hence, the ninth and tenth Amendments:

> Amendment IX.
> The enumeration in the Constitution, of certain rights, shall not be construed to deny or disparage others retained by the people.

> Amendment X.
> The powers not delegated to the United States by the Constitution, nor prohibited by it to the States, are reserved to the States respectively, or to the people.

Unfortunately for us, these two Amendments have been heeded little by those in power. As government grows, the other rights retained by the people are gradually ignored and nullified. And even where the powers of the several states increase, the power of the people to enforce their rights in relation to them seems to diminish. We've already noted that Democracy is an ill-conceived way to ensure our rights. The vagueness of the ninth and tenth Amendments reflects this. How are the rights of the individual supposed to be upheld against a government that's funded through coercive measures and that uses coercive measures enacted by a majority or plurality to regulate other people's property?

So, where exactly does this leave us? What are we to make of the Constitution—before a couple hundred years of executive practices, legislation, and adjudication were piled on top of it? Most of the Constitution is dedicated to outlining the managerial and procedural aspects of a representative government. Though the text may strike many practical Americans as mind-numbing legal babble, its brevity is a very nice walk in the park compared to, for instance, the Federal Register, in which tens of thousands of new pages are generated *each year*.

The Constitution basically contains such things as the following: the government's composition, terms of office, election (and electoral college) voting details; the legislative authorities of the bicameral Congress (House and Senate) as well as the President; the nature of the Executive Branch, which outlines the President as Commander in chief, his duties and responsibilities in relation to his cabinet, judges, Congress, and foreign States; the nature and jurisdiction of the Judicial Branch and the duties and responsibilities of its various courts; the legal relationship between and among the several States and Citizens to the Federal government; the procedures of Congress for further Amendments; the nature of the Constitution being "the supreme Law of the Land"; and, finally, its ratification.

Though the Constitution seems quite methodical in its presentation, one might notice that many of its specifics, and even its general structure, are more or less arbitrarily determined. If a representative government is to be formed, then someone has to make up its quantitative and qualitative rules, and these are probably as "good" as any.

While a full critique of the Constitution would certainly require a book in itself (and lots of strong coffee), it's important to focus on its major flaws in relation to our liberties, specifically its enabling of the coercive powers of government. Article 1 Section 8 shall serve our purposes well here, for it specifies many of the essential aspects of what our so-called limited government has permission to do. This is what folks mean, among other things, when they advocate governmental adherence to the Constitution:

> Clause 1:
> The Congress shall have Power To lay and collect Taxes, Duties, Imposts and Excises, to pay the Debts and provide for the common Defence and general Welfare of the United States; but

all Duties, Imposts and Excises shall be uniform throughout the United States;

The power "To lay and collect Taxes" is equivalent to theft, because the services aren't solicited by individuals and the funds aren't voluntarily contributed. To call expropriated wealth "revenue" is really an insult to earnest businesspersons everywhere.

The "common Defence and general Welfare of the United States" is perhaps the largest national abstraction possible. Might this be why the Pentagon and Congressional bills squander hundreds of billions of tax dollars each year?

The U.S. budget is approaching three trillion dollars. Needless to say, this isn't the sort of Federal government that the Framers intended, but this clause certainly provides for it. The government's special road to hell continues to be paved with "good intentions."

Additionally, the idea that "Duties, Imposts and Excises shall be uniform" exposes the absurdity of fair thievery.

Clause 2:
To borrow Money on the credit of the United States;

Perhaps at times it's wise for a person or company to borrow money, but for a government to do so merely adds more theft to its list of already despotic actions. After the coercive practices of taxation and regulation, the victims have little else to "give." A State-controlled banking system and a printing press thus enable such things as meddling with interest rates and inflating the money supply, hence devaluing the people's wealth.

Clause 3:
To regulate Commerce with foreign Nations, and among the several States, and with the Indian Tribes;

To "regulate Commerce" means to interfere with free trade, plain and simple. Though the Framers may have intended this clause to mean something else (like preventing state governments from impeding commerce), all three branches of government have taken it upon themselves to apply it to nearly every conceivable behavior, including things grown on your own property and used strictly for your own consumption. In short, now nothing is safe from regulation.

And of course, the U.S. government's regulation of the Indian tribes began with a trail of tears (and blood), broken promises, and violated treaties; it continues with many of their descendants impoverished by statist welfare programs.

> Clause 4:
> To establish a uniform Rule of Naturalization, and uniform Laws on the subject of Bankruptcies throughout the United States;

While initially pretty straightforward, "a uniform Rule of Naturalization" has turned into an onerous regulatory bureaucracy that thwarts millions of industrious people's attempts to move to America and make a living here.

People have a right to trade their labor like any other value, good, or service. To regulate such trade is therefore to regulate people's freedom to associate and freedom to travel. Today's fervent rhetoric against "illegal immigration" reflects the prevalent notion that law should be obeyed regardless of its infringement on individual rights and lack of logic. If anything, people's anger ought to be directed at the welfare State and at the police State required to enforce "our borders," both of which continue to expose the ills of Communist thinking.

Property owners ought to be able to determine who can and cannot travel on their property. Fortunately, by definition, the market highly favors those who invite and promote commerce with fellow travelers and residents, and it tends to disfavor those who isolate themselves from such commerce.

And what about bankruptcies? They should be left to customary law precedents, whereby being absolved from one's debts would be something to work out with one's creditors. Governmentally authorized bankruptcy is a deterrent to sound money management, be it by an individual or by a company.

Clause 5:
To coin Money, regulate the Value thereof, and of foreign Coin, and fix the Standard of Weights and Measures;

"Uncle Sam," the entity that taxes the People, is now authorized to make more money and dictate its value in the marketplace. This is especially handy when further taxes become unpopular; treasury bonds are handy too, of course. Governmental officials would rather us not understand the real nature of money and currency.

In order to avoid confusion, let's examine some definitions that draw the necessary distinctions. Money is a commodity, such as gold or silver, generally recognized and accepted in the marketplace as a universal medium of exchange. It's typically shaped or organized for accurate assessment and ease of transfer, for example, minted. Money has various properties that contribute to it being widely accepted. These include being scarce (making it relatively difficult to increase supply), portable, durable, equally divisible, non-counterfeitable, and esthetically or culturally appealing. Money that also has non-monetary uses, for instance, for industrial purposes, provides additional value in the marketplace, which may or may not contribute to its advantage over other types of money.

Currency is a note or coin, or digital representation thereof, that may or may not be redeemable for money. But it's nonetheless recognized and accepted as a universal medium of exchange for use in non-barter transactions. Money-backed currencies, such as paper receipts or certificates, facilitate transactions in which physical transfer of the money they represent (historically, gold and silver stored in banks) proves burdensome. After all, it can be a real pain to lug around a bunch of metal pieces.

Fiat currency is governmentally controlled currency that's issued monopolistically and prohibited from being redeemable for money. Because of its coercive character, fiat currency exposes a couple facts: It hasn't been recognized and accepted voluntarily by the marketplace, and any voluntarily chosen market money and/or redeemable currency would drive it out of existence. Thus, fiat currency requires a legalized monopoly in order to prevent its own demise, as well as to promote its recognition and acceptance as a universal medium of exchange.

Not surprisingly, for these reasons, fiat currency tends to be seen by most people as simply "money." Over time, understanding is lost about the voluntary roots of money and its preferential selection by the marketplace, as well as the tremendously negative economic effects of fiat currency. The American dollar, the basic unit of fiat currency in the United States, has now lost nearly all of its initial value. Originally it was a governmentally regulated money coin that designated a specific quantity (typically silver) or a currency note redeemable for a set quantity of either silver or gold under governmentally controlled bimetallism.

The government plainly has no valid business determining the medium of exchange in an economy. That's the market's job. Individuals in the marketplace determine, based on supply and demand principles, what the media of exchange will be and their values in relation to other goods and services. Typically, throughout history, the market has chosen metallic standards such as gold and silver.

> Clause 6:
> To provide for the Punishment of counterfeiting the Securities and current Coin of the United States;

This clause grants the biggest counterfeiter of all the ability to punish others who wish to play the same game. All thieves must be arrested, except those with the power "To lay and collect Taxes, Duties, Imposts and Excises" and "To coin Money, regulate the Value thereof, and of foreign Coin, and fix the Standard of Weights and Measures;"

> Clause 7:
> To establish Post Offices and post Roads;

This one probably doesn't need much comment, only to mention that it gave rise to the phrase, reflecting the horrific behavior, "Going postal." Granting the government a monopoly on mail delivery makes about as much sense as granting it a monopoly on baby delivery.

Anyone care to stand in *that* line?

In regard to post Roads, true to some of the Framers' concerns, federal and state established roads have been a regulatory bonanza for government (NHTSA and DOT are two examples) and a huge cost for Americans. Immense traffic congestion and around forty thousand fatalities from auto accidents annually (millions suffering lesser fates) demonstrate one more thing that government has no business doing.

> Clause 8:
> To promote the Progress of Science and useful Arts, by securing for limited Times to Authors and Inventors the exclusive Right to their respective Writings and Discoveries;

It turns out that this clause was destined to stifle progress in the arts and sciences. Confusion over who actually owns what and what rights people have in relation to their own possessions has produced brigades of attorneys and battalions of court cases to sort out the non-sortable litigious mess. We'll address this extensively in another chapter, so it's sufficient to say here that the market should decide how to freely honor creators and innovators, as it does everything else.

> Clause 9:
> To constitute Tribunals inferior to the supreme Court;

Naturally, justices of the Supreme Court can't preside over all cases in America. In fact they only hear a small fraction (less than a couple hundred) of the many thousands of cases that make it to their docket each year. Of course, it makes great sense to delegate authority and "outsource" when it comes to settling disputes and dealing with wrong-doers (tortfeasors). If only the high Court and the lower courts dealt solely with those types of cases. Unfortunately, that's like asking a lion to become a vegetarian. More often than not, courts do Democracy's bidding, which involves continually violating other people's freedoms and property.

This also raises the big questions of authority and jurisdiction. Why should any particular court have the final say? How many appeals should be permitted? What are the costs and how are fees determined? How can the right to a speedy and just trial be reconciled with a legalized monopoly of law? What happens when a particular court itself commits a tort? Who judges the judges? As noted in other chapters, only a free market of legal professionals can answer these questions to any reasonable degree of satisfaction. What America has presently is an injustice system. In the coercive world view of most judges, up is down; right is left; 2+2=5; innocent is guilty.

> Clause 10:
> To define and punish Piracies and Felonies committed on the high Seas, and Offences against the Law of Nations;

Again, the questions "Under whose jurisdiction, and at whose expense?" arise. And the answers "Government's jurisdiction and at the taxpayer's expense" ought to raise at least one eyebrow by now. The idea of punishing piracy seems understandable enough. Anyone who robs, pillages, or plunders, with or without an eye patch and a hook for a hand, is a bad guy. But the idea of "Felonies" begs the question of the validity of statutory law.

You've probably noticed that governments are adept at calling all sort of things felonies, in order to fine people and lock them up, or kill them when they don't submit. Real criminality, however, entails violating other people's rights, which means initiating force against their persons and/or property.

> Clause 11:
> To declare War, grant Letters of Marque and Reprisal, and make Rules concerning Captures on Land and Water;

Interestingly, the last few Presidents have found this clause inconvenient for foreign policy purposes, so they've just ignored it and proceeded to embark on various military missions (though they themselves never enter into harm's way). The last time Congress officially declared war was way back in 1941 against Japan and Germany. All subsequent wars of the U.S. military were fought in violation of this clause. Many pundits today think it's outdated or unnecessary, but the Framers knew the immense danger of placing national war-declaring power into the hands of a single person in the executive branch of government. The Commander in Chief is supposed to conduct war, not make it.

Nevertheless, this just deals with the surface details. The *real* issue, again, involves jurisdiction and expense. Who exactly are those who declare War and grant Letters of Marque and Reprisal, let alone the CIA and NSA, accountable to? And who are the people who follow their orders accountable to? More often than not, war, which is essentially large-scale legalized killing, is devised by its planners for their own purposes and their own ends—one end being more control and power over the citizenry. Indeed, as Randolf Bourne noted, "War is the health of the State."

The character of Odysseus in the film *Troy* had a memorable assessment of this issue: "War is young men dying and old men talking." The character of Achilles in the same film put it this way: "Imagine a king who fights his own battles. Wouldn't that be a sight?"

So goes war over countless centuries. As long as the leaders in government can *take* their "revenues" rather than earn them through profits (the opposite of "war profiteering," by the way), they'll always cast longing eyes toward military adventurism. As long as someone *else* has to pay the bills, in both blood and money, they'll continue to draw up schemes of greed, conquest, and destruction—and say it's for our freedoms, the security of the nation, the good of the people, the safety of our children, and other such collectivistic nonsense.

U.S. Imperialism, Global Empire, Pax Americana, the World's Policeman, the Warfare State, Big Brother—call it what you like—its so-called leaders have taken America far from its intended moorings as a peaceful nation "entangling alliances with none," in Jefferson's words.

> Clause 12:
> To raise and support Armies, but no Appropriation of Money to that Use shall be for a longer Term than two Years;

Again, at whose expense and under whose jurisdiction, in accordance with the principles of private property and individual rights?

Clearly, two years is simply too short a time span for rulers who desire to satisfy the hunger of a giant military/industrial complex. Staggeringly large military or "defense" appropriations are now commonplace, as are standing armies.

Clause 13:
To provide and maintain a Navy;

Same questions: At whose expense and under whose jurisdiction? Currently, the U.S. Navy treats its sailors to tours around the world, harboring for years at numerous foreign ports, flying sorties and launching million dollar missiles now and then—all at taxpayers' expense.

Clause 14:
To make Rules for the Government and Regulation of the land and naval Forces;

This clause follows from the others, but it still begs the main questions. Given the rules and regulations that government imposes on the market, we can expect the ones drawn up for themselves to be no less nonsensical. Nearly anyone who's spent time in the military will attest to its wastefulness, inefficiency, and plain wrongheadedness.

Clause 15:
To provide for calling forth the Militia to execute the Laws of the Union, suppress Insurrections and repel Invasions;

Many of the federalist Framers were concerned about the potential for more insurrections like that of Shays's Rebellion in Massachusetts, which was eventually halted by a State-organized militia. Daniel Shays and others were successful, however, in freeing many farmers from debtors prisons and many more from being bankrupted in courts through land foreclosures, which were induced by excessive litigation fees and high property taxes imposed by the Massachusetts' senate (composed primarily of commercial interests). It's an interesting story in its own right, and it exposes once again the problems of representative government, which imposes taxes and is not accountable to people but rather mainly to special interests. Naturally, such a government will seek ways to preserve itself and its interests, at the expense of liberty and justice.

Nowadays, of course, there's no need to call forth the Militia, because the Air Force, Army, Navy, Marines, Coast Guard, National Guard, and Reserve are already in place performing their assorted duties. The principle of State preservation is the same, from dictatorships to constitutional Republics.

> Clause 16:
> To provide for organizing, arming, and disciplining, the Militia, and for governing such Part of them as may be employed in the Service of the United States, reserving to the States respectively, the Appointment of the Officers, and the Authority of training the Militia according to the discipline prescribed by Congress;

What's called "national defense" now occupies over 130 countries around the globe. Troops are stationed in countries in which battles were fought many decades ago, as well as in places where battles have never been fought. The National Guard and Reserve have been sent to help occupy Iraq, creating still more irony. This is all supposed to make the world safe for "freedom and Democracy." Investigate for yourself the number of foreign actions taken by U.S. military forces as well as covert operations, for example by the CIA. Try not to be too surprised. After all, it's for the good of the people, you see.

> Clause 17:
> To exercise exclusive Legislation in all Cases whatsoever, over such District (not exceeding ten Miles square) as may, by Cession of particular States, and the Acceptance of Congress, become the Seat of the Government of the United States, and to exercise like Authority over all Places purchased by the Consent of the Legislature of the State in which the Same shall be, for the Erection of Forts, Magazines, Arsenals, dock-Yards, and other needful Buildings;

Washington D.C. Which do you prefer at this point: District of Columbia or District of Criminals? Does anyone serious believe that George Washington would want his name associated with the present organization—or for that matter, the buildings? The prodigious Greco-Roman architecture in D.C. tends to evoke feelings of permanence and even reverence, but history has demonstrated that *ideas*, not architecture, ultimately create permanence and reverence.

> Clause 18:
> —And To make all Laws which shall be necessary and proper for carrying into Execution the foregoing Powers, and all other Powers vested by this Constitution in the Government of the United States, or in any Department or Officer thereof.

Oy Vey. I wonder if the Framers had a sense of shame while approving this clause. Although, when you're in the coercive power and corruption business, there's no need to impose any serious restrictions upon yourself, or any serious consequences for violating the ones you do impose. Instead, it's carte blanche with the "elastic clause." Yes, that's because "necessary and proper" has been used to justify all kinds of legislation and actions that would undoubtedly make most of the Framers shake their heads in disgust.

By now it's probably most apparent that rules and orders written on paper, no matter how well-conceived and crafted, don't necessitate people's adherence to them. One key to understanding the Constitution is that it's only as effective as the integrity of those who believe in its ideas. Yet there are really two issues here: the content and the adherence to that content. The foregoing analysis of Article 1 Section 8 demonstrates that the content, irrespective of how it was intended at its creation, has deep and irrevocable flaws. These flaws have clearly been exploited by those who don't care about how big and intrusive government gets; or rather, they only want it to get bigger and more intrusive. Those who attained office soon found all kinds of powers and wealth at their disposal, and they deliberately sought to exploit those features.

Once government enacts the power to tax, the unjust game begins.

It's then a tug-of-war between the rights-respecting and the rights-violating aspects of the citizenry and their elected representatives. But this game isn't a fair one. It takes place on an uneven field, and those who strive to take the moral high ground are soon outnumbered by those below. They're easily pulled down into the political muck.

This is demonstrated by all the debates in America about the problems of government and how to deal with them. There are policies and studies galore, but no real solutions: campaign finance reform; further regulations against lobbying; a presidential line-item veto; term limits for legislators and judges; reduced pay and benefits; bipartisan investigative commissions; a flat tax; a fair tax; a national sales tax; tax cuts and tax credits; supply-side economics; new "cutting-edge" programs for this or that; competitive bidding on governmental contracts; improved "streamlined" regulations; "deregulation" (in name only); and, always *more funding* and practically *never less spending*; oh, and let's not forget..."leave no child behind"—or is it standing?

Indeed, very few individuals propose the only just and moral solution that would be like a knife cutting the rope in the relentless game of tug-of-war, sending all the rights-violators tumbling to the bottom. The power to tax is the power to acquire wealth ultimately at the point of a gun. That is the evil essence of taxation, and of the State. If you don't oppose it, then you leave humanity open to an unending source of despicable behavior and exploitation.

The Framers knew that the game they were devising required taxation in order to be played. Maybe their main hope was that things wouldn't get too out of hand, that is, out of the hands of the citizenry and into the hands of oppressive government. The Framers knew that coercive power tends to corrupt even the noblest of character. The separation of powers and various checks and balances were the safeguards they imposed. To protect against despotism and runaway corruption, they depended on the people to be vigilant in thwarting attempts by those in power to circumvent these supposed safeguards.

But even the most vigilant citizenry won't be able to monitor all the things happening within the large bowels of government, nor stop the relentless flow of corruption. Americans have neither the time nor the energy, nor the real capacity to do something about it—so long as they believe that the Constitution has legitimate authority. The game will always be rigged in favor of the State and those who desire to wield its power.

Whether or not they ever meet their representatives, let alone influence some of their decisions, most people rightly feel that politicians and bureaucrats will *never* have a positive impact on their lives. So, most of us move onward in the pursuit of our own happiness, yet resigned in the certainty of "death and taxes." Those involved in politics, on the other hand, continue to see nothing but opportunities—opportunities to pander, to make promises, to gain riches and power, to achieve fame, control, and still more control.

Our Constitutional Republic is mainly in the business of three disrespectful things: monopolizing the money supply and printing dollars out of thin air, thereby inflating and devaluing currency; taking wealth from you through taxation rather than asking for it through voluntary trade; and, telling you to do things that you never agreed to, using force whenever you disobey.

The sad fact of the matter is that the Constitution, like Democracy, also contained the seeds of its own destruction. It was essentially the most civil way to allow for the most uncivil things to be done to people. Democracy, representation, taxation, and regulation are all affronts to private property and the idea of self-ownership, which happen to be the topics of the next chapter.

III

WE HOLD THESE TRUTHS TO BE SELF-EVIDENT(AFTER A BIT OF INSPECTION)

Freedom In A Nutshell

Let's now explore the answer to the underlying questions of this book. What is, and how do we achieve, a political environment of 100% freedom, that is, a country of complete liberty?

As you might suspect, the answer to these questions can be revealed in just two words: Privatize everything. Once done, then private interests will interact as each sees fit in the marketplace of goods, services, and ideas. Contracts and voluntary exchanges will become the orders of the day. Since consent between and among individuals is the assumed principle, the freedom to contract or not to contract with others will be respected as one's inherent right. This follows from the fact that each of us is a sovereign entity. Each of us is capable of making our own decisions and acting on them. This includes exercising the right of self-defense, or bestowing that right to an agent of our choosing.

Self-Ownership

Liberty-oriented, or libertarian, ideas have existed for many centuries in various forms. Yet they gathered serious momentum, conceptual refinement, and outward expression primarily in the last couple centuries. The notable insights of Adam Smith in economics and John Locke in political philosophy, for instance, led their intellectual successors in the New World to formulate a more mature vision of individual rights. We could say that the idea of individual sovereignty reached budding adolescence with Classical Liberalism.

As mentioned, the framers of the U.S. Constitution applied their understanding of rights only partially to certain types of people and to certain types of actions, based on irrelevant and arbitrary distinctions. Basically, if you weren't a white male land owner, chances weren't too high that you'd be respected as an individual with equivalent freedoms. As also mentioned, half the population wasn't granted the freedom (or rather, the "privilege") to vote until the turn of the twentieth century. Yet, as we've seen, voting is its own form of tyranny. There's a special irony in *choosing* one's *rulers*, don't you think?

Women throughout vast reaches of the globe still face oppression and terrible predicaments, as do many other people who are also grouped based on insignificant differences. In America, even though honorable men such as Thomas Paine attempted to enlighten others about some of these inconsistencies, the idea of rights in most people's minds still had some growing up to do.

In fact, anyone who's studied the history of individual rights will notice that the idea's implementation has never reached political maturity. So, the question arises: What would allow individuals everywhere to see rights for what they are, that is, to see them as natural and reason-based rather than government-based? Simply put, self-ownership.

You own yourself. You probably take this for granted, for you see slavery as the evil alternative. Unfortunately, there's such a thing as partial slavery, which is how humanity lives today—and sadly, it's somewhat by our own choosing, ignorance, and misunderstanding.

Sure, we may be convinced that we will protect ourselves and our possessions from would-be intruders, but it's a whole other ball game in the realm of politics. We usually play hardball when it comes to defending our friends and family, and personal possessions, against criminal behavior. But we play the weakest game of whiffle ball when it comes to defending our individual rights as sovereign beings who understand self-ownership against State officials.

If we don't integrate the idea of absolute ownership of our minds and bodies, we leave ourselves open to major exploitation by illogical political systems and the persons who run them. And for the record, *every* political system presently enacted by Homo sapiens is illogical—

that is, each and every one contradicts the truth of self-ownership.

It turns out that only big-brained hominids can formulate and understand the concept of ownership in the legal sense—and then proceed to ignore it. Chimpanzees and monkeys, for instance, can display systems of reciprocity and can even express emotions of fairness and injustice. But we've yet to see any law offices in the jungle or, for that matter, chimps in suits perusing court documents. While other primates do have a sense of various things being favorable or unfavorable to them relative to others, they can't make the necessary conceptual connections to the idea of self-ownership. Because they aren't creatures of reason and have little, if any, self-reflective capabilities (as evidenced by behavioral and brain studies), they naturally have little to say on the subject of law and advanced political systems.

Because human beings can reason with the precision of an immense vocabulary of concepts, we are the only known species capable of fully resolving disagreement and conflict through, for instance, mediation and arbitration. We can solve interpersonal problems peaceably by using our rational faculty, rather than the crude methods employed by non-reasoning primates. Even though the highly sexualized Bonobo chimps do have interesting ways to minimize conflict, such dispute resolution is not exactly practical for us. One can imagine commerce and trade ceasing on account of an assortment of particularly unwelcome genital handshakes.

And that's precisely the point of self-ownership. Because we can reason, we remain keenly aware of how we can choose to deal with each other: either through consent or coercion. Consent is based on the idea that you have total dominion over your own mind and body, and that others have total dominion over *their* own minds and bodies. We can't have it any other way without running into a big contradiction. We cannot, with a reasonable mindset, only apply the right to self-ownership to some people but not to others. Since we all possess and use reason and therefore make independent decisions, there's no logical or practical justification for applying the principle of self-ownership in a discriminatory or inconsistent fashion.

Self-ownership is a universal principle, just like the principle that humans are creatures of reason. You have willful (volitional) control over yourself. Obviously, to claim that human beings don't have willful control over themselves is to be willfully inconsistent. Thus, you are free from others laying claim to you. Because you own yourself, others by definition may not infringe on your domain.

Of course, we must take into account those unable to perform self-willed actions and even those unable to make choices. As babies, we all emerge from a state of relative helplessness into full-fledged, conceptual, volitional beings. Some people, a small minority in the adult world, remain dependent on other adults for care and safety, like children must rely on their parents. One of the many great things about our species is our ability to acknowledge the rights of those who are less independent and act on our desires to help them. Indeed, none of us would be alive if that weren't the case.

Property Is An Extension Of Self-Ownership

So, what are the implications of owning yourself? For us to see ourselves as absolute owners, we must begin to apply this principle to any social circumstance—as well as extend it to things outside of ourselves. Though that may sound simple enough, applying the concept to cultural and political institutions that have vast influence over our lives can be demanding.

Ownership in general essentially means rightful possession, either by first use or by consensual transfer of what one possesses to another. Ownership also entails future use and/or disposal of that which is possessed. The idea of ownership stems from the idea of self-possession. In order to further your life and pursue your happiness, that is, in order to function in the world as a reasoning person, you *must* claim things outside yourself (not merely your comb and toothbrush) as your possessions. Even ascetics who harbor disdain for earthly goods must claim the food they chew and swallow to be theirs and not someone else's. If based on nothing but sustenance alone, ownership is a very good thing.

As mentioned, everyone in a semi-capitalist society such as America seems to take ownership and property for granted. After all, what would all those mortgage payments be good for? And all that stuff in the garage and crammed into closets? Or how about the large (or small) sums of money in the bank? Or that newly purchased office furniture?

We do presume to own things, a lot of very cool and useful things. Private property is in fact the lifeblood of the marketplace, and our lives in that marketplace represent the beating heart of commerce and trade. Capitalism is basically an extension of our reasoning minds.

Staking claim to something can be as trivial as your sunglasses or as profound as a multi-million dollar company and the sizable chunk of real estate it sits on. Without the ability and the right to claim these things as your own—by virtue of first use, possession, or consensual transfer from another—you have scant ability to live and prosper. You also have little ability to create *value* in these things. What can't be traded in the marketplace has little, if any, benefit to anyone. What can't be owned can't be properly used, improved, or traded in the marketplace.

Moreover, without private property, no prices can be ascribed objectively through the interaction of buyers and sellers coming to mutual agreement, based on their knowledge of the trading environment. Without private property, prices aren't really possible, no matter how many bureaucrats in their perches of power believe their decrees to be better substitutes. Lack of objectivity in pricing inescapably leads to supply shortages. We should never forget that government rations things by having us all stand in line.

Unfortunately, many things on Earth are presently either unowned or they're "owned" by various governments. As Ayn Rand wisely noted, "public property" is a contradiction in terms; thus "private property" is actually a redundancy. "Public" supposedly means everyone, even though only a handful of people may have actually consented.

If government prevents private ownership to be ascribed to something, various people will abhor this vacuum. Like a pack of hungry, very impolite wolverines, interest groups will vie for the biggest, juiciest share of the unclaimed bounty. The rest of us will be left standing on the outside looking at the spectacle, wondering how we lost out or how so many people could be so short-sighted.

The only way certain domains—of land, sky, and bodies of water—can remain prey for those who spurn private ownership is if government uses coercion to prevent rightful claims from being made and delineated among owners. When the State denies individuals possession and use of private property, the political process has taken over. What could have been someone's property is now subject to all sorts of absurdities and dire consequences, one of these being what economists call "common pool" problems. Unclaimed areas usually become a free-for-all for users and abusers, where it's first come, first served and little accountability concerning the ecological effects.

Case in point: the oceans, which comprise roughly two thirds of the Earth's surface. They aren't owned by anyone. So-called territorial waters are merely collectivistic boundaries ascribed by those political officials in charge of enforcing statist dominion. After all, one sure way for those in government to regulate something is to prevent anyone from owning it. Then, what isn't permitted is forbidden.

As an environmental consequence, most populations of large fish are so loaded with mercury that daily consumption might make you forget your own name, or at least where you put your car keys. Okay, so the effects may not be so dramatic. While there seems to be no convincing evidence for ill effects on most of us, small children and pregnant women are still told by experts to limit their consumption of mercury-laded fish. Nevertheless, the pollutants that accumulate in big fish (being at the top of the aquatic food chain) are indicators of oceanic conditions.

As another indicator, rubber duckies and all kinds of less cute trash wash up on shores of remote islands, carried there by ocean currents. Massive crude oil spills destroy ecosystems for years, even decades. Large portions of coral reefs are dying and turning brittle white, from both natural and human causes. Storm drain, sewage, and run-off waters that are loaded with fertilizers and assorted man-made chemicals generate a proliferation of more primitive organisms such as blue-green algae. These organisms negatively affect the health of other species' populations and create detrimental toxins along coastal regions. Whole communities of sea creatures are decimated by overfishing. The destructive practice of bottom trawling has ecological effects similar to, or worse than, clear-cutting on land. I could go on, but I'm sure you get the point. Regardless of whether the news media exaggerates (or fantasizes) the global causes and effects, the local effects are noticeable, and they're harmful—as well as mostly preventable.

Yet the perpetrators act as if they don't realize the natural consequences of their behavior, as if it's acceptable, for instance, to dump all sorts of waste into unclaimed waters, not to mention into the air (or into low earth orbit, where it's becoming a veritable shooting gallery of parts). This is, of course, all thanks to lack of ownership and non-enforcement of private property rights.

Unfortunately, the present legal consequences don't involve restitution, reparation, and cease and desist orders. Those would be the consequences resulting from private property rights, that is, market-based solutions. We don't expect our neighbors to empty their trash cans on our front lawns, or into our swimming pools, nor would they dream of such behavior. This is because property owners are normally understanding and respectful of each others' rights. Similarly, if persons owned the oceans, they wouldn't tolerate pollution or ecological destruction of their waters. They'd run tight ships, and demand others do likewise, especially if they infringed on or despoiled their property. The same principle applies to all other bodies of water or realms of sky.

Even on assumed privately owned land, government does little to assist enforcement of property rights. For example, owners who've been harmed by industrial waste and toxic landfills, or even noticeable freeway pollution, face seemingly endless litigation and court costs.

Of course, expecting the government to come to your rescue and enforce your rights is oftentimes like expecting an orangutan to help you write a legal brief (no offense to orangutans; they can't help it). Even the highly venerated U.S. Constitution allows government to take private property for "public use" if it serves a so-called compelling public interest. Public interest usually means anyone's interest except your own. When the State takes property, the owners are supposed to be placated when they're given "just compensation." But no compensation can be considered just when the unjust power of Eminent Domain is used. Similarly, property taxes are another major way governmental officials violate your property rights. Having to pay rent to the State for owning something unquestionably mocks the nature of ownership.

To reiterate, the solution to all these issues of unreason and injustice is to ascribe property rights fully to all places, both claimed and unclaimed. Then, we could achieve some semblance of accountability and legal recourse to property rights-violations. Again, you don't let people pollute your property, because it's *your* property.

The same can't be said of governmental stewards, the military, various public property exploiters, and some corporate executives who think that the rights of private property owners need not stand in the way of maximizing their own and their shareholders' wealth.

Yet, you might wonder, if there were no public property or regulated private property (through, for instance, zoning laws), what about issues of untidiness or ugliness that might affect adjacent property values? Few neighbors currently use their own front yards as landfills, not because of coercive laws, but because most people don't enjoy living in filth and devaluing their own property. Those eccentric owners who have junk cars gathering rust on their own property, for instance, might face disgruntled neighbors (depending on the neighborhood), public shame, or even ostracism. As a result, many of these "collectors" wisely live in less populated areas where there's less potential for conflicts.

The typical bureaucratic response to this issue, that is, forcing them to do things with their own property, contradicts the nature of property rights. We must appeal to reason, so that respectful relations can be maintained and furthered. Present city ordinances and zoning laws (and regulations galore, as we'll see in the next chapter) are giant leaps in the opposite direction of individual rights. They're coercive attempts to control other people's actions and property, actions and property that have infringed on *no one's rights*.

Also, everyone is always free to live in a deed restricted area, in which covenants ensure no eyesores. As many people do today, you can choose to live in a gated community, or in a place governed by a Homeowners Association (though be wary of fascist-like HOA boards and their excessive fees and fines).

Ever wonder why primitive people and those in communal arrangements have experienced so little material progress? Economic progress can only happen if one has something to trade, and that something has to be produced and properly packaged for sale. Now, who's going to do the work, and who's going to gain the benefits? Well, in a free society of self-ownership and property, everyone who does the work gains the benefits. Each willing participant trades value for value in win/win, mutually beneficial transactions and interactions. This represents societal cooperation at its best.

Yet some who have nostalgia for primitive cultures, or who believe in the alleged (never exhibited) benefits of Communism, for instance, bristle at the idea of extending private ownership to things beyond personal effects. Sure, they may endorse the idea of having your own clothes. But they prefer, instead, non-ownership or communal ownership of resources and various fruits of your labor. Never mind that historical evidence and present day politics are totally unfavorable to them; Communism has yet to show that it works, let alone that it's moral. "But, damn, it's good in theory!" some say. Given our earlier analysis of *The Communist Manifesto*, one immediately wonders, "good" in what sense?

Non-ownership or communal ownership fosters conflicts over resources. Additionally, the *value* that could be created in those resources (capital) remains dormant. Aside from the irresolvable disputes generated among individuals and groups, this predicament soon leads to widespread lack of motivation to achieve anything. Communism, in all its variations, is the ultimate demotivator. "What's the point?" becomes its guiding rhetorical question. People who find ways to "work" the system are typically those who wield the most power via the State, and they get the spoils. The rest merely eke out an existence; they live on the brink of nonexistence.

As we discussed earlier, few people today recommend a full-blown Communist prescription for society. Yet many may advocate a powerful monopolistic organization of individuals to monitor, control, and regulate what should be done with both owned and unowned domains.

This is the general idea of government, or the State, in which the underlying principle of Communism holds constant sway.

The extent to which some individuals are denied by other individuals their full right to acquire, use, and/or dispose of property is the extent to which capital accumulation is hindered, productivity is diminished, prices rise, goods and services become more scarce, and opportunities for commerce wane. Private ownership, in contrast, leads directly to value creation, free exchange, productivity, and accountability.

The long, sordid history of thuggery, both personal and political (which ultimately is personal) has continually dismissed the principle of self-ownership—in favor of the contradictory idea that violence is a workable way to deal with others. Statist mentalities reach for threat of force and punishment to affect behavior and solve perceived problems. Terms like the "common good," "general welfare," "public interest," etc., attempt to disarm people who would otherwise have enough good sense to call this what it is—coercion—and deal with it appropriately.

Still some claim, "Why should you be so selfish and greedy and so against this kind of sharing?" Notice that political "sharing" is a euphemism for being forced out of one's own time, money, and property for the supposed good of others or the group. And the person who demands the sacrifices of others never claims to be selfish himself.

Since you own yourself, naturally you need and ought to benefit and learn from the actions you take and the choices you make. To sacrifice your own interests for the sake of other people's interests (or vice versa) would be to act in contradiction to your nature. You need to care for yourself before you can care for others, after all. We must be individuals first and (willing) helpers of other individuals second, if we so choose. Thus, we should pay no attention to the intellectuals of all creeds and adornment today who tell us that helping others requires sacrificing our rational self-interest. Nothing is nobler than, or preferable to, living according to your own values, based on your own judgment.

Living a consistently self-interested ethics doesn't mean being irrationally selfish, that is, being callous or harmful to others, or to yourself for that matter. You ought to embrace your needs and desires to be with and enjoy others and bestow good things on them, as well as your need to be your own best friend. Only if you value yourself and others honestly, according to your enlightened and objective self-interest, will you rid yourself of making sacrifices and the ensuing resentment.

Everything generally boils down to the economics of your own life and desires based on your values, that is, what you have time and energy for, and what you perceive as serving your own life and well-being—in other words, what gives you the most enjoyment, satisfaction, challenge, or comfort. Contrary to statist dogma, a free market, which naturally coincides with our rational self-interest, greatly fosters helping others. Common business activities such as creating jobs, developing and offering products and services that people want, or simply doing volunteer work or making charitable contributions (which depend on wealth and resources created by capitalism's massive productivity effects), all entail mutual benefit, be it monetary or psychological. Even miserly persons who keep their money under their beds help the economy far more than the State; misers take money out of circulation, instead of inflating, devaluing, and regulating it.

Remember that we have two main choices in dealing with others, and one of them ain't very nice. We can realize that nothing will get accomplished without creating values in our lives and in the marketplace, and that values can only be properly created through ownership. Or, we can attempt to prevent people from creating values and sidetrack whole societies in the direction of stagnation and destroyed opportunity.

Our planet is one of relative abundance, an abundance that depends not only on our technological know-how, but also on the ethics human society lives by, or suffers and dies by, as the case may be. Given the economic laws that operate no matter what we decide, it's painfully obvious that those who choose wrongly aren't very concerned with human health, happiness, and thriving. Rather, they embrace a moral code that sets humanity against its own nature—in order to impose their particular version of "the good" on the rest of us. Of course, the institution of the State enables them to defy the ideas of privatizing everything and honoring owners' freedom to create and exchange values with others.

Perhaps some are troubled by others doing things as they see fit in society. After all, their choices may run counter to the majority or to those who seek to control them. They may threaten the goals of power-seekers everywhere who want others to do things *their way*.

Some even contend that if the free market were actually allowed to be free, then the rich would get richer and the poor would get poorer, and those with the most wealth would have the most power to rule over others with ruthless cruelty. How remarkable! This ridiculous depiction of unfettered capitalism actually resembles that of any third-world dictatorship, which is the furthest from unfettered. Not surprisingly, the commonly proposed solution to this alleged scenario (tyranny by the rich and powerful) is brimming with irony: Grant coercive power to an organization that doesn't depend on profits, but instead expropriates wealth from the willing and the unwilling alike and prohibits and permits things as *it* sees fit, that is, arbitrarily.

There's no other way of respectfully dealing with fellow human beings than by respecting their reasoning nature. Many in our society seem to think that force is preferable to persuasion, that if *they* were in charge, they would make the world a better place. What they've failed to realize is that their plans for a better world were doomed from the beginning, on account of using an incorrect means to achieve a better world. To reiterate, the end doesn't justify the means when the means run counter to individual rights and the principle of self-ownership and by extension private property.

To initiate force against innocent persons who've not done as one wants is to reject any sort of consistent form of morality. No matter how much we may wish it weren't so, we can always disagree with each other. Each of us must be able to make our own choices. No one outside your own experiences is better equipped to make informed decisions for you. Moreover, for others to intervene in such an affair is to contradict human functioning—choosing to prohibit choice.

One big difference between a central planning statist and the individual decision maker, aside from their codes of morality, is the vast gulf between their respective levels of available, local knowledge. The statist planner/regulator in any guise (town, city, county, state, or D.C.) only has guesses about how individuals would make choices in the marketplace. Most of the time we can't even guess what sort of choices our friends are going to make. So, there's less than a snowball's chance on

Mercury that central planning bureaucrats or policy wonks can make optimal decisions for each and every person in the particular way that each person knows best.

This is reflected in the joke about two Communist planners. They were scheming about how to effectively control aspects of industry and trade and allocate labor and resources accordingly. In the course of their conversation about how to implement this special form of insanity across the globe, one said, "But of course, we'll have to leave one country alone, let it remain capitalist." "Why in the world would we want to do that?" asked the other. "Because we must have a way to determine what our prices are going to be!"

Again, prices are set by the interaction of buyers and sellers in the marketplace. The law of supply and demand is something that can't be messed with—not with impunity. The invisible hand of the market, as Adam Smith outlined a few centuries ago, is a hand that needs no master. This is because, on the grand and complex scale of entire economies filled with extensive divisions of labor, intricate specializations, and innumerable consumer interests and preferences, *no* substitute exists for personal decision making. No one can think and act for you, either as a producer or as a consumer—unless you prescribe specific courses of action through consensual contract. Even such a contract with agents who act on your behalf requires you to make individual choices based on your personal context that no one else can properly ascertain.

Living in the marketplace as autonomous decision makers, no matter how extensive or intimate our social networks may be, is the only way we can and will become fully responsible and independent adults. As creatures of reason, being responsible and independent—psychologically, intellectually, and financially—are very healthy things. Actually, they're indispensable. To live otherwise is akin to a bird trying to fly without extending its wings.

Let's now look at the general organization of laws in America that attempt to deny us the responsibility and independence of adulthood. Where do you suppose they're leading us? Well, it's definitely not into the same valley as the land of milk and honey. More like Mordor with its assortment of Ringwraiths.

IV

THE IMMORALITY OF POLITICS

I was watching a panel discussion on C-SPAN awhile ago, in which a person declared that the Democracy movement needs to join forces with the anti-corporate, anti-capitalist, and anti-globalization movements. If that isn't a loaded proposition, I don't know what is.

First of all, we've already considered what Democracy is, be it representative or popular. Those in the citizenry who think that they can get government to perform their particular version of aggression on the rest of society ought to consider what that means morally. Basically, it entails using force rather than persuasion, force that's funded by further force, reflecting the preposterous claim that a popular majority or plurality can influence politicians to do something good via immoral means. Such a process is not rational, moral, or just.

Naturally, many Americans are frustrated with governmental intrusiveness, waste, corruption, and ineptitude. Rarely do most people wholeheartedly endorse the particular policy direction of government during any given election term. Yet, few ever challenge the immoral means of government. Instead, like the person on C-SPAN, they challenge the right of people to be productive and freely trade, that is, capitalism and globalization. They'd rather use the tools of government to structure commerce as *they* see fit, not as the actual participants in trade see fit.

Close inspection reveals that the various Democracy movements, which advocate "taking back" their governments, are simply dissatisfied people wanting to impose their values on the rest of society (and the world). Seldom do they speak of liberty in the rational sense of being individually free in the marketplace to make your own choices with your own property. Instead, they speak of corporate greed and corporate injustices, and then they run to the State in search of remedies.

Corporations: The Semi-Good, The Bad, And The Ugly

Let's delve into the nature of corporations a bit, starting with their semi-good aspects. True to form, the current anti-corporate ideology reflexively makes Wal-Mart one of its main targets. Some think that the largest retailer in the world is too big and should be restrained through more regulations; there was actually a show on CNBC in 2005 about this. Wal-Mart is the largest retailer primarily because people who seek affordable goods favor its particular assortment of products and prices. Otherwise, it would be just another Kmart. Basically, people working at Wal-Mart engage in voluntary trade with their customers, trading value for value.

But what about, for instance, Wal-Mart's "exploitation" of cheap labor in China, or the advantages it obtains from the lack of workers' rights and pollution regulations there? This question obviously over-looks the pervasive state of poverty in rural China, which tends to make working in a factory in the city more appealing. Most people on the other side of the planet don't like being dirt poor and living hand to mouth either.

Of course the Chinese government remains guilty as charged. It's tyrannical system keeps hundreds of millions of Chinese impoverished. And some of its rights-violations and aggressions against free speech, free press, and property in general are on a par with the worst totalitarian regimes throughout history. However, this isn't exactly Wal-Mart's fault or responsibility.

Wal-Mart's executives simply use the economic disequilibriums that currently exist throughout the world to their advantage. Chinese labor and manufacturing costs are much lower than in the U.S. If Wal-Mart didn't capitalize on this situation, its competition surely would continue to. Further, the more capital investment in manufacturers that Wal-Mart extends overseas, the faster those companies can become part of the developed world. Over time, costs should seek equilibrium. More economic wealth tends to enable more freedom, and vice versa. Eventually, more efficient and effective technologies for dealing with waste and pollution in China will arise. The Chinese State may or may not hinder their implementation.

Regarding Wal-Mart contributing to "trade imbalances" and "outsourcing," those who believe that they should keep their particular jobs despite market pressures and market changes will be perpetually dissatisfied. Their calls for all sorts of regulations, as well as union pressures for Wal-Mart to alter its employee relations, seek to make Wal-Mart less productive, less competitive, less satisfying, and more costly to its customers. Regulations interfere with more productive business methods, essentially market processes that seek higher and higher levels of productivity. From a moral standpoint, of course, regulations also violate individual rights and property rights. We also need to keep in mind that the money people save by shopping at Wal-Mart is used in all sorts of other ways that benefit individuals, the economy, as well as other industries.

But that's mostly the economic side of the business of international trade, not of the corporate structure itself. As usual, the political side is much less savory. If only the anti-corporationists, anti-capitalists, and anti-globalizationists would make this necessary distinction. Perhaps the most difficult thing for all of us who grew up in statist economies to recognize is the difference between a free market and an unfree one. A free market, that is, capitalism, is thought to exist presently, and it's typically blamed for all sorts of economic troubles. Much of statist indoctrination, so-called public education, consists of informing students about the market's various failures and how government's job is to step in and fix things or make things right.

Similar to the time of Marx and Engels, business and trade aren't taking place in a free market world. Unfettered capitalism is so far from present that proponents of today's marketplace often do more harm than good to the cause of liberty. Businesses everywhere are tangled in a seemingly unending web of governmental interventions.

However, corporations more resemble the web-spinners' *helpers* than their hapless victims. The corporate structure is actually a "legal fiction" created by laws and molded by successively more ridiculous court rulings, and then maintained by governmental officials and their cronies on Wall Street and elsewhere. Corporations exist legally for various purposes that have changed since their inception. Originally, they were granted by state governments to do "good works" for the "general welfare" of the state (definitely a deal with the devil). Big companies become corporations today typically to lower overall business owners' liability and acquire more capital at lower risk and cheaper rates of interest.

Corporations are treated as individuals in and of themselves ("corporate personhood") with rights granted to them by government, and with an existence apart from the original private company's owners. Most of today's major corporations have quite intimate relationships with law makers and regulators. Thus, they've become extensions of the statist system, which enables them to use governmental force to gain competitive advantages over others in the marketplace, or to simply shut out competition entirely (as is the case with various local utility monopolies).

So-called free trade agreements between rulers of States reflect the major influences of multinational and transnational corporations. Many corporations tend to be notorious for shirking responsibility and externalizing various costs to governments, which of course externalize those costs to the people. Corporations also foster separation of ownership from management (and ownership from labor), which doesn't bode well for personal and professional accountability either. Corporate ownership by still other corporations as well as stock ownership by mutual funds and pension funds, that is, by investment corporations, are also invariably State-facilitated arrangements. Such is the bad and the ugly of corporations.

Of course, limited liability is especially appealing in today's corrupt and unjust justice system. Yet few businesspersons realize that to submit to the State through the corporate structure is to slap Lady Liberty in the face. Even though various liability/insurance policies can be set up by businesses, these should not make investors immune from, for example, the consequences of bad debt or defaults, or irresponsible and immoral management. The best check on these consequences resides in heeding the inherent free market risks in doing business and making investment decisions.

Moreover, can you think of a good reason (other than financial, of course—and there's the political rub) for a competitive company to formulate such cumbersome things as articles of incorporation, bylaws, and a board of directors, as well as ridiculously burdensome accounting procedures? These are essentially governmental hoops to jump through in order to attain a specific tax and regulatory status. Anyone with good business sense understands that these devices can severely misdirect one's energy and hinder managerial decisions. They can also give investors a false sense of security, encouraging them to think that government has designed it so that they'll be protected. But regulations are no substitute for freedom to make good and bad decisions.

When the two founders of Google went public, for instance, they realized that this issue of choice would become compromised. Essentially, they wouldn't be able to make quick, rational decisions on the fly anymore. They were going to become constrained by a committee of board members and their shareholders, and thus less streamlined and less flexible from a managerial standpoint. Contrary to corporate dogma, a managerial standpoint is one of the main considerations for business viability and, thus, satisfied customers; it's not to maximize shareholder wealth.

We must acknowledge the fact that the State has basically won when businesses use statist mechanisms to do business. Fascism and corporate welfare then become effectively entrenched, and business is done by permission and assistance from bureaucrats, both political and corporate.

In a just legal system, this unprincipled, pragmatic behavior would definitely fade away, and reputation and responsibility would be greatly revitalized. Currency that's grounded in, for example, the gold standard, would be readily available at market rates, determined by buyers and sellers at market-created and market-regulated—meaning consumer-regulated—financial institutions.

Certainly, agencies such as the Securities and Exchange Commission and the Federal Trade Commission represent the giant elephants in the room in today's securities and investment banking markets. Until these beasts are slain, along with the other beasts in the room—the U.S. Treasury, Federal Reserve System, and all its assorted financial and legal instruments—we can only speculate how financial and big business markets would shape up. Currently, they are a cesspool of corruption and a labyrinth of legal complexities, devised by politicians, regulatory officials, securities lawyers, and their accomplices on Wall Street, essentially financial enterprises in the business of lobbying for governmental policies and regulations in their favor—in order to become even more *filthy* rich.

The general legal framework involving our print-on-State-demand fiat currency fosters, among other sordid things, an over-extension of credit and accumulation of debt. The average CEO's multi-million dollar salary and stock options ought to make one follow the money trail in these matters. Additionally, the various exchange rates for American and foreign fiat currencies reflect what happens to monies controlled by governments.

This takes us back to the Wal-Mart phenomenon, arguably the largest business on the planet. Perhaps a major factor in people shopping at Wal-Mart for the lowest possible prices is the nature of the present economy. Big box stores in general have thrived as people have found it more cost effective to be "prosumers," or do-it-yourselfers, rather than paying for professional services or for better customer service and higher quality products, which smaller businesses might offer.

Standard of living and real wages haven't really increased over the last few decades, when you crunch the numbers in a fair way, and personal debt (both credit card and mortgage) has ballooned into the many trillions of dollars; a negative savings rate accompanies this unfortunate situation. So, a couple significant things are probably helping to keep the American economy from overtly tanking: advances in computer and information technologies and Wal-Mart's enormous economies of scale, which depend heavily on the former; their finely tuned computerized inventory and cost management systems are case studies in efficiency.

Maybe in the truly free and much more prosperous economy of the future, more consumers would shift their focus away from price as the primary factor in their buying decisions, to other aspects such as impeccable quality or a sublime shopping experience. Or, more consumers may base their purchasing decisions on the reputations of each manufacturer's employee or supplier relations (and relations with other States). However, successful companies such as Wal-Mart, absent their corporate structure, might likely respond to these shifts in consumer preferences. The free market always encourages businesses to become as efficient as possible, which entails implementing the technologies to do so.

Well, that's the mixed bag of corporations. Rather than clamor for more regulations on them (in the name of social responsibility, community interests, and environmentalism) activists should seek the discontinuance of State-created corporate structures entirely. Those who malign corporations must first challenge the institution of the State and its practices that have spawned them. After all, we can always decide *not* to do business with various corporations, and they won't come to our doors demanding unearned money. The same can't be said of the State.

Let's explore the nature of regulation further. Although, at this point, you might want to put on some rubber gloves and firmly affix a gas mask.

The Sand And Molasses Of Statism: Regulation And Preventive Law

Ah, the alphabet soup of regulatory agencies: The IRS, FDA, EPA, USDA, DEA, FBI, DHS, NSA, CIA, FBATF, ICE, SEC, FTC, OSHA, TSA, NHTSA, DOT, FEMA, etc.—ad naseum. If only we could keep them stored in a glass jar somewhere, as a showcase of not-so-well-intentioned iniquity. Then again, maybe such a jar just belongs in the trash can.

A simple Web search for statist regulatory bodies will reveal the entire list of ingredients in the alphabet soup. It's a concoction potent enough to make your eyes water and head ache, filled with countless departments, committees, boards, commissions, bureaus, services, administrations, authorities, corporations, institutes, offices, and agencies. Sorry, no Ginsu knife set is offered with this mess of goods. But wait, there is indeed more, because this is only a quick mention of what's on the federal level. We shouldn't forget the state, county, city, and town organizations in all their busybody forms and fashions, intent on meddling in all aspects of commerce and trade—from whom and where we can buy a gallon of milk, to how much money gets taken from us in taxes with each gallon of "boutique" blend of gasoline we pump, to what sort of media content we can see (endless murders and violence on TV, fine; naked people, typically a no-no unless they're being murdered, of course). Trillions of dollars are spent performing these "services" for the public. The various governments of the United States devour probably half of the many trillions of dollars circulating in the American economy. And since our medium of exchange is printed by the State, it thereby demonstrates that it can do more than just regulate our monetary system. It can fully communize it!

Ronald Reagan famously noted how government views the economy: "If it moves, tax it. If it keeps moving, regulate it. And if it stops moving, subsidize it." Perhaps those in government are most aware of its methods of operation. President Reagan definitely had first-hand knowledge.

Regulation attempts to replace the judgment of property owners and free market processes with the judgment of bureaucrats. Not only is this like pouring sand and molasses into the gears of a finely tuned machine. It also leads to the creation of machines that are less efficient, less functional, nonfunctional, or that produce the opposite of what one wants—Rube Goldberg contraptions gone haywire. Many great machines never even get made, which is the end of the road of the destruction of capital by government.

Preventive law is the mainstay of regulatory bodies. After all, who could regulate if there were no laws to generate all that sand and molasses (as well as the regulatory bodies themselves)? Preventive law, that is, enacted legislation that seeks to prohibit or direct behavior of individuals in the marketplace before they do anything "wrong," equates to deeming people perpetually guilty. "Guilty" under such a legal system has virtually nothing to do with injuring others or infringing on their rights.

Thinking of installing some plumbing or electrical work in your new home? You're supposed to study the laws (building codes) first, and don't forget the inspectors. Thinking of hiring a couple new workers for a project? You're supposed to check into what the Equal Employment Opportunity Commission and the U.S. Citizenship and Immigration

Services (and various others) have to say about that. Thinking of selling a new product or service? You're supposed to investigate how many governmental agencies are in charge of that particular line of work, and the reams of forms to fill out, rules to abide by, and fees to pay. Thinking of purchasing a weapon for extra security? Well, with any luck, you'll be able get out of *that* tangle of red tape alive.

Of course, once you inspect the laws in any particular area of your life, you quickly realize that you're only looking at the foot of the legal monster that looms above you. So here's the bottom line: If you're thinking of doing something—anything rights-respecting—maybe it's best *not* to see how many laws you're going to break, lest your plans are foiled.

Unless you stay in bed all day, you're likely to violate some regulation on some level during your routine activities. Essentially, under a regulatory system, aka the nanny State (no offense to real nannies), people aren't allowed to make independent decisions. They're instead given governmental mandates with penalties for disobedience. This is the nature of regulatory control, and it's supposedly for the common good, once again. Hence, rather than administer justice for particular right-violations, which is the sole purpose of a legal system, regulation focuses on preventing certain courses of action that law makers and bureaucrats have declared unacceptable. Law makers and bureaucrats then rely on law enforcers to do the dirty work of aggression for them.

If those in government strictly focused on the issue of justice instead of trying to control people's lives, they'd face a considerable downsizing of their workforce. Certainly those in a regulatory system wouldn't want to design it to create more efficiency and higher productivity—to ease up on the influx of sand and molasses. Obviously, only those in the marketplace who rely on profits and customer satisfaction have such goals in mind.

Preventive law is an inversion of the concept of justice, because it creates myriad crimes out of nowhere, crimes that violate no one's rights or property. This stands to reason, because government is an entity that pretends to operate outside the bounds of property rights (it being "public property"); naturally, all its regulatory edicts reflect its lack of jurisdiction in the realm of other people's property.

Ultimately, regulation thrives in a society that either agrees with its contradictory premise that some adults must treat all other adults as non-adults, or that fears too much the consequences of non-compliance, which ultimately entails rejecting one's status as an autonomous, self-owned adult.

The key question then is this: By what right, by what code, by what standard (to reiterate an Ayn Rand character's words) do these organizations of people believe that what they're doing is just and proper? One of their answers might be "By the consent of the governed." Fortunately for the governors, most of the governed are too busy working and playing to really care about the immense rights-violations being perpetrated on their persons and property. It seems easier to conform.

As mentioned earlier, one could argue that the laws and regulations in a country are basically reflections of the ethics of the general populace. If the general populace believes that being dishonest or unreasonable is helpful in order to run a business, for example, then that belief will be reflected in how regulatory agencies operate (guilty until you prove your innocence). Even the apathy that people show towards governmental corruption reflects their view of the virtue of integrity, at least on the political level, the level where most people remain resigned in the belief that nothing can be done.

I'm not going to bore us by citing more of the sordid and voluminous details of the Washington racket and our closer-to-home rackets. Many astute libertarian and even conservative thinkers have covered that ground like a herd of angry buffalo. Not even the most virulent weed could survive such a thorough trampling. Yet, those in Washington and those who support them in the several states act as if they're immune to such intellectual stampedes. They proceed onward, routinely smug in the thought that they're doing the public's duty—and that people are following their orders.

Well, all really bad things must come to an end sometime, especially if they've been created by humans. No better time than the present, as far as we're concerned.

Basically, the State's regulatory programs manifest a huge contradiction operating in our society—that people don't have full right to use and/or dispose of their property as they see fit; instead politicians, bureaucrats, judges, police and others in institutions of "authority" are to intervene in some form or fashion in virtually every human exchange and interaction. Supposedly, we should be comforted or at least kept from rebelling by being told that this is for our own good, or that we can't comprehend the valuable reasons for such interference. Death and taxes...right.

Moreover, governmental regulations act as smoke screens between companies and market assessments of their credibility. Because most people assume the nanny State is watching out for their interests, they fail to put company claims about products and services to the accountability test. Naturally, in a truly free market some organizations would be keen on providing such tests in an independent fashion, much like Consumer Reports and Underwriters Laboratories attempt to do today.

Without regulations, companies would have to take full responsibility for their trades; regulatory agencies couldn't interfere with their thorough evaluation by the marketplace. Further, without the great leveling effect that regulations have on competition in the marketplace, in which every business is supposed to conform to the same rules, consumers would find many more choices regarding who they do business with. Stagnant companies that favor the status quo because of their governmentally regulated market positions would have to change, or lose customers.

Yet, we are told that the market sometimes fails, that the market is inadequate for addressing true human needs, and that some market processes are distasteful, corrupt, bad, or wrong. Again, people are "selfish and greedy."

For Whom The Market Fails

For whom does the market fail? That's the question overlooked in these various false accusations. Who exactly *is* the victim in *voluntary* exchanges of goods and services between and among volitional beings? Clearly not the individual decision makers in the marketplace, who obtain what they want and pay for it. Since society is composed of countless such individual interactions, it certainly can't be society that's harmed. And since the alternative to voluntary exchange is forcible exchange, and forcible exchange violates rights and therefore choices, it can't possibly be a better way to "get things done" in society. Again, to accomplish things by coercing or destroying the very entity capable of making rational choices—a human being—is to contradict the human method of functioning, in favor of something witnessed on The Animal Channel during predator-and-prey night. In the realm of rights and ethics, there's simply no room for such glaring inconsistencies. Self-ownership and its moral implications for property aren't open for debate.

But the institutions of government, being one massive coercive redistribution scheme, dare not pursue this line of logic. That would be equivalent to saying that each individual is sovereign, would it not?

Only one correct answer exists to the question of who is harmed by the market: those who want to impose their wills on others. If one's method of operation is to force others to do things, then banning that method is definitely going to cramp one's style. Town, city, county, state, and D.C. officials rely on regulatory opportunities to take from taxpayers through bloated salaries, pensions and welfare benefits, cronyism, private kickbacks, etc. Regulation can also satisfy various power and control cravings or even lessen feelings of occupational unimportance, by constantly monitoring other people's occupations.

Does anyone seriously believe that unjust power doesn't tend to corrupt even the most well-intentioned and honest individuals? If the money you're spending doesn't come from your own bank account or even your company's bank account, what incentive will you have to monitor the balance? Further, if you can print and loan yourself funny money and adjust its rates of interest (essentially, it's time value) why care about financial responsibility?

Consider this: If the market were allowed to be free, that is, if individual choices and property were fully respected, then there would be no need for public policies, politicians, elections, bureaucrats, lobbyists, ridiculous rules and regulations, and, for that matter, 90% of the news! Obviously then, the unrefined sensibilities of those who would otherwise wield coercive power would be harmed; their "well-meaning" desires to control others would be thwarted; and, their supposedly grand plans for society would be nixed. They wouldn't have the option to run the unjust organizations of the State anymore. Further, all the intellectuals who spend most of their waking hours analyzing, theorizing, recommending, and justifying "better" governmental policies or maintaining the status quo would be left up a specific creek without any paddles.

If only they realized that something new and brilliant awaits everyone who chooses to be productive and live by their own efforts or, under certain circumstances, by the charitable efforts of others who are free to offer help (rather than forced to offer unaccountable, indirect help through taxation). The marketplace welcomes those who take responsibility for their actions and function as independent beings—as adults—able to make good decisions for themselves. Again, a free market provides things in *abundance* for anyone who accepts the trader principle.

It's no surprise that the wealthiest economies in the world are also the freest economies, or at least they're still running on capital accumulated from past economic freedoms, such as our US of A. The poorest people in the richest countries are better off and have many more opportunities than those in less free countries. A truly free market will offer the poor and the not-so-poor a standard of living that they can only yearn for now, as well as enable them to migrate more easily to ever higher levels of income. In contrast, the more controlled an economy is, the more difficult it is to move up the income ladder.

Imagine A Free World

We really can't overestimate how much regulations negatively affect our lives, liberty, property, and pursuit of happiness. In this day and age of computer gadgets and every (presently) conceivable technological gizmo within reach of individuals with even modest incomes, you might think it's possible to exaggerate this point.

But my point is not that we can't afford many of today's conveniences. Most people can afford an assortment of devices for connectivity, productivity, and entertainment. Instead, my point is that we could afford *so much more* if we had a non-regulated economy and monetary system that was basically immune to inflation, devaluation, and eco-nomic recessions and depressions (the so-called business cycle). In other words, by now, our current state of knowledge and technological capabilities would be *far* more advanced, perhaps similar to living a few hundred years in the future! Today, for instance, many tech savvy persons desire better Internet access and Web capabilities. While ubiquitous WiFi with more bandwidth and convenient interfaces would definitely be great in so many ways, why settle for less?

Imagine quick remedies for the injuries and diseases that currently ruin people's lives. Imagine perfect health for you and your loved ones, defying the typical aging process at the cellular level. Imagine everyone being rich (clean rich, not filthy rich) and able to afford, for instance, without incurring any debt, spacious, custom-designed, energy-efficient, self-cleaning homes. Imagine gourmet meals in the time it takes to press a few buttons, or utter a few voice commands. Imagine the time you'd save to spend on whatever really fun and challenging things that you probably have on "the back burner."

Imagine faster, safer, more affordable and convenient travel to most places on our planet. Imagine an altered landscape of transportation with nonpolluting engines. Imagine no more traffic jams. Imagine flying cars. Imagine luxury vacations in Earth's orbit or sightseeing on Mars, for instance, a trip to the top of the Mt. Everest-dwarfing Olympus Mons or to the abyss-like edges of Valles Marineris. Imagine a week-long astronomy class on the dark side of the moon. Imagine spectacular and thriving cities of new commerce and entertainment on (and in) the oceans.

Imagine human-simulated computer mentors that could answer nearly any question posed by learners of all ages. Imagine personalized computer "therapists" that could appropriately sense your moods and help you gently relieve stress, or amplify your happiness, through a variety of ingenious methods. Imagine being able to be immediately connected to anyone who shares similar experiences, desires, interests, talents, or goals. Imagine a much more informed, interested, harmonious, and happy society (the kind central planners can only dream of —or rather, have nightmares about). Imagine the synergistic effects of these and many other wonderful progressions and innovations. I'm sure you have your own variety of great things to add to this list. Regardless of whether or not they're presently achievable, many brilliant advances will certainly be achievable in our lifetime, once we generate a society of complete liberty.

And even despite political changes for the better, such technological advances may be somewhat inevitable, given the human discovery process. According to proponents of extropianism and transhumanism (future and human potential philosophies), which include artificial intelligence researchers and optimistic theorists such as Ray Kurzweil, this century will actually be the one in which humanity moves past its prior scientific obstacles and engineering difficulties. Kurzweil's vast, future-oriented technology website covering all aspects of this argument is www.kurzweilai.net. He and many other futurists assert that a "technological singularly" will occur once computers surpass the computational abilities of our own brains, a point in time beyond which it's anybody's guess as to what amazing innovations will arise.

In relation to these fascinating ideas, John Smart, who's incidentally a friend of mine in southern California, has developed the Acceleration Studies Foundation (ASF), an organization dedicated to analyzing such predictions and various future-related trends, so as to help people better understand and potentially benefit from them. www.accelerating.org and www.accelerationwatch.com are Smart's websites, which contain a wealth of information. The members of ASF realize that people who are keen about what's possible in their lives tend to alter the economic and social landscape for the better. Such people enthusiastically and responsibly embrace each new beneficial human achievement. In other words, they're prepared for the future, and they're happy about change.

By the end of this century we just might have radically new energy devices, thousand year lifespans, and virtual reality machines that simulate anything convincingly. These, of course, would be in spite of the government's regulatory system, not because of it. Moreover, to think about all the persons who are currently suffering and dying—as a direct or indirect result of our politically created conditions—makes this insight even more poignant. We simply don't have centuries or even decades to deal with the extremely important political problems that face us.

Technology basically empowers you to pursue a better, healthier, more productive, and more fun life. Regulation retards this empowerment. Retardation is the name of the government's game, coupled with destruction of possibilities and thwarting of individual choices. The various dystopian worlds we tend to see in science fiction movies are usually the result of some combination of futuristic technologies and modern day regulatory thuggery. This is obviously a very bad mixture. To leave power in the hands of those who are unaccountable is to invite an Orwellian police State into our lives. A nanny State is deplorable in itself, but a police State with advanced technologies to monitor and control Americans is absolutely intolerable, especially for those who understand individual rights and seek a better future for everyone.

Effects Of Government On Producers And Consumers

As a result of fearing the worst about government's potential dissolution, some might feel inclined to run to its rescue. Some are quick to overlook the unavoidable political contradictions of statism by listing all the services that government offers its "customers." Okay, so let's examine the idea of customers a bit more. We should first reflect on the fact that whatever the government does that's considered useful, the market can do it better, at a fraction of the cost. With government, there's no profit motive; consequently, there's no proper allocation of resources and management of costs.

Whether or not we're consumers of governmental services, the control of our property through taxation and regulation hurts each and every consumer of any product or service. It also hurts the homeless, because they typically live on the no-man's land of public property, which is entangled by a welfare bureaucracy that encourages self-disempowerment and dependency. Consumers represent all who participate in a market economy, spanning all levels of income.

Certainly, producers are the prime movers of any civilization. Inventors, designers, researchers, engineers, entrepreneurs, industrialists, as well as all those who directly and indirectly assist them, contribute to enormous increases in productivity and innovation, regardless of a civilization's stage of development. They create an economy whereby more work can be done more quickly with less labor and resources and capital investment, thereby creating more money for reinvestment and thus more capital for creating still other goods and services. Capitalism, after all, is the economic system of free trade that generates more and better items for the production process—more capital that facilitates more products and services in the market. A great deal of time is saved in this process, time that can then be spent on many other activities.

Advances in productivity are really something to behold. A glance at our world's population statistics and mortality rates over the last few centuries reveals the power of capitalism—or rather, semi-capitalism. As we've noted, we also see the effects of a free market most readily in the technology sectors, particularly computers and information systems, as well as the biotech fields that make use of them. The Internet and all the industries involving information technology contribute to massive productivity effects. One might even contend that they provide a counteracting buoyancy to the giant lead weight of government around our economy's neck; without them, we might not be able to keep our heads above the waters of economic ruin.

Each producer, from a graphic designer to a peanut farmer, is also a consumer. Aside from basic economic laws such as supply and demand, the prices and available variety of what we can consume are determined by two things in our present society: what government has done to our money, and what government has done to impede, redirect, or stop the flow of information, goods, and services in the marketplace.

The State can only be a negative on the economy—which means that it can only be a negative on our individual lives. It doesn't matter if we're picking produce in southern California or composing a symphony in Michigan. The potential for profit, saving, and investment is greatly diminished in an economy that's prevented or diverted from what it would otherwise do—*freely trade*.

But many still don't believe this. Given that the vast majority of us attended State-run schools, it's not very surprising. Some act as if there were a viable alternative to private property and voluntary exchange, as if there were some middle-of-the-road approach that doesn't cause us too much trouble. Invariably, they want to be able to use the State's tools of force—which, again, translate into guns pointed at resistant people and jail for the nonconformists at some point—in order to create their version of a so-called fair and level playing field. Those who want to impose economic "fairness" through politics usually don't care how they achieve it or what this idea really means. It certainly doesn't mean using rational tools of persuasion and example.

Schemes Of Villainy

Some people don't see the benefit of trading in a free and voluntary market. Probably while the ink was still drying on the final draft of the Constitution, unscrupulous individuals brought their particular "interests" to government to gain advantages. Here's an apt quote by the eloquent 19th century legal scholar Lysander Spooner, writing to then President Grover Cleveland (the 22nd and 24th president). It should give us an idea of how far we *haven't* progressed politically:

> [Competing interests]...will be "persistently" clamoring for laws to be made in their favor; that, in fact, "the halls of national legislation" are to be mere arenas, into which the government actually invites the advocates and representatives of all the selfish schemes of avarice and ambition that unprincipled men can devise; that these schemes will there be free to "compete" with each other in their corrupt offers for government favor and support; and that it is to be the proper and ordinary business of the lawmakers to listen to all these schemes; to adopt some of them, and sustain them with all the money and power of the government; and to "postpone," "abandon," oppose, and defeat all others; it being well known, all the while, that the lawmakers will, individually, favor, or oppose, these various schemes, according to their own irresponsible will, pleasure, and discretion,— that is, according as they can better serve their own personal interests and ambitions by doing the one or the other.
>
> Was a more thorough scheme of national villainy ever invented?
>
> Sir, do you not know that in this conflict, between these "various, diverse, and competing interests," all ideas of individ-

ual "rights"—all ideas of "equal and exact justice to all men"—will be cast to the winds; that the boldest, the strongest, the most fraudulent, the most rapacious, and the most corrupt, men will have control of the government, and make it a mere instrument for plundering the great body of the people?

A better way of describing the situation can't be found. Spooner was a fierce opponent of injustice, and there was plenty of it in America throughout the 1800's. In many respects it's gotten much, much worse.

Between the years 2000 and 2005, the number of registered lobbyists in D.C. doubled, to over thirty-four thousand. Have you ever heard of K Street? It's the place where lobbyists (many formerly "connected" bureaucrats and politicians) hang out to feed at the State's trough and peddle their influence.

The billions spent on lobbying and the money that politicians pocket is disturbing to say the least. Most contend it's the cost of doing business with the State. As the well-worn phrase notes, politics is definitely war by other means. The absolute power granted to the institutions of government through taxation and monopolization becomes alluring to those who dispense with free market principles and decide to make immoral deals instead. Politics in midstream becomes a way of life.

The greatest disaster is the effect all this has on capitalism's producers and consumers. Many businesses and groups lobby to pass legislation in their favor, to grant subsidies, or to prevent competition. Big businesses, especially corporations, have a long track record on this account. Very few have ever lobbied for more competition, that is, a freer marketplace. Once again we would be wise to follow the corrupt money trails here. Usually, the well-established corporations seek to maximize their market share by way of all-expense-paid vacations and other perks for bureaucrats and legislators, as well as specially devised last minute insertions of pork—rather than through voluntary association with potential customers. After all, if government is the biggest bully on the block, and it makes all the rules, then you either join it by buying it, or beat it by defying it.

Few ever entertain the latter possibility, of taking a moral stance on behalf of reason, liberty, and the ideas of self-ownership, personal sovereignty, and property rights. Even the companies who solely lobby to remain competitive, for example, by getting their tax burdens and regulations reduced, soon find themselves in a sick world of compromise, corruption, lying, and pleading—as if they never had a right to exist for their own sake.

To make money is definitely not worth the sale of one's soul; a lucrative deal is not worth the forfeiture of one's mind and moral life. Imagine if those in business (and business schools) decided not to concede the statist premise anymore. How long do you think the corrupt system would last then? Not very long. Or, what if consumers fought for their inherent right to engage in trade and commerce unimpeded by the State's instruments of force? Would this not expose the con game of various special interests that use government to regulate under the guise of promoting such things as "public safety" or "consumer protection" or "a level playing field"? It assuredly would.

This is a really old racket that goes back to the guild system (a topic of the next chapter), which excluded cheaper and better competitors' goods and services from the market. The same phenomenon can be found with the opponents of "globalization," or free international trade. Similar to those in developed countries, local producers in most developing countries organize and lobby for laws to prevent competition from entering and offering more appealing products and services at better prices. Political corruption runs rampant, and a toxic combination of a Fascist and Socialist police State perpetuates itself. This creates entrenched class or caste societies with little outside investment and choices in the marketplace. "Poverty, filth, and wretched contentment" (to borrow from Nietzsche) become the norms. Panhandlers and peddlers of all wares who live at merely subsistence levels become commonplace; entire economies stagnate in a depressing status quo.

Incidentally, this is the main reason why "The American Dream" remains unattainable for most people throughout the world, regardless of how plentiful their natural resources are. In statist guild systems, outright political and business corruption, constant bribery, strong arm police tactics, and kangaroo courts reign. Instead of going from rags to riches, nearly everyone's rags get dirtier and more torn. Rather than being able to produce, save, invest, and consume, most are relegated to barely surviving, left bowing in homage to their present day feudal lords.

So, all of us are unfortunate consumers of politics, and the vast majority of us on the planet get the really raw end of the deal. Although the rawness tends to be especially noticeable in poorer and developing countries, the developed world reinforces their bad ideas and behaviors.

Politicians love to talk about the ills of special interests, attempting to assure a dissatisfied public that they themselves aren't part of the problem. It's such an unpleasant aspect of politics that Ross Perot was really able to tap into Americans' frustration about it (as well as the debt and deficit) during his first run for the presidency. He might have actually won the 1992 election if he hadn't stepped out of the race for a few months prior to that November Tuesday. Perot based his campaign on a promise to get rid of lobbyists in "thousand-dollar suits and alligator shoes" walking the halls of Congress, as well as on a pledge to deal with the immense federal debt piling up. He wanted to run the Executive branch like a business, for he himself was a successful billionaire. Needless to say, this resonated with the American public. Heck, I even voted for the guy, back in my naive days, of course, a year before reading *Atlas Shrugged*.

Upon reflection, however, Perot's rhetoric exposed one of the biggest fallacies about government. Even if you have the most consistent political principles (and Perot certainly didn't, for instance being *for* various taxes and regulations and *against* aspects of global trade) there's a fundamental difference between the way a business works and the way government works: Businesses seek profits and rely on good reputation, whereas government forcibly takes money from its "customers" and depends on its coercive monopoly status to stay in "business." Not even the most erudite business owner can manage such an immoral organization properly.

The only proper thing to do is to devise a plan to close up the whole coercive shop and ask one's workers to find productive work—in a marketplace now yielding plentiful opportunities for creative projects as diverse as one's interests, passions, talents, skills and abilities. Only then will both producers and consumers be free to gain and keep values as they see fit, according to *their own* needs and interests.

V

ENDING AUTHORITARIANISM AND MODERN DAY GUILDS

Since all statist policies are interrelated, let's analyze their nature by dealing with three that affect us severely in one way or another: the drug war, prescription drugs and devices, and regulatory licensure in the health care industry.

Thou Shalt Not Alter Your State Of Mind, With Exceptions

The so-called War on Drugs has been an abysmal failure. It has failed to curtail the supply of and demand for illicit drugs. It's also failed miserably to respect rights, though that assuredly wasn't its goal. Each individual has a right to purchase items from others and to use those items as he or she desires, while respecting the rights of others. Any government that attempts to deny this simple fact by making certain items illegal to purchase and possess, simply drives this aspect of the free market into the black market.

Thus, the bigger the drug war becomes, the worse conditions on the black market become. People who work in the supply chain of illicit drugs, from growing or manufacturing them to delivering and selling them, have to spend time and resources eluding capture by the drug warriors and literally fighting for market share through gang-related turf battles, as well as bribing cops. Supply costs thereby increase drastically, and drugs become incredibly more expensive than they would be in a free market. The high prices in a black market for otherwise cheap substances encourage both dealers and users to do many immoral and unjust things, in order to keep doing business and keep getting their fixes. But this isn't the half of it.

By far the worst effects of the drug war are the consumption of billions of tax dollars, further corruption of police and other governmental agencies, and substantial increases in rights-violations inflicted on the entire citizenry, as well as drug suppliers and users. Many innocent people are harassed, spied on, searched, and generally disrespected—and of course their time is wasted in the process. Others less fortunate are falsely accused and arrested, falsely convicted, injured or even killed, and their property is ruined or seized. Police and DEA officers generally commit these egregious rights-violations with impunity. In the police club, where monopolized and tax-funded membership has its privileges and immunities, paid leave is considered a strong penalty for harming or killing innocent people. "To protect and serve—those in charge" is plainly their real motto.

Of course, those actually involved in the black market of illicit drugs face the brunt of the drug war; the rest of us are considered collateral damage—as are all innocents in all wars. A sizable percentage of all drug law offenders (up to a quarter or even a third, though the statistics are hard to pin down because crimes such as theft are categorized as non-violent) have committed no aggression on their fellow citizens, no physical violence or property rights infringement. Those who have aggressed against others are arrested and incarcerated primarily because of robbery for drug money, drug deals gone bad, and fights over turf.

Drug law offenders' prison sentences may also be more severe than sentences for criminals who've been convicted solely on the basis of aggression against others and their property. Around a quarter of inmates in state prisons and about half in federal prisons in America are there because of drug related offenses. That translates into many hundreds of thousands of people, or millions if you count the entire corrections system, including those on probation and parole—all stemming from prohibition laws. Disputes over the statistics don't really matter, though, because the principle of individual rights still stands: Even if *one* person's life is ruined and he or she is put in a cage for doing something in which there's no complaining party (*no victim*), then members of the justice system, particularly judges, police officers, and jailers, reveal *themselves* to be the real criminals.

As the drug war has stepped up its enforcement over the last few decades, inmate numbers have increased in concert, and so have prisons, prison guards, probation and parole officers, administrators, and corrections facilities. Many of these groups, after all, have big unions with highly motivated lobbyists.

Clearly, there are two types of people who really want to continue the drug war: people who work in law enforcement and people who sell drugs. Curious bedfellows aren't they? Both drug warriors and drug dealers make their living from drug prohibition. Meanwhile, politicians constantly mouth platitudes about keeping the streets safe for our children.

The demand for drugs obviously drives the supply; without a demand, there would be no market for suppliers. Prohibition just creates extra difficulties and costs for suppliers, and hence, higher prices for buyers and, in turn, higher profits for dealers. But the drug warriors don't care about these basic economic facts. They care about the immorality of those who sell, buy, and use certain drugs, similar to the alcohol warriors during *that* failed attempt at prohibition. Since they see such behavior as immoral, no amount of economic arguments will change their minds, especially when they're making their living via prohibition laws. Ironically, they don't see their *own* behavior as immoral and unjust, even though it involves violating people's rights in the most intense manner. Such is the nature of governmental force.

I recently heard a drug prevention advocate during a radio interview say that he didn't care how much the government spends on the drug war—it's for the good of the people! In other words, he didn't mind the previous hundreds of billions of tax dollars used, and he doesn't mind squandering billions more to fund his crusade to supposedly make the world a better place. Of course, he never said anything about contributing any of his own money. The stupidity in his viewpoint was not in wanting to make the world a better place. Rather, it was in trying to prevent people from making voluntary exchanges and ingesting certain substances; it was in wanting to initiate aggression against those he deemed immoral. This is the sort of hypocrisy that turns morality on its head.

Here's a revealing international fact: Despite Iran's Islamic government's draconian laws against anything deemed immoral, such as drugs, it's considered to have the highest per capita use of heroin. Ultimately, legislating morality, in the name of whatever religious dogma, can never achieve the desired results. Forcing harmless people to do things, or not do things, against their will is itself the primary immoral act. To deny people's use of their own judgment (hypocritically judging their judgment as faulty) only fosters more immorality.

Drug users, including users of alcohol and tobacco (and other things deemed ingestible), aren't persuaded to behave differently or to adopt new values by being disrespected, injured, killed, or thrown in cages and kept there for years. People who use drugs may or may not be addicted, and they may or may not understand what's truly required to live "the good life." But if there were no prohibition on certain substances, people would have to take full responsibility for their own choices. Whoever desired to influence their choices would have to refine their skills of persuasion.

The end of prohibition will entail the end of the black market and all its terrible repercussions. (Of course, all other black markets, such as for prostitution and gambling, ought to be ended as well, for similar economic and moral reasons.) The prices of drugs will then become vastly lower, offering little value to drug dealers as well as to their antagonists, the drug warriors. People could purchase drugs not only easily like they do today (even in prisons, which provides absolute proof that prohibition doesn't work), but also safely and inexpensively.

Even though drugs will be much cheaper and available for sale at drug stores, for instance, drug usage initially won't be much different than today's (regular usage of around five percent for marijuana and around one percent for other illicit drugs, which is considerably less than regular usage of alcohol, statistically a far more dangerous substance). Yet after ending drug prohibition, everyone's rights will be respected in this realm, and people will be free to seek treatment without fear or punishment. Over time, the percentage of users will probably decrease, on account of no more huge financial reasons to push drugs on people and no more allure of forbidden fruits—no more rebelling against authorities who seek to control people's behavior.

The more responsibility people assume for their choices, the better their choices become. Self-ownership fosters accountability for one's thoughts and actions; it discourages passing the buck. This leads us directly to the big topic of pharmaceuticals.

Thou Shalt Not Take Full Responsibility For Your Own Treatment— Authorities Will Handle That

Prescription drugs and devices are another example of that bane of a market economy known as regulation. Regulation is insidious and sometimes its consequences don't seem as noticeable as prohibition laws and their ensuing black market effects. Regulations actually create gray markets, ones in which people's choices are restricted and altered, which adversely affects prices, supply, distribution, and demand for goods and services. As a result, many consumers seek back-door, oftentimes illegal, avenues for more accessible and cheaper goods and services. You've probably heard of persons buying their prescription drugs in Mexico or Canada, or traveling to India for surgery (medical tourism) performed at a small fraction (about a tenth) of the price in the United States.

Like the drug war, those who strongly advocate regulation of prescription drugs and devices are typically those who benefit financially from it. After all, if you didn't have to go to your doctor (of any specialty) to obtain a prescription, and could just make purchases directly, it would certainly cut out the middle man. Of course the middle man, primarily a creation of lobbyists such as the American Medical Association (AMA) and the American Pharmacists Association (APhA) says that you need him, that he's for your own good, for your own safety. To further emphasize this, he leaves you no choice but to have him help you.

It's really quite incredible—full-fledged adults in a technologically advanced, information-filled civilization are told that they must be forced to do things that are beneficial for them. The racket of prescription drugs and devices is maintained under the guise of helping us, but in actuality it prevents us from making our own sensible decisions. This naturally lessens our responsibility to make appropriate choices, and it places a false kind of responsibility in the hands of State-stamped medical authorities. It soon becomes a cycle of self-fulfilling prophecy:

The authorities are in charge of pharmaceutical and medical treatment, essentially of our well-being, so we're supposed to follow their guidelines and allow the State to tell us what to do; then, we reflexively accept what the authorities tell us, relinquishing our needs for critical thinking, self-reliance, and independent judgment; it's all being taken care of by authorities, so why take responsibility?

Meanwhile, the Food and Drug Administration (FDA) makes sure that doctors can't perform or prescribe, and pharmacists can't sell, anything that hasn't been adequately tested. "Adequately tested" means many years of R&D, trial phases, and hundreds of millions of dollars spent in concert with meetings with FDA supervisors.

This is again purported to be for consumers' own good. Of course, it's difficult to convince all the millions of people who've suffered and died on account of the FDA's regulatory hindrances. This certainly gives renewed meaning to the phrase "killing you with kindness." Even though persons are needlessly suffering and dying on a daily basis because of this regulatory agency, drug and device companies continue to obey its directives. The tragic impact on those desiring immediate treatment can't be overestimated.

Such regulations also tend to deprive medical companies of their ability to take full responsibility for the quality and efficacy of their products and services. Why think independently when the Feds are micromanaging your business or feeding you with tax dollars!

Naturally, the consumer market for medicine in this political climate suffers enormously. A perversely structured third party payment system is a direct result of governmental regulation. The health care insurance industry is a fantastic case study in intrusive meddling by the State. Of course managed health care, poor hospital service, and obscene prices, along with assembly-line doctors who're frustrated by unmotivated patients and mounds of paperwork, necessarily follow. Prescription drug benefits for the elderly (among others) put the icing on the health care-welfare cake.

Drug companies, patients, doctors, health care workers, administrators, and insurers need not remain mired in this system of unrelenting unreason. They just need to identify and understand the real causes of this mess, so that their solutions don't merely compound the problems, which were themselves created by prior "solutions." Rather than calling on government to make things better, they need to advocate allowing the free market to increase competition and customer satisfaction, decrease prices, innovate quicker, simplify and streamline all realms of health care. Doing so will foster a much more fulfilling environment for patients and providers.

Thou Shalt Not Do Business Without Joining The State Guild—Licensure

This again takes us directly to the issue of guilds. One of the things typically instituted in any profession, predominantly at the state level, is a mandatory system of occupational licensure. The government makes it illegal to practice without a license, which is obtained through a state-controlled, profession-managed process. Clearly, this is the modern day version of the mercantilist guild system. Professionals seek to restrict the supply of potential competitors—and thus your choices as a consumer in this market—by becoming the equivalent of grandmasters who determine the nature of the practitioner's path from apprentice to journeyman.

Again, like any other governmental regulation, licensure is always claimed to be for the good of consumers. Fear-mongering tactics have become commonplace: "You wouldn't want to be treated by someone without a license, would you?" "At least with a licensed professional, you know whom you're dealing with." "You should find a licensed professional." And let's not forget the bureaucratic argument: "Government contracts require that we hire only licensed professionals, so we must enact licensure in our state, or else we'll have to hire licensed people from other states!"

In truth, the only proper judge of whether a service has been rendered properly is the *consumer of that particular service*. If the customer is happy, then the opinions of others, irrespective of their declared level of expertise, are hardly relevant. Even in the case of fraud that's alleged by outsiders to the transaction, justice can only be achieved by convincing the customer that he or she has been wronged and should therefore seek restitution. In other words one should use reason, not the force of preventive law. In today's market, for example, consumers of faith healing, therapeutic touch, and homeopathy no doubt pose a major persuasive challenge; oftentimes their *belief* in the effectiveness of the service is the only thing that matters to them. Then again, perhaps the ills of State-controlled medicine encourage people to seek market alternatives where they're allowed to exist, that is, where they don't seriously encroach on State-controlled medical turf.

Few consumers realize that licensure is just another political scheme that, among other very bad things, dramatically increases the costs of health care services. Because all practitioners are ordered to comply with the rules and regulations as set forth in law—which typically require many years spent in governmentally funded and accredited graduate schools, supervision at state-designated workplaces, state board exams, and various professional fees and continuing education mandates—a license to practice represents an enormous conglomeration of direct and indirect expenses. These expenses have to be recouped somehow. And guess who gets stuck with the bill? Consumers. Because licensed practitioners face no competition from non-licensed practitioners, higher prices are guaranteed to consumers by the State. I don't suppose anyone cares to say thank you.

Health care services shouldn't be immune from market forces and the need for successful business practices. Reputation for quality service is the key to good business, and this is no different in the health care industry. Licensure tends to replace professionals' reputations in the eyes of their customers with governmentally enforced stamps of approval. This obviously dilutes the power of reputation in the marketplace and lessens the responsibilities of professionals to their customers.

Simply put, you can't provide a quality service if your main focus is not on your customers' needs and their level of satisfaction (business 101). The creation of artificial, coercive barriers to entry for competition is not in line with quality service. Using special interest groups in concert with the force of government isn't good customer service, by any standard. Creating a virtual guild system that scoffs at efficiency, accountability, and affordability isn't good customer service either.

For practitioners to follow a regimented, caste-like system of professional qualifications and requirements makes a mockery of individual initiative and personal responsibility, as well as independent creativity. This, in turn, discourages many educated and motivated people from entering and practicing in particular professions—professions that they would otherwise enjoy. Consequently, supply of health care options decreases, which drives up prices. Diversity of opinion and expertise narrows, which restricts innovation and efficiency in these particular sectors of the marketplace.

Needless to say, mostly those who agree to conform and obey authorities become practitioners, which doesn't bode well for consumers either. Would you rather go under the knife of a bureaucratically controlled guildmaster, or a self-controlled, reputation-oriented, profit-driven professional? Again, the more a person relies on his or her own judgment in making decisions based on immediate information, rather than based on the collective pronouncements of a bureaucratic process, the better those decisions will be. Happy and free professionals tend to produce happy and healthy customers. Unhappy and unfree professionals tend to produce unhappy, and sometimes dead, customers.

The practice of health care, be it physical therapy, psychotherapy, nursing, dentistry, general medical practice or medical specialty (for example, neurosurgery) ought to be treated no differently than any other market industry. That is, it ought to be left alone, unfettered, free to operate based on the law of supply and demand. Unfortunately, the influential professionals within these practices, like those in many other occupations, have convinced themselves and most of the public that their coercively based system is rather good for everyone.

Such a system soon becomes the opposite of what was intended, which was to make excellent health care available and affordable for everyone. Then again, maybe that wasn't the intention. Politicians' and lobbyists' standard policy position to create a "universal health care system" represents an even more foolhardy attempt at alleged customer service. It's a move from semi-Socialism to Communism within this industry. We only need look at Canada to witness the effects of such a system, where people are now clamoring for private, free market alternatives to being put on the government's waiting lists.

Some really bad things would be guaranteed if statist health care were fully implemented in America: Government would now have an endless supply of new problems to fix without the proper tools to fix them—with more regulations and more red tape for still more bureaucrats to wrap practitioners in (mummy fashion, this time); more favors would be dished out to various conniving interests, wasting still more tax dollars; and, government would ration the ensuing health care shortage and bloated demand by having you sit in an exceedingly long line of uncomfortable chairs. Definitely no express check outs here. As political humorist P.J. O'Rourke has quipped, "If you think health care is expensive now, wait until you see what it costs when it's free." Naturally the only proper solution is to fully deregulate and privatize this market.

So, when the market of health care is freed from statist control, what will really happen? Will many charlatans take advantage of the newly unregulated and unlicensed occupations, preying on gullible and naive consumers? Will many people die from improper drug dosage and usage conflicts (all too common in hospitals today, by the way)? Will doctors not be able to make a good living because of too much competition?

Just like any other aspect of the economy that's allowed to function in accordance with the unencumbered choices of individual buyers and sellers, we will witness the opposite of people's initial fears and misguided economic concepts. Motivated entrepreneurs in medicine and health care in general will revitalize its possibilities for efficiency and innovation—which necessarily include customer service and satisfaction. Assuredly, revitalized consumer watchdog groups and groups of consumers themselves will provide strong checks on any fraudulent practices. Educated opinions spread quickly via the Internet. A just justice system will assist those who might be wronged and enforce judgments for restitution and reparations. Quacks will become an endangered species, only surviving (as they largely do today) on the money of customers who blindly believe in their particular brands of snake oil.

Unregulated insurance companies will charge rates in line with their clients' levels of risk, and most people will realize that catastrophic health care coverage will be more than adequate to cover their potential health care expenses; the newly low prices of general care and routine visits (and even many surgeries) wouldn't justify more expensive insurance plans.

Notice that, on account of governmental control and regulation of health insurance, consumers currently try to have their insurance companies pay for every conceivable medical expense. These include things that free market insurance could never insure, that is, things in the realm of personal control, things not accidental. Undoubtedly, the high costs of health care (and the regulations fostering them) promote such irresponsible behavior.

Also, today's focus is mainly on damage control, or treatment, instead of preventive health care measures and vitality programs. In a free market there will be no financial incentives for these suboptimal practices; they'd be much too costly. People will thus be encouraged to pay more attention to what they put in their mouths and how they treat their bodies. Doctors, imagine having educated and motivated patients! To follow the recommendations of the State-controlled dietary establishment and "The Food Pyramid" is a poor substitute for paying attention to the research and evidence, or at least seeking out reputable people and organizations who do. (In this regard, a book for laypersons that I can recommend as a starting point in evidence-based nutritional understanding is *Living the Low Carb Life* by Jonny Bowden.)

As for persons burdened with chronic illnesses, even their costs will decrease dramatically, mostly on account of a big rise in the number of health care providers, and therefore treatment options, as well as new business models and technological innovations. Additionally, private charities will spring up in many areas that are now usurped by governmental "benefits," such as Medicare and Medicaid. Because bad (government) money drives out good (market) money, most indigent persons are currently abandoned in a system of carelessness, callousness, and ineffectiveness. The government's so-called safety net has many sizable holes in it, and it's only a couple feet above the ground, which makes for quite hard landings. The moral of this sad story is twofold: Trust a typical politician or policy wonk less than the distance you can throw him or her, and never leave something so valuable as your health (or anything else, for that matter) at the mercy of a committee of bureaucrats and lobbyists.

Now, how about the fate of those relatively high incomes that physicians and other professionals currently receive? Although a free market of health care services will certainly reduce the pay rates of many practices, it will also substantially reduce the costs, in both time and money, of entry and operation of businesses. Therefore, what really matters for professionals in *any* industry is their standard of living.

Rather than years wasted in the authoritarian grip of regimented higher education and then in stale, red-taped organizations, innovative and smart apprenticeship programs will be the order of the day for practitioners in businesses everywhere. People learn much more by doing things according to their interests than they do by memorizing information, following overbearing orders, working inhuman hours, taking board exams, and defying common sense in the workplace. Not only do these things jeopardize the health of patients, but they also tend to weaken one's potential for career happiness.

It's an understatement to say that a truly free market will have greatly beneficial effects on everyone's living standards, enabling us to buy and enjoy much more with less money. Competition in any industry brings out the best in all aspects of supply and demand of goods and services. This is because productivity and capital are increased, and people are free to do more things with their newly created time and money—which fosters a continuous upward cycle of opportunity. A free market generates an ever larger and more wealthy middle class, which means that luxury item wish lists can be fulfilled by nearly everyone willing to be productive.

The general point of regulation—be it licensure or any other trade barrier, foreign or domestic, such as tariffs, quotas, duties, taxes, restrictions, special privileges, etc.—is that it hurts both buyers and sellers. Neither sellers nor buyers have the right to use laws to benefit their particular interests. That would mean using aggression instead of persuasion, force instead of reason. Such behavior may be fit for other primates, but certainly not us. Yet writing and enforcing unjust laws is definitely the most widely used and most unacknowledged form of violence by our species.

Rather than favoring regulation, people should seek *free market* methods to distinguish themselves. This mainly boils down to price and quality of product or service. If your prices are relatively low and your quality is high (or sufficient for the job), then you've got a winning combination in the eyes of most consumers.

VI

ENDING MODERN DAY LETTERS PATENT

Having covered the nature and value of private property and what a free market means for us, as producers and consumers, sellers and buyers, we now come to the important topic of "intellectual property." On this issue, we must again sweep aside the traditional and conventional notions, along with all the vested interests trying to maintain the status quo, especially amid a digital age.

Historically, letters patent were enforcement of monopoly privileges by a legal authority, be it a monarch or other form of authoritarian regime. These documents officially granted exclusive rights to those creators of inventions who were able to obtain them from those in power. Currently, intellectual property (IP) is enforced via patent, trademark, and copyright laws.

The primary claim for IP is that particular creations must remain the originator's property—not only the items in the originator's possession, but also the conceptual processes and structures manifested in items sold to others. In other words, monopolistic privileges concerning patterns of information, be they original, rediscovered, or even duplications (from independent sources at different times) are declared property and thus under one's exclusive control in the marketplace by the force of the State. Today's legal notion of IP seeks to stop and penalize others who use, copy, distribute, sell, alter, or improve upon these conceptual innovations in the marketplace, when they don't get permission from the lawfully declared owners.

Obviously, the fundamental issue of debate over IP concerns whether it's actually a valid form of property and, thus, whether its reproduction and manifestation in the marketplace by others without the purported originator's consent or "license" is a violation of property rights. In the realm of the intellect, the free-ranging and creative place of ideas, should property rights actually be claimed, not to mention granted and enforced by the State? Does ascribing such rights make any sense, based on what we know about property?

Closing Pandora's Intellectual Box

To reiterate, we claim property to avoid conflict with others and thus better enable value creation in the marketplace. And we establish rights to our property either by way of first possession or voluntary transfer from someone else. After all, it's hard to create and trade myriad goods and services when no one knows exactly who owns what, or when the State claims ownership.

Property boundaries are delineated basically through both property usage and possession. Notice that we can establish technical boundaries of utilization of our own property, whereby overstepping those boundaries would infringe on the property usage of others. As renowned libertarian scholar and economist Murray Rothbard noted, we basically homestead specific technological units for our particular purposes. Radio transmitters are a prime example; the owners only broadcast at specified frequencies or wattages that they have negotiated—either through contract or prior use—with other owners of electromagnetic spectrum usage. Clearly, establishing such property boundaries is essential to avoiding conflicts. However (no surprise here) presently such free market property arrangements have been impeded and heavily regulated by the Federal Communications Commission (FCC) and various judicial decisions.

You can rightly assume that what resides in your own brain is your property, whether or not you're an inventor, composer, or author—just as the rest of your body is your property. Clearly, someone would have to trespass on your property and do a coercive brain scan in order to gather this decidedly private information. But only by keeping information to oneself, that is, in private form and shielded from the marketplace can one declare conceptual information to be one's own. The right to privacy, along with this private knowledge, stems from property rights and their established physical boundaries in relation to others.

The notion of property of the intellect existing in the marketplace, however, is basically a contradiction in terms. As outlined, property is something that's claimed, used, and possessed as an extension of self-ownership. Property rights ultimately mean the freedom of action to use and/or dispose of certain owned items and to do various things in relation to them. Property rights do *not* mean the freedom to prevent others from duplicating what you own, unless that duplication creates conflict of usage and possession of your property, as in identity theft, which involves fraud (which we'll deal with in detail later).

Clearly, tangible items have all sorts of uses and capabilities that are conceptualized and exploited by reasoning minds. For example, you own the contents of your diary because the book of blank papers is yours and the ink adds something tangible to the item; the words within it also demonstrate how you can put it to use. The same could be said if the ink were in the form of the language of musical notes, that is, a song.

When intellectual information that's manifested in tangible items and processes makes it to the marketplace, such as a story or song or even mining processes or the sequencing and use of particular genes, it's quite obviously no longer for the creator's eyes only, and no longer in the creator's possession. Others are then exposed to this information via these items and their innumerable uses. One would have to initiate force to dictate to others what they can and cannot do with the intellectual information that's now in *their* brains. In other words, because what's claimed to be intellectual property is simply a pattern of information manifested in a tangible thing—specifically information that can be reproduced by others without conflict—one can't enforce the terms of its replication and dissemination once it reaches the marketplace, that is, once information has been duplicated by other brains and transformed into tangible expression by them. That would essentially be trying to control the property of others.

To put it another way, after a person exposes ideas, products, and services to the marketplace, he or she has no right to prevent others from reproducing or duplicating those same things—even if that person was the one who truly created or discovered them. One only has the right to control *one's own* particular products and services in which that information is embodied, that is, one's own capital resources and inventory (rightful property).

When other minds become aware of information, it basically goes from being private property (because trespass would be required to glean it) to being in the public domain, or marketplace. That's the way a free market works. No force is initiated by either buyers or sellers. Both realize that property rights apply to all aspects of tangible items they own and the various uses they choose to employ with them.

The Legal Jungle Of Patents, Copyrights, And Trademarks

For many of us, having been subjected to innumerable FBI warnings and "all rights reserved" clauses, or even been called pirates or thieves by members of the IP establishment for sharing files on the Internet, all this may be a rather new way of looking at the subject. So let's explore it further.

The current understanding by courts, lawyers, and law schools of IP and its licensing is essentially arbitrary, as well as complicated and confused. For instance, where does one idea or a small set of abstract ideas (typically not copyrightable) end, and a series or string of ideas (such as a poem) begin? Sure, one might say "Ideas themselves are not copyrightable; only their manifestations in specific combinations are," but where do old ideas end and new ideas begin?

This leads us directly into the thickets of patent law. Where exactly does the discovery of an idea, a better mouse trap for instance, transition from being "obvious" (and therefore not patentable) to "unique" or "original"? How many actually unique inventions are there, in which the creator didn't utilize or build upon any other ideas or processes already known (and perhaps even claimed as IP, what's called "prior art")? And what happens legally when many people arrive at the same idea independently—or when one person makes a discovery one week, month, or year before someone else?

Instead of answering these questions in a logical manner by rejecting the notion of IP entirely, the State imposes its laws as the politicians, bureaucrats, judges, and lobbyists have outlined. In the midst of the enforcement of various versions of IP, parts of copyright are legally declared to be free to use under the specified conditions of "fair use." And formerly copyrighted material is at some point declared to be in the public domain. Patented ideas, plants, and designs expire at a variety of designated times, while things trademarked can be renewed indefinitely through payment of fees. How come?

In this environment of legally enforced intellectual "property" in the marketplace, where does one draw the line concerning what's in the public domain? Some say for educational purposes only. Does this mean strictly a school or library, or what? Moreover, how long should one be able to enforce exclusive rights to IP? Plant and utility patents, 20 years? Design patents, 14 years? Copyrights, 70 years after the author's death—or, 95 or 120 years after publication—or should we revert to the original 14 years—or, in perpetuity? Can a crustless peanut butter and jelly sandwich really be patented and the exhaust sound of a Harley-Davidson motorcycle really be trademarked? Apparently they can. According to whom? According to the U.S. Government's Patent and Trademark Office, by arbitrary fiat, of course.

Witness also how patent claims are written: specific enough to assert something supposedly novel, and yet broad enough to discourage others from even thinking about offering any specific or general improvement without risking patent infringement. So much for encouraging creativity and innovation, or Constitutionally promoting "the progress of science and useful arts."

It's understandable and completely natural that copyright, trademark, and patent holders and filers have their self-interest in mind. No one wants his or her works misused, and individuals certainly don't want to lose out monetarily. Of course, I'm also aware of this mindset, being a previous holder of copyright (it's the default legal status unless one disavows it), and having filed for both a provisional patent and trademark as an entrepreneur a few years ago. But upon serious inspection, it turns out that IP enforcement isn't actually in our rational self-interest. A free market of ideas most certainly is. IP claims backed by lawyers and governmental guns do nothing to foster a free society of respectful interaction. As in all economic activity, persuasion and reputation should replace force as a means to gain and maintain market share.

Of course, many people who stand to lose their existing monopoly privileges might be horrified or incensed by the preceding paragraphs. Their stance goes something like this: "I will allow people in the marketplace to use duplicates of *my* creation so long as *I* can exclusively control their use, copying, and distribution." In other words, they want to enforce and retain exclusive right to license alleged property in a widely distributed fashion, rather than to just sell it and see it released into the public domain. But there's nothing inherent in an idea or string of ideas, big or small, complex or simple, that warrants a claim of property rights. Though I'm sure each of us has declared something to be "*my* idea" before, we know that it's possible for others to formulate (and improve upon) the same idea as well. Everybody has ideas; it's the nature of human consciousness to have them and put them to good use. Unlike valid forms of property, ideas aren't scarce; they can be reproduced without conflict. Just as in other aspects of business, protectionist rackets can't logically serve our economic interests; in fact, they stifle commerce and hinder economic opportunities.

Again, copyright, patent, trademark proclamations, and their legal implications concern, by definition, reproducible items offered in the marketplace. Proclamations such as "end-user licenses" aren't objectively valid because what's being claimed as property actually isn't. So, one logically can't mass produce and enforce blanket contracts on buyers that attempt to censor their minds and control their behavior. This obviously applies to the various license "agreements" we encounter at points of purchase (excluding warranty information and return policies, of course). Contrary to popular and legal belief, we aren't in any valid sense signing an IP contract when we buy copyrighted, patented, and trademarked items.

All reproducible items in the marketplace are necessarily marketable items, not someone's intellectual property. To the degree that others become aware of the information contained in these reproducible items (in a rights-respecting fashion) they may reproduce them at will. We, as property owners and producers, have no right to artificially create scarcity through licenses that aim to prohibit or restrict duplication and dissemination of information in the public eye. It turns out that most products or services can be duplicated, depending on the reproduction technology that's available and one's skills and resources at reverse engineering. We'll address more of the economic significance of this shortly.

Duplication doesn't entail any theft of property—only utilization of the particular information pattern found in the product or service. Thus, human beings only have the choice of whether or not to keep their creations secret. Of course, this doesn't mean that someone else won't think of the same things and bring them to market. Supply will meet the demand.

The Nature of Contracts

So, you might wonder, what about contracts in general? Again, everyone has a right to what they possess or have acquired voluntarily. In addition, each of us can devise agreements in order to prevent potential conflicts from arising with others in the use of our own property. Loaning and leasing are examples of contractual stipulations placed on the use of one's property by others, via negotiation and signed agreement. And as mentioned in a previous chapter, covenants between property owners are another example of preventing conflicts and outlining behavior that affects or can affect one's property rights; real estate easements are yet another example. For instance, people can contract with one another to ensure that no one will build anything prohibited by their signed deed restriction.

Trade secrets and their protection by nondisclosure agreements as well as "contracts not to compete" curiously represent attempts to keep the contents of one's mind and the nature of one's creations, private after being exposed to others. Similar to covenants and deed restrictions, these contracts reflect the desire to direct the behavior of others in the use of their own property. Nondisclosure and no-compete agreements seek to prevent others from disseminating certain knowledge that they have (or will have) gained from the property owner. A contract binds others (who choose to be bound) to this secrecy and outlines the penalties imposed for revealing and/or exploiting certain information. Thus, such a contract represents an agreement between parties in a working relationship that concerns a thing or process, that is, a pattern of information not to be reproduced in that context.

However, here's the kicker with these types of contracts: Such processes can obviously be duplicated by others who *aren't* involved in the contract and therefore have no working relationship to uphold. This necessarily leads to problems of enforcement as well as determining exactly how others who weren't parties to the contract acquired the same ideas.

Exclusivity agreements, in contrast, involve signing parties who agree to do business only with each other, according to specified provisions, hence contracting to restrict duplication of business processes instead of ideas. Conditional contracts are somewhat similar. For example, we're probably all too familiar with (and perhaps frustrated by) the ones we sign with the purchase of our mobile phones. Most corporations' wireless communications plans have a two-year contract, which stipulates that the discounted phone price (or "free phone") and the monthly rate apply *only if* the customer gives them two continuous years of business. Otherwise, fines will be imposed, that is, "early termination fees," usually amounting to a couple hundred dollars.

These kinds of contracts are a bit representative of the unspoken mottos of many "pragmatic" and regulated corporations, four of which now provide roughly eighty percent of the wireless market: "The hand is quicker than the eye"; "Which shell is the pea under?"; and "Never give a sucker an even break." The marketing push for sales often overrides fully informing, and thus fully satisfying, customers. A simple solution for businesses to avoid costly litigation and bad reputations is to make sure the customer is aware of the trade-off involved in signing the conditional contract: short-term gain but potentially long term pain (cheap phone but you're locked in with us for two years) versus short-term pain but long term gain (expensive phone but the ability to switch anytime without an early termination fee). Customers who select the latter option then pay the actual phone price up front, which is typically a few hundred dollars, and either pay month-to-month or buy their minutes as they go. However, this still doesn't overcome the problem of potentially not being able to use your new phone if you switch service providers, which is another corporate-created shell game. You'll have to see if you can "unlock" your particular brand of phone and install a new SIM (subscriber information module), which of course means spending more money.

We can of course thank the FCC and its maze of regulations for most of this trouble. Lack of competition and therefore lack of consumer choices in the marketplace of wireless telephony and other radio technologies are the result of State-licensed, State-controlled, and State-prohibited use of electromagnetic spectrum. Without clearly delineated property rights in this area of the market, which includes presently unlicensed spectrum, FCC rules and corporate cronies of central planning bureaucrats continue to commit their injustices on consumers and potentially innovative competitors. Local governments also hinder placement of towers, which of course contributes to weak signals and dropped calls. Clearly, electromagnetic spectrum property rights ought to be established via homesteading, that is, making use of available bandwidth as well as transmission and reception technologies. Just as necessary is the ability to sell that property to other entrepreneurs in the market, who can employ new methods that are currently stifled by FCC licensure and regulation.

We of course always have the discretion to breach our contracts, though with the associated penalties. Such penalties can't include simply forcing performance of the contract, which would obviously make it unbreachable. Bodily harm also can't be a proper penalty for contract breach, for instance, being dropped into a vat of boiling oil for not performing your contractually stipulated obligations. Torture is a form of pure evil, no matter what you've agreed (or not agreed) to do.

We don't possess the right to enslave ourselves, nor can others enslave us. This would contradict the rational, chosen nature of contracts, rendering them unconscionable. In most cases, monetary damages seem to be the only reasonable penalty for breach of contract, which enable payment to *others* who are willing and able to finish or repair and restore what was contracted. A free market system of contract insurance, with accompanying ratings of individual customers that reflect their contract history, would help prevent breaches as well as mitigate damages. Insurance for agreements that involve a lot of time, labor, money, and capital investment, the loss of which would otherwise be difficult to recoup, can be quite useful. Agreeing to the assignment of penalties for breach may also give the contracting parties greater confidence about their firm business intentions to work together.

Having said that, there are some valuable rules of thumb in the business world that also insure against such risks. Regarding trade secrets, for instance, if you don't want your secrets to become public, then keep them to yourself. Or, if need be, tell your secrets to persons you can unreservedly trust. In any event, leaked secrets may be one of the natural costs of doing business. No matter how many crafty contracts we've had our attorneys draft and our associates and employees sign, in an attempt to control their behavior, risks are unavoidable in business. By now it should practically go without saying that such risks won't entail destitution, because of the nearly endless business opportunities in a truly free market.

Granted, in long-term business relationships, as well as long-term neighbors, it's important to minimize potential for losses. But the more we associate with and reside next to people of honesty and good character, that is, people of virtue, the better our working relationships will be. These valuable human qualities ought to *precede* contracts which, after all, can be breached anyway.

There also seems to be a degree of folly in wanting to *make* others do certain things, in this case to keep secrets under threat of penalties. Such contracts may themselves erode trust and respect in the working relationship. When dealing with others in a company, it's clearly most beneficial to rely on trust and the honor system. Distrust and dishonesty are corrosive to any relationship—human interaction 101.

Inescapable risks are of course part of doing business with others, but the more we respect others (and the more they respect us), the less risk there will be in doing business with them. Distrust of others often becomes self-fulfilling prophecy, as authoritarian old-school managers and antagonistic labor union bosses (who rely on political pull) continually demonstrate.

On the other side of the contract, there are probably some things we ought not agree to. If we believe that we're entering an agreement that creates a relationship of drastically unequal power (typical of standard form contracts), we should think carefully before we sign. Adhesion contracts, for example, are those that leave us with no choice concerning the terms and no room for bargaining. If a brief reading of the contract's extensive fine print makes you feel like you've mysteriously entered a law library, then at least make sure the basic terms are reasonable—and that you can effectively argue against the unreasonable terms in the fine print, if need be. True to form, the corporate-influenced and governmentally controlled legal system makes the nature of some agreements really problematic. Restriction of market choices is the statist game, after all. Therefore, it's imperative to discover the reputations and level of customer satisfaction of those with whom we might contract.

How About IP In Perpetuity?

Having covered the essential nature of contracts, let's now resume our discussion about the invalidity of IP. What if government weren't in charge of granting and enforcing such "rights"? Are there any other approaches that try to avoid the governmentally created contradictions?

As far as I know, the only internally consistent approach to claims of IP is that of Andrew Galambos, a free market anarchist who favored the processes of the marketplace and private legal agencies instead of government. Many who've studied the writings of various libertarian thinkers might have heard of his version of intellectual property. Basically, Galambos believed that inventors should be able to enforce exclusive rights to their discoveries, and thus the information embodied in things exposed to the marketplace, for however long they wish. IP would thus exist in perpetuity for the declared owners. Private enforcement agencies would ensure compliance, and a free market-created "Clearinghouse" would supposedly inform everyone who used another's IP to whom they'd need to pay royalties (assuming the IP holder wanted to license it).

I'm not sure if Galambos drew any definite lines about what could and could not be legitimately claimed by individuals as IP—perhaps whatever one proved to come solely from one's own brain. I do know that students of his lectures were advised not to discuss his ideas in detail outside the classroom (they even signed nondisclosure agreements concerning this). Not surprisingly, this makes for difficult, beating-around-the-bush conversations with his former students.

The Galambos interpretation has internal consistency, to be sure, in that it leaves the determination of IP duration to the discretion of the alleged holder of it, rather than to the capriciousness of government and lobbyists. But it asserts a notion of property that extends beyond the simple right to privacy, one's right to possessions against trespass (as well as to working relationship contracts that seek to extend that right, however misguided they may be). Hence, Galambos' form of IP can't be considered morally valid or, for that matter, practically enforceable. To reiterate, no one has the right to prevent others from reproducing the information patterns they've observed in the marketplace, even if such patterns are avowedly original. They only have the right to seek justice for commissions of fraud.

The great thing about the free market is that it encourages trading values, swapping ideas, and spreading information. This leads to further cooperation, capital accumulation, increases in productivity, and more economic opportunities for everyone. The extensive network of commerce in society is the direct result of the flow of information and the sharing of knowledge. Entrepreneurs depend greatly on insights gained from their experiences in the marketplace of ideas, goods and services. No one, no matter how intellectually and psychologically independent, creates in a vacuum. Individual minds build on the prior works of other individual minds. Teams and groups of people add to the synergistic effects. The result is a vibrant economy filled with virtually endless avenues for creative expression and money making.

If there's a demand, then a better drug, a catchier tune, or more efficient vehicle will be supplied to the market. The notion that new ideas would never reach the public without IP is simply erroneous. It not only attempts to make the end justify the means—restricting competition in order to make money—but it's also contrary to the nature of a free market. There's little payoff in keeping one's innovations to oneself indefinitely, even though accumulating venture capital and effectively taking a product to market can indeed take some time.

Distribution, marketing, and perhaps the honor of being distinguished as the original creator, all determine how well one's work will sell on a free market. Mainly, it's about distribution and marketing, which typically lead to successful sales. Yet many creators today don't want to heed this business truth. They're lured instead by the government's coercive mechanism of IP—even though over 95% of patents never turn a profit. The lottery has been called the poor man's tax, so perhaps the patent process ought to be called the inventor's wishing well. It's a deep, dark well at that, filled with many coin-catching IP lawyers. Certainly, there are much better uses of our time, money, and creativity.

The copyright racket is similar. Millions of authors and composers have waited and waited (and waited) for royalty checks to trickle down to them from licensing entities such as the American Society of Composers, Authors, and Publishers (ASCAP) and Broadcast Musicians Inc. (BMI). The big record labels and their special interest strong arm, the Recording Industry Association of America (RIAA), also contribute to today's chaotic, extremely litigious, and unjust legal framework. And let's not forget the Motion Picture Association of America (MPAA), which back in the day, actually sued to ban video cassette recorders. They're now involved in a whole host of lobbying efforts regarding DVDs and issues of "Digital Rights Management" (DRM). Remember those FBI warnings? These are new and improved ones designed to prevent "unauthorized use."

Creative Commons, And So On

Unlike these organizations, we now know better than to ask government and their abettors to do us any favors, to grant us any special corners on the market. In contrast, Net labels, open source record labels, free software licenses (GNU General Public License), and "copyleft" licenses ("all rites reversed") are examples of free market responses to governmental coercion and corporate copyright schemes. Creative Commons (founded and chaired by Lawrence Lessig) offers licenses as well as public domain dedication to creators of online content. These are now somewhat viable alternatives to typical end-user licenses, though they still have to maneuver through copyright laws.

The Creative Commons (CC) license offers a range of options, from simple fraud protection, which requires that credit be given to the author, to prohibition of commercial use. Of course, it still relies on copyright law for making such restrictions; so, to that extent, it's an intermediate point on the way to complete liberty in the marketplace of ideas.

Nonetheless, as long as licensees (buyers and users of an author's works) follow specific disclosure guidelines, all works under CC license grant the following freedoms: to copy the work; to distribute it; to display or perform it publicly; to make digital public performances of it (for example, webcasting); and, to shift the work into another format as a verbatim copy. Obviously, this is a big enlightened step forward in the realm of property rights. Once you buy something, it's yours to do with as you please. Common sense wins in the end!

In the marketplace of goods, services, and ideas, anything that *can be* reproduced or duplicated using one's own effort and ingenuity typically will be. This necessarily includes patterns of information. Notice that I've repeatedly mentioned "reproduced" or "duplicated." This is key, because certain tangible resources can't be reproduced; one can only transfer possession of them. Real estate is a good example. One's own self is another, as well as specific contracts, including legal documents pertaining to yourself, in which duplication would be fraud (counterfeiting being a form of fraud). Any attempt to occupy or possess such property of another without consent is theft, the initiation of force, essentially the height of social conflict.

As noted, products of the intellect are inherently reproducible, so bringing further goods and services based on them into the marketplace doesn't cause the loss of one's property. There's no theft, and there's no attempt at forceful occupation of one's property. Thus, there's no conflict. Only by attempting to possess and use another's property, or use a non-reproducible item, without the owner's consent, can a person commit a rights-violation. Such a rights-violation can involve visible, tangible property, which importantly includes documents that assign ownership, such as titles, deeds, bank notes, or money deposit receipts. Duplication of these legal documents by those not representing the property of the particular person or organization would be counterfeiting. Additionally, we have no right to possess and use "invisible" property of others without their consent, such as using *occupied* frequencies of the electromagnetic spectrum, which are aspects of reality that more tangible property, such as a transmission tower, makes use of.

In determining what are valid property rights, the proper distinction doesn't concern visible versus invisible, or tangible versus intangible property. The proper distinction concerns reproduction, possession, and use without conflict *versus* reproduction, possession, and use with conflict. It's as simple as that.

Human ingenuity really determines what can be established as property. For instance, by switching from solely analog to analog plus digital on the FM radio band, more streams of information can be transmitted; each channel can then carry a few additional signals. Advances in technology can obviously create many new forms and facets of property. Internet domain names are just one example of all the technological properties created from the Internet. Since the Internet employs a universally recognized addressing system, someone can't duplicate your domain name address with impunity; that would be a case of trying to possess your piece of (virtual) real estate without your consent. Further, the various owners of the Internet backbone and server networks don't permit such conflict.

This is why identity theft is clearly an instance of fraud: The thief claims to be the actual person who's authorized to make particular transactions, in order to unjustly use that person's property and privileges. Of course, duplication of names is commonplace in most cultures, but the name must coincide with each unique person and his or her particular property, according to specific standards of verification. There may be many John and Mary Smiths out there in America, but they don't presume to be the same person with the same property and privileges. Fortunately, nearly all people want to avoid such confusion and hasten to resolve it, which is one reason why we use middle names and specify our addresses. Of course, assigned numbers coupled with biometric identifiers would also help to prevent any confusion of identities in a prosperous future of many more people on this planet. However, such choices must always be left to individuals, not governments. As long as the State presumes to be in charge of personal ID cards and numbers, and as long as it imposes such things as drivers' licenses and Social Security numbers, we should be very alarmed. Such information is being used to deny our basic freedoms to travel and function independently in the marketplace. States, especially police States, make a point of keeping track of people in order to gain more control and power over them—always for "security" reasons, of course.

How The Market Performs Without Intellectual Property

In a truly free market, which is governed by an understanding of objective law—that is, law based on individual rights—what you create with your own brain and transform into goods and services is also yours to sell in the marketplace. The profits from these sales are assuredly your property, as is the inventory that you've yet to sell. But the creations of your own brain, whether truly original or not, can't remain your property as information patterns within the goods and services you've sold to others.

Fraud is basically an issue between the buyer and seller, directly or indirectly involving the original creator. Absent today's IP enforcement, companies that produce knockoffs might face fraud charges if they didn't make it clear to customers that their $10 "Nikes" (with the accompanying Swoosh on the side) for example, were made by a different company than the $100 actual Nikes—though typically the price difference is a dead giveaway, just as it is for all those "Ray Bans" and "Louis Vuittons" on street corner shops. Of course, the main reason people buy knockoffs is to save money while creating an illusion of high fashion. On account of this, there's little incentive for most buyers to bring charges of fraud, for that would entail getting their money back from their cheap purchase and forking over many more dollars for the real McCoy.

Nevertheless, few companies would last long if they tried to sell knockoffs as the originals, that is, as products or services coming from the original producers and sellers. Valid charges of fraud by just a handful of customers might make such business practices quite risky. Moreover, market pressures to avoid confusion will naturally discourage many companies from using identical trademarks and service marks. It's just not good business to be continually mistaken by your customers for another company. Though imitation can be the sincerest form of flattery, most businesses try to avoid damage to their finances as well as reputations through misleading buyers about their actual identity. Yet, companies might find many creative uses for previously monopolized marks, and they'll be free to do so, even though they won't be free from encountering charges of fraud by irate consumers.

Clearly understood and delineated property rights are the only way to avoid confusion and conflict in civilization. In a society that fully respects ownership, conflict and its legal consequences are avoided by not trespassing on legitimately claimed property. One who first possesses property, or receives it through consensual transfer, determines how it's to be used and/or disposed.

Today, people commonly try to defend (or oppose) the modern day approach to letters patent by way of arguments about use and profits. Those strongly in favor of IP are backed by the Constitutionally authorized Patent and Trademark Office and legions of lawyers, both governmental and corporate. They contend that without IP, no inventor or businessperson could make a profit: As soon as their products hit the market, others would piggyback on companies' R&D investment and flood the market with cheap knockoffs, such as generic drugs. Hence, for the sake of business, profit-making, and capitalism, IP must be recognized and enforced—ultimately, at the point of a gun.

Such a stance obviously overlooks the fact that many business sectors today make enormous profits without direct reliance on IP enforcement. The fashion industry and most service industries are prime examples. Ironically, however, many try to bolster their arguments for IP by pointing to the heavily regulated and very corporate pharmaceutical industry, as if their huge investment costs were a free market phenomenon. The many years and hundreds of millions of dollars (actually approaching a billion per drug) spent on research and development in the FDA trial-and-approval process aren't actually necessary. Additionally, more competition in the realm of creating and selling products that relieve suffering and prevent deaths won't stifle money making. Clearly, some moral premises need to be checked here. Some IP advocates also point to the millions spent on actors and film production in the corporate-controlled movie industry, as if good flicks with skilled actors require skyrocketing budgets. No matter how many fear its artistic repercussions, a free market without IP won't reduce us to only watching clips on YouTube.

On the other hand, those who mostly reject the calls for strong enforcement of IP (fortunately a good share of the creative, free software and open source techie crowd, as well as quite a few non-union artists and musicians) contend that information needs to be free and that people shouldn't be restricted in its use; instead, people should be allowed to sample, tinker, create, and duplicate. For instance, a software engineer's version of digital hell is likely one in which he's not allowed to use, modify, and distribute source code for further development. And a consumer's version of digital hell is often one in which she can't copy media to other devices that she herself owns.

Preventing people from reproducing and innovating various products and services truly impedes economic progress. In addition to frustration over the use of one's own property, it yields much less innovation, fewer choices, and higher prices. It also means tremendous amounts of energy wasted in legal wrangling and disputes involving purported intellectual property rights infringement. Many businesses even expend much energy and resources on securing patents they'll never use, in order to prevent others from entering particular areas of innovation—so-called defensive patenting.

The arguments for intellectual freedom in the marketplace are indeed correct, while arguments for some version of IP, be it the government's or Galambos', are mired in hopeless contradictions. The reproduction of goods, services, and ideas reduces scarcity and, hence, it lowers prices and creates many more values in the marketplace; it also greatly diminishes litigation. These facts reveal that there will be many more opportunities for profit-making in a free market without IP. But that, of course, is a utilitarian argument, and what must logically accompany arguments about utility or consequences, are rights-based, principled arguments.

IP proponents essentially want to control what's already been sold. Obviously, the "property rights infringement" that advocates of IP are referring to ultimately boils down to the loss of *sales* of their goods and services, that is, potential profits from unknown buyers. Clearly, the money presently in the pockets of consumers is not the property of producers. It only becomes a seller's property after a transaction has been made. Once you purchase a product from me, for example this book, the entire book is yours to keep, alter, even to copy and sell as you like. You'll notice that I've released it into the public domain. Since it's your book, *your property*, I have no right to tell you what you can and cannot do with it. Plus, maybe many more people will read these valuable ideas if you help in the distribution process. Grass-roots, word-of-mouth marketing is thereby facilitated.

Others have no right to stipulate what people can and can't do with their property. Moreover, we must be careful not to start thinking that labor, in and of itself, has economic value. That would be embracing the labor theory of value, brought to us mostly courtesy of Marx and Engels. For example, if I spent the rest of my life (and thus resources and money) writing a philosophical treatise on the pure, undeniable pleasure derived from eating freshly baked chocolate chip cookies, should I expect to profit from it? Perhaps only in my dreams. What if I baked and sold the actual cookies? Most probably, I would make some money. What if no one had ever heard of such delicious cookies? In other words, what if I were the original creator of the recipe? Would I then have the right to forcibly prevent others from baking the same kind of cookies, so that I could coercively maintain a monopoly on my cookie market? Of course not. What if I had negotiated contracts with those suppliers and workers who might otherwise exploit my trade secret? Regardless of the inherent problems in enforcement of such contracts, this still wouldn't stop anyone else from doing some clever cookie reverse engineering and competing with me.

The same principle applies to all "recipes," be they words on pages, the mechanical and electrical structure of a computer, the design of an aircraft, the parts and workings of a turbodiesel engine, the composition of a drug, or the sequence of genes for production of a particular protein. The most interested and enterprising individuals in an innovative and continuously changing marketplace will determine the future manifestations of this information.

Productivity is a valuable end. Labor can be a means to that end, but it's not the end in itself. If labor were an end in itself, then a thousand workers digging a 10 foot deep, mile long trench with shovels would be preferable to one person digging it with a fifty-ton excavator.

The excavator frees up those 999 other men to do all sorts of other things, to expand productivity in countless ways. It also frees the excavator operator, after a few days work, to begin the next project. Moreover, the excavator represents many other types of work that the would-be shovelers can do instead—from the production of crude oil and refinement of its diesel fuel and hydraulic oil, to the forging of steel and the tooling, machining, and assembly of thousands of parts for the heavy equipment. And let's not forget the engineering know-how and design elements that must be employed to create a dependable product that construction companies want to buy and use; countless innovations follow from these trial-and-error processes. This all helps explain why hydraulic power is favored over muscle power these days.

There are always costs in doing any kind of business, costs to any use of capital and expenditure of labor. And it just so happens that duplication is a potential risk one faces with products and services that are easily copied and disseminated. Advances in technology tend to make many more things easier to reproduce. This is a really good thing, because it yields more for everyone, thus raising everyone's standard of living. Perhaps the technological apex will be reached with the perfection of nanotechnology, the ability to rearrange matter at the molecular level for design and fabrication of nearly anything. For instance, if everyone had a special nano-machine that could construct a new automobile from a pile of scrap materials in a few seconds, then the big automobile manufacturers would certainly have to switch to a different line of work—maybe to the manufacture of "new and improved" nano-machines, ones that could make *flying* cars instead. Just as most horse-drawn carriage manufacturers found a different line of work after the introduction of automobiles, so too would auto manufacturers find new ways to make a living. Free markets are about change, after all—and we humans are especially good at adapting to changes in our environment.

At some point a few thousand years ago, the wheel was invented. If those in the Galambos' school had their way back then, we'd all be paying royalties to the legally declared heirs, the descendants of the wheel inventor, every time we turned a wheel. Many of us would thus try to use our wheels surreptitiously, only rolling them in the darkness of night. Others might settle for less suitable polygons, such as decagons or even dodecagons in order to avoid royalty payments. Envision this scenario in a marketplace of *billions* of brains, each creating and declaring things to be their own intellectual property, and you can begin to fathom the deepest meaning of legal chaos, confusion over ownership, economic distortions, slowing of innovations, as well as rights-infringements.

Again, anything that *can* be reproduced in the marketplace likely *will* be reproduced in the marketplace. Humans are in the business of making stuff—better and cheaper stuff, including plastic that lasts beyond our own expiration date (nod to George Carlin). Reproduction is not theft, by definition, unless it involves the government's printing press, which as you know is another story about fraud on the grandest scale imaginable.

Basically, it's up to buyers and sellers to sort out what's highly valued in the marketplace. It's probably a safe bet that most people desire to honor the "real deal," or the originator's product or service, rather than individuals or companies selling so-called knockoffs. At the very least, most people believe that it's bad manners not to give credit where credit is due, that is, when appropriate; obviously, most things we think about and do are not so novel. Many people exhibit brand loyalty, which may be fostered by better customer service, delivery options, and ease of returns. And many are willing to pay a premium for these things.

In fact, most people are happy to pay original content creators. Music is one clear example, as long as gratuitous middlemen keep out of the way. GarageBand.com and eMusic.com for example, are a couple websites that enable independent musicians direct access to their audience; and, they offer songs as MP3 file downloads (which is a non-DRM, versatile format). Nonetheless, the popularity of Apple's iTunes Store has arisen not only because of the cool designs of iPods, but also because of convenience and selection. Of course, it's heavily influenced by the RIAA and the big record labels, so instead of selling open MP3 files that can play on any player you might own, the songs are in AAC format with Apple's version of DRM called FairPlay; among other things, this allows songs to be duplicated only to other iPods.

Peer-to-peer file sharing is still widespread on the Web, which shows that the price points for iTunes songs are still too high and their inherent DRM device restrictions unwanted. Nevertheless, many consumers find it more convenient to "legally" acquire music in the single-song purchase fashion, rather than buy shrink-wrapped CD's in record stores. In contrast, podcasts on iTunes and many other websites are offered as MP3's. They are free to consumers (podcatchers) and feature either limited or no advertisements. While podcasting represents a fun hobby for many in this burgeoning field of infotainment, the main business model at present relies on user donations. Many independent artists and musicians are turning to this too, as they give listeners many free songs to encourage monetary contributions.

It turns out that most people, when they can afford it, desire to reward original creators; they know and appreciate hard work when they see it. This will especially be the case in a future economy that fully respects individual rights and, as a result, has enormously more wealth (gold standard, no taxes, no regulations, etc.). Still, what people value on a free market is their own prerogative. Obviously, the cheaper the duplicates, the more likely that poorer people will be attracted to them; this would definitely be the case with generic drugs throughout the developing world. Entrepreneurs and inventors therefore need to adjust their business models accordingly, to acknowledge people's freedom to innovate and compete, which ultimately benefits everyone.

VII

THE DEMISE OF THE STATE

Prudence, indeed, will dictate that Governments long established should not be changed for light and transient causes; and accordingly all experience hath shewn that mankind are more disposed to suffer, while evils are sufferable than to right themselves by abolishing the forms to which they are accustomed. But when a long train of abuses and usurpations, pursuing invariably the same Object evinces a design to reduce them under absolute Despotism, it is their right, it is their duty, to throw off such Government, and to provide new Guards for their future security.

Thomas Jefferson   *Declaration of Independence*

If it's impossible to run government like a business, if governmental regulation prevents and punishes voluntary trade between and among consenting adults (and children), if government uses arbitrarily devised and enforced statutory law instead of natural, objective, individual rights-based law, and if government relies on immoral, unjust means to stay in business, then what exactly is it good for?

Surely Thomas Jefferson would find the present state of political affairs atrocious, an intolerable form of absolute Despotism. Consequently, what does this imply for us in the voluntary marketplace? What if we refused to continue suffering such evils? What if most people realized that it is their right, it is their duty, to throw off such Government, and to provide new Guards for their security? What if we suddenly replaced Government with something that was actually moral and rights-respecting—that is, with the unmatchable, uncompromising methods of a free market system?

Unfortunately, even the talented likes of Penn & Teller can't perform that fantastic of a magic trick, at least not before our very eyes. But let's consider the hypothetical scenario for now. Later, we'll discuss some real life solutions, practical options, for getting rid of the status quo, that is, for uprooting the current rot and planting some beautiful freedom flowers.

A Fully Privatized System

Under a fully privatized system, new businesses and entrepreneurs don't navigate financial and regulatory mazes in order to compete with established, already-conforming-to-the-racket-and-lobbying-for-more-favors-and-less-competition businesses. Banks are no longer shills for the fascist welfare-warfare State, and interest rates are accountable to the market, not to the Federal Reserve System overlords and the nobility of their various monetary subsidiaries. Free markets are actually free, and the people benefit enormously. Our standard of living—our purchasing power as well as economic opportunities—thus skyrockets.

Dispensing with government therefore entails euthanizing some quite sacred legal cows. Simply put, taxes and preventive law are laid to rest, leaving only death the last certainty for us, to be further held at bay by the biotech field and medical innovations. Remember the alphabet soup of regulatory agencies? They're government's way of maintaining control and overseeing affairs that they've no business controlling and overseeing.

Without the ability to expropriate money from a populace that's no longer subservient, the institutions of government atrophy to a point of splendid emaciation, and then death. As government withers, people thrive. We then witness marketplace hypertrophy, an advanced economy on steroids, with no toxic side effects.

Without the State's power to tax, which is derived from coercion and people's compliance, we finally say goodbye and good riddance to unaccountable government. Without taxation, we finally say "Welcome to the land of milk and honey" (no offense to the lactose intolerant and to diabetics like myself, who of course would be cured through new biotech advances).

This leads directly to the question of how real accountability is created for the services that government supposedly attempts to provide us. Well, that's easy: You vote with your money! This is the real, meaningful, and direct power that each of us possesses, and it's indeed the genius of a free market system, a system of self-governing capitalism. We pay only for what we want, and we get only what we pay for. If we believe we're not getting a good deal, then we stop payment and do business somewhere else.

This is the real "check and balance" of the marketplace. Actually, there's no logical or effective or efficient substitute. You can try to make a country of laws but not of men, but men will make and maintain laws in accordance with their enforced monopoly organization called government. Therefore, the only thing that can prevent corruption, theft, waste, and injustice is to abolish their funding and look elsewhere.

A legalized monopoly on anything in the marketplace, especially a legalized monopoly on the use of force—and especially one that *takes* money rather than *makes* it (and I don't mean with the printing press)—is a prescription for absolute power and absolute disaster. It means disaster for individual rights, private property, liberty, and the pursuit of happiness. And in some cases, it means suffering and death to multitudes of people. Upon some reflection, one wonders how such a diabolical system could ever be entertained, let alone implemented and continually upheld, by rational adults.

As long as people exchange values in a voluntary manner, by means of their own decisions, there's no need for instruments of force. The only type of force warranted in a free society is *retaliatory* force. Reasoning beings have a need to rectify injustices and ascribe consequences for wrongdoing. And since the only moral instruments of force stem from the right to self-defense and defense of one's property, these instruments must be enacted either on one's own or by a chosen agent of retaliatory force, based on efficiency and reputation, or price and competence. One could call these "legal agencies," but for all intents and purposes they more accurately are called insurance companies.

Free market insurance companies will likely become the new

Guards of our future security that Jefferson spoke of, though he wisely left them to our imagination and ingenuity. What they'll be insuring is our right to live and flourish in an environment of liberty that respects property rights, an environment of complete liberty. They'll make sure that whatever rights-violations have occurred are rectified with reparations for damages and equitable restitution. Nonetheless, individuals will always be free not to purchase such services; no one may impose on others who live peacefully.

Notice that this will be fully possible only when private property is ascribed to every possible domain. Again, there's no alternative if we desire to live in lands of peace and prosperity governed by respect for ownership, rather than deference to authoritarian and arbitrary power structures.

As the Austrian economist Hans-Hermann Hoppe has keenly noted, insurance companies in the business of defending rights will have every incentive to minimize risks to their clients and to exact justice when faced with a probable claim, following from a rights-violation. Those with the best reputations for competence will be in most demand. Remember, the people have decided to no longer tolerate Despotism or suffer evils. As noted by Homer in the *Iliad* a few millennia ago (and by Achilles in the film *Troy*), there are no pacts between lions and men. When some men take on the manners of lions, there can be no appeasing them.

Let's also keep in mind that today's corporate insurance companies have big offices on K Street. It's no wonder; insurance is one of the most heavily regulated industries in America. We, as consumers of all forms of insurance, suffer considerably as a result. Higher prices, convoluted, almost unreadable policies that nearly require a team of lawyers to decipher, and substantially reduced choices face us daily. Additionally, insurance companies are prevented from making all sorts of practical business decisions, and many of the bigger corporations have lobbied to attain corners on the market and become immune to various market pressures (surprise surprise).

The thought of replacing the coercive operations of the State with respectful free market processes is probably unsettling for many who are accustomed to the status quo, either as rights-infringers or, ironically, as their victims. In any proposal of radical, principled, political change, some tend to fear the worst, and they tend to overlook their present yokes and chains. Let's examine a few typical concerns.

> If government essentially does things by pointing guns at people, how in the world can you give this power to more than one organization? You will never be able to keep an eye on so many powerful organizations!

Does giving absolute, or even "Constitutionally constrained," power to initiate force to one organization somehow solve the essential problem of Government? No, it does not. Does allowing legal immunity for one group of aggressors against the sovereignty of individuals make a political system of justice? Most certainly, it does not.

Instead, monopolistic government creates the very problems that it's purportedly designed to solve. Rather than creating law and order, it fosters lawlessness and disorder by incorporating the initiation of force as its method of operation. Instead of being accountable to citizens, it throttles them with unjust laws and expropriates and controls their property. Instead of protecting our rights, it lays a wretched foundation for criminality in society by taking revenue rather than making profits, and threatening everyone to conform to it's collective, irrational will, as well as put up with its huge lack of customer service.

In short, the State creates massive roadblocks to peace and prosperity. Even if government were strictly relegated to the use of retaliatory force and protection of individual rights (under Laissez-faire capitalism) this would contradict it's nature as a legalized monopoly that forcibly bars other organizations from competing, organizations that can perform the service of justice better, perhaps far better, as well as much cheaper.

The ideas of voluntary payment and rights-upholding agencies follow from the principles of justice, individual rights, and contracts. Since anyone has the right to self-defense and to rectify wrongs done to him or her, anyone can delegate enforcement of that right, or become an agent to enforce such rights for others. Logically, no one has the right to enforce a monopoly of rights-based agency on others. None of us may tell others what's good for them and then proceed to force them to accept it. In other words, individual rights come *before* government, not the other way around. The concept of liberty precedes any actions to ensure it.

Organizations of people in the free market (not ones who currently use political pull) get powerful because they satisfy consumer wants and needs. As soon as they start failing at this job, they lose market share or even go out of business. People spend their money on products and services that best suit their needs, rather than on one-size-fits-all models. Therefore, the power really resides in those who decide to spend money, not in those who compete for earning it.

> Won't there be numerous overlapping jurisdictions in which violence is used to resolve jurisdictional disputes, not to mention biased judgments in cases for clients of particular insurance companies? After all, when governments disagree, they tend to go to war. Why would private enterprises, who get paid by whoever is rich enough to buy their favor, be any better? In fact, wouldn't they be worse, creating a land ruled by warlords and Mafia-type thugs?

Such reasoning partially illustrates why we remain in our present form of Despotism. Jefferson was so right when he wrote that "all experience hath shewn that mankind are more disposed to suffer, while evils are sufferable than to right themselves by abolishing the forms to which they are accustomed." Apparently, we need to be *fully* enslaved by the State before any real alternatives are worth considering. Of course, by then our fates would be permanently sealed, similar to being stuck in quicksand up to your neck before attempting to extricate yourself or call for help.

In matters involving human thought and action, one must strive to avoid context-dropping as well as confirmation bias, which means only looking for what one wants to find and finding only what one is looking for. Actually, in politics it's often worse than that: The things found are merely creations of one's own mind. Needless to say, objectivity is thrown out the window, head first.

Scientists are probably most keen about these reasoning pitfalls, at least in their own disciplines. But immense and widespread governmental funding and influence tends to noticeably impair their better judgment. Nonetheless, an astute scientist tries to adhere to the rigors of the scientific method, such as performing controlled (especially double blind) studies to better pinpoint causal factors and rule out extraneous variables.

We don't have all the laboratory tools of the scientific method at our disposal in politics. We can't put randomly assigned groups of the citizenry in a controlled environment and subject them to experimental legal procedures. What we *can* do, however, is consider the massive weight of the evidence regarding present legal procedures, both statist and voluntary (such as arbitration and meditation). We can also use our knowledge of history, sociology, economics, philosophy, and psychology in order to derive an objective understanding of human nature. Doing so allows us to arrive at logical and practical political and ethical principles as well as sound conclusions.

In the case of insurance companies being representatives and defenders of our rights, we have to examine the essential incentives and disincentives to resolve jurisdictional and judgment disputes fairly and peaceably.

Obviously, in order to make the transition to a society of complete liberty, most people must agree to it. Most people need to understand these concepts and behave accordingly. This tellingly explains why we're not there yet. Most today either don't have knowledge of a better way for people to interact politically, or they defer to those who are influential and in positions of power to make their decisions for them. We certainly suffer the consequences of each, although showing deference to irrational authorities is much harder to overcome than simple ignorance. Thus, the ideas of justice and property rights that complete liberty so potently addresses are not recognized and staunchly advocated by most people. Instead, we have numerous variations on the same theme of injustice—statism—circulating in the political and moral world of "memes," a term coined by evolutionary biologist Richard Dawkins, which refers to ideas or practices transmitted to others in a culture.

However, as new memes about complete liberty begin circulating more widely in the American population, we'll witness a great political inoculation, a resistance to injustice and authoritarianism. The veil of ignorance will be lifted and the large wall of power structures will then begin to crumble.

Those who believe in property rights, the sovereignty of individuals, and voluntary contracts also believe in the tremendous value of justice. A society of predominantly rights-respecting people forms an impenetrable network of liberty-oriented memes, which are translated into their physical manifestations as legal agencies. In such an environment, people simply don't tolerate—in particular, they don't *pay for*—biased or unjust services rendered by insurance companies, or by any other type of competitor.

Companies of villainous intent therefore can't gain a foothold on the free market. It's certainly no coincidence that the Mafia and warlords thrive in unjust and chaotic political environments, where various black and gray markets, and few free markets, exist. Inherently collectivistic in nature, these tribal mentalities impose, with whatever weaponry at their disposal, their stagnating forms of rules and punishments on people. An advanced civilization of voluntarism and unfettered capitalism naturally fosters the opposite environment. Rights-respecting people are vigilant with their pocketbooks and their opinions in empowering their agents to prevent the rise of any rights-violating groups and companies. Bad organizations hence encounter severe viability problems in such a context.

As for war, remember that war is typically the result of disagreements between the actions of States, specifically their leaders' self-serving and nationalistic choices, which then drag the tax-burdened and well-regulated populace into the bloody battlefields. In a society of rights-respecting people, funding dries up for such a destructive process. Given that a large military is incredibly expensive to operate and maintain, very few individuals or organizations have the resources to create a war machine. No war can occur without funding, and soldiers tend not to venture across borders without pay and benefits and/or a drive for revenge.

In a society of rights-respecting people, where "politics" is a thing of the past, there are no financial or ethical incentives to fight other insurance companies, let alone other, less enlightened nations. Companies are obviously encouraged to minimize their costs and discouraged from being less efficient. Competition for price, quality, and moral reputation, like in any other realm of business, serves as the ultimate inhibitor of corruption. Service to the customer is even more important in a system of complete liberty. Any deviation from the principles of justice on the part of an insurance company would spell disaster to its reputation and bottom line.

I've deliberately saved the idea of overlapping jurisdictions for last. Interestingly, this issue has been a central sticking point for those who favor voluntarily funded, yet still monopolistic, government (Laissez-faire capitalism). The philosophical debate of "anarchism versus minarchism" continues on forums and email lists throughout the Web. This issue has also been addressed in many other libertarian books that explain the contradictions in a "voluntary" State and the unparalleled merits of Anarcho-capitalism, which is another term for complete liberty.

The key thing to remember is this: Companies that operate in the same so-called jurisdiction are no different *in principle* than people in physical proximity to each other. All are capable of exercising their right to self-defense and defense of their property. Your right to self-defense doesn't interfere with my right to self-defense. Your right to contract with a particular agent of rights-protection doesn't conflict with my right to contract with a different agent of rights-protection. Your right to seek restitution for torts done to you doesn't interfere with my right to seek restitution for torts done to me. Individual rights and their enforcement, by definition, can never be in conflict.

Insurance companies simply serve as professional, contracted agents who agree to exercise the more complex and less immediate aspects of the right to self-defense, pursuant to a rights-violation, on behalf of those who decide to pay for their services. This is a crucial example of division of labor and specialization in the marketplace. Just as few of us spend our time and resources growing our own food and building our own houses, few of us will want to spend our time and resources protecting our rights.

Rights-defending insurance agencies will focus on issues of justice. They'll provide security and enforce remedies when security has been breached. These are their selling points and means of gaining customers. As in any industry that requires universal standards in order to function properly across competing platforms, insurance companies naturally institute generally agreed upon rules of operation and engagement with other parties. These assist them when they're faced with confusing or missing evidence and contradictory claims by their clients and clients of other companies.

Insurance companies will definitely incorporate much of customary law precedents as well as arbitration and mediation methods, which are obviously non-statist, common-sense ways of restoring victims and upholding property rights. It's in their business interest to make law simple and efficient. The principles of due process, evidentiary investigation, fair and speedy trial, objective judgment of whether force was initiated (and by whom), and appropriate restitution and/or reparation will generally govern their practices. In a just legal system, the accuser (or their insurance company) will pay compensation to the person falsely arrested and accused (or heaven forbid, falsely convicted), which provides an incentive to minimize lengthy trials and wasted resources. Hence, today's various irresponsible lawsuits will be markedly reduced and, of course, the State's practice of holding individuals for days, weeks, months, or even years without trial will be eliminated.

In situations where companies are at loggerheads, where they can't reach an equitable resolution, their standardized procedures will still be followed. A previously agreed upon and outlined appeals process to third party courts will safeguard against corruption and unresolved conflicts. Moreover, the accused must retain the right to choose a third party justice service, which enables the most fair and equitable judgment and resolution, that is, objectivity in law.

Again, it behooves all companies involved to insure not only against risk to their respective clients, but also against risk to their working relationships with other companies. Because each company will profit by insuring against potential rights-violations and by enforcing correct and equitable judgments, all companies seeking a share of the market have every incentive to settle conflicts peaceably and with minimal cost, according to a uniform system of justice.

So, what is the specific legal nature of a society of complete liberty? What are the universally agreed upon principles, that is, the principles honored to enable standardization? Further, what laws will best promote our happiness? Let's proceed.

VIII

LAWS THAT PROMOTE OUR PURSUITS OF HAPPINESSES

Pursuits of happinesses laws? Though Congress is totally unfamiliar with them, there can indeed be such laws. I use the plural form of both words not to make grammarians grimace, but to emphasize that there's more than just one pursuit to more than one form of happiness. A society of complete liberty allows for everyone's version of earthly bliss. As long as we respect the rights of others, we're free to do as we please to promote our own joy as well as the joy of others. Fortunately for us, the laws that can promote these pursuits are very few, very understandable, and very exact in their meaning. Nothing more and nothing less is needed.

The only laws that can promote each person's pursuit of happiness are those that administer justice on individuals who attempt to restrict or erase people's freedoms through the initiation of force. That's the universal principle. Law is a method of outlining consequences for violating the rights of individuals, penalties for infringements on one's person and property. Rights-violations reflect the plain fact that the victim wasn't a willing participant. To force someone against his or her will can only be justified if that someone started the aggression. In other words, the only proper laws are those that employ retaliatory force.

It would certainly be nice if every single human being decided to deal with every other human being solely by means of reason. We are, essentially, rational animals. But with today's prevalent authoritarian institutions of non-reason, which are bent on indoctrinating each new generation, the reality is a bit different. Disagreements also happen in the natural course of trade and social interaction. Some people lack the coping skills necessary to seek peaceful resolution. Others think that committing fraud helps their bottom line. However, the fact that respectful and enjoyable relationships are the overwhelming rule in the marketplace of most societies, not the exception, is a testament to the general goodness and virtue in humanity.

Clearly, once we remove the unquestionably biggest rights-violator that constantly pretends it's not a rights-violator, or doesn't care that it is—the State—we can immediately expose and eventually clean up what's left of criminality.

Law should be readily known and understandable to everyone in society, to all consumers and producers, to average people. Laws must be outlined in common sense, reasonable, fair and equitable terms. And the laity ought to be the moral bulwark of such laws. If it's not, then we're in big trouble. A country soon becomes run by statist intellectuals and unjust courts and legislatures who rely on their countless thought-less enforcers—enforcers who depend on people acquiescing to their widespread tactics of coercion while rationalizing that it's for maintaining law and order, the common good, general welfare, future of our children, and other such falsehoods. Clearly, if we don't understand the proper nature of law, then we'll end up with some variation of what we have today. Laws reflect basic moral premises, after all, and being treated like slaves to the State assuredly demonstrates this.

The moral premise embedded in the hundreds of thousands of laws passed and enforced by local, state, and federal governments in America is simply this: The individual good must be sacrificed to the purported collective good. In other words, the demands of a collection of individuals supposedly trump the rights of any particular individual. When stated this way, the premise can't stand scrutiny. Because only individuals have rights (only individuals can have thoughts, feelings, and make decisions), no rights of a collection of individuals can override those of a single person. Again, rights can't be in conflict with each other, by definition.

In order to avoid contradictions, and their ensuing political insanity, laws must be based on the principles of justice. And justice demands that restitution and reparation be granted to victims of initiatory force. Additionally, imprisonment must sometimes be reserved for violent individuals who've caused physical injury or repeated damage to property. Imminent threats to rights-respecting individuals mustn't be allowed to continue in a just society.

What About The Bill Of Rights?

In a market of complete liberty, which is governed simply by property owners and insurance company policies, crime will be reduced to a mere scintilla of what it is today. Property owners will determine the appropriate and reasonable rules on their property. They will also understand the legal and financial consequences of violating the rights of, or simply mistreating, those who were invited to engage in trade there. Even in circumstances of trespass, property owners are always wise to err on the side of assuming good intent on behalf of trespassers; only wanton destruction of personal property or threat to life and limb justifies immediate use of retaliatory force. And the amount of such force should be only that which is necessary to prevent further wrong-doing.

Despite various statist-oriented claims to the contrary, we have nothing to fear from private property owners. Actually, as we know from our myriad personal experiences, and by virtue of the preceding chapters, we have everything to gain from them. They are, in fact, us. As long as the State isn't in our lives, strong moral and economic incentives tend to ensure people's rights to their persons and property, and to travel. For property owners to do otherwise, of course, would mean loss of business and widespread ostracism, especially in ever more cooperative, coordinated, and information-connected societies.

Obviously, expression of contrary viewpoints would have to take place on available property. Since everything will be privately owned, including streets and sidewalks, this would amount to simply getting permission from a particular owner—rather than today's hassle of City Hall permits, assorted regulatory hurdles, and State-designated "free-speech zones" for protesters.

More importantly, notice that people today mostly rally to show their support or dissent for some aspect of what coercive government is doing, or not doing, to or for them. After all, the restrictions supposedly placed on government by the Bill of Rights were considered necessary to ensure that people's various actions wouldn't be prohibited by political whim. What a failure this has been.

The freedoms to assemble peaceably, to complain to government, to speak your mind, to publish at will, to worship as you please, to have weapons, to maintain your privacy, to prevent troops from calling your house their home base, to have a fair and speedy trial in accordance with the rules of justice and due process, are continually assaulted where the State reigns supreme. A legalized monopoly on force always leaves people concerned about losing more of their freedoms. In a system of complete liberty, however, these freedoms aren't in jeopardy anymore; they're restored and assumed as matters of fact. A land that embraces the principles of self-ownership and non-initiation of force upholds people's freedoms, rather than threatens them.

Again, the Bill of Rights was crafted in an attempt to prevent government from restricting or erasing your freedoms. Additionally, some of the Amendments in the Bill of Rights have no relevance or necessity in a private context. Obviously, the freedom to do whatever you please can only be fully exercised either on your own property or on a consenting person's property. While many commercial property owners may make rules restricting various rights outlined by the Bill of Rights, they're usually reasonable and prudent ones, such as "Leave your guns at the door, gentlemen" or "No disturbing other people's experience in the theater, please." There simply aren't many economic or moral incentives to do something unreasonable and imprudent in relation to people's rights; businesses don't want to drive away customers, after all, and hardly anyone desires to be disrespectful in commerce.

Owners have to earn their money by providing things that others want, like, enjoy, and appreciate. Humans are definitely social animals, and trade for mutual benefit tends to break down all disrespectful barriers. Complete liberty thus creates a legal context in which bigoted persons could no longer wield the collective tool of the State at individuals seen as members of various classes and groups, which government typically spends a lot of time categorizing and appealing to.

In those cases in which a commercial property owner's rules are more stringent than some consumers find acceptable, such rules will be immediately contrasted with more appealing ones by other owners. The competitive nature of the marketplace to provide customer satisfaction and safety rewards the decent and the tolerant. It disfavors the ridiculous. Most commercial development projects are prime examples of this. They satisfy genuine human desires and needs. Amusement and theme parks, museums, concert halls, stadiums, business and science centers, cruise ships, skyscrapers, and shopping malls all tend to cater to what's satisfying and preferable in the eyes of consumers—be they families and kids, art and music lovers, sports enthusiasts, honeymooners, tourists, businesspersons, or shoppers. Such places earn people's respect as well as admiration.

Welcome To The Bill Of Law

We're now going to follow the excellent lead of Michael van Notten, who was a libertarian Dutch scholar versed in international law, in order to illustrate how beneficial and straightforward law will be in the future —and how your Bill of Rights freedoms have been a meager governmental consolation prize, one that's continually reduced over time.

Van Notten wrote an excellent article titled "Bill of Law," in which he outlined a legal system without coercive and monopolistic government. And there's no need to have a Doctor of Jurisprudence degree with a Black's Law Dictionary in hand to understand it. Since most of law school concerns nonessentials and political context-dropping, to study the following actually saves us the better part of three years and many tens of thousands of dollars. We can forget about maneuvering through those whirling, cognitive death blades in higher academia. Van Notten outlined practically everything laypersons as well as scholars need to know regarding the legal framework of a free society. Whether the property is predominantly owned (and subdivided) or leased (which van Notten favored for more diverse and wholesome communities), the same sensible laws apply in order for liberty to flourish. They represent the legal foundation of a new libertarian world.

Below is his entire article. It will be good to use as a reference in your quest to enlighten others. I've made only a couple caveats, which you'll find enclosed in brackets. Sadly, Michael van Notten is no longer with us to assist in this profound journey of debate and persuasion. He was spearheading a libertarian nation project in Somalia before he died in 2002. (Somalia has yet to achieve what he envisioned, of course. Currently, various political and religious factions are still fighting for control, and the U.S.-backed Ethiopian military has been directly involved in the ongoing struggle to impose a U.N.-sanctioned government. In other words warlords, tribal mentalities, and statist powers continue to impose their non-libertarian views on a war-torn population, and the U.S. government and the U.N. continue their meddling.)

BILL OF LAW

We, the founders of the free nation, in order to guard the freedom of those who visit or settle in the free nation, do hereby affirm the following principles, rights, and rules of procedure. We expect every person in the free nation to abide by these fundamental laws.

The procedural rules given here are intended as a starting point for the development of rules for maintaining and enforcing natural rights. These rights do not change, but the procedures for maintaining and enforcing them can be continually improved.

Any person offering judicial or police services in the free nation shall be free to specify more detailed rights, obligations, and procedures than those included here, provided they are consistent with the natural law described hereinafter.

Natural Law

Natural law describes the natural, voluntary order of human society. This law is timeless, unchangeable, and universal. It takes priority over any other law, including constitutions and contracts. It acknowledges the right of every person to live a life that is governed by his own goals and opinions. Natural law serves to prevent and resolve conflicts between people pursuing contradictory goals. It stipulates that every person shall be free to dispose of his rightfully acquired property and shall refrain from disposing of the property of others without their permission. It permits all activities that do not violate someone else's person or property.

As a matter of principle, a society based on natural law should be maintained by means consistent with that law. These means will then generate—under the disciplines of profit and loss, supply and demand, and peaceful competition in the free market—the information required for discovering the optimal way of protecting natural rights.

Legal Principles

I (natural rights)
Every person shall be free to:
1. form his own opinions;
2. control the actions and labour of his own body;
3. use any object not belonging to others and make it his property;
4. make voluntary agreements with others; and
5. defend these freedoms.

II (natural obligations)
Every person shall respect the rights of others, and therefore refrain from:
1. using force or threats thereof against peaceful persons or their rightfully obtained possessions; and
2. disposing otherwise of other people's property without their permission.

III (remedies)
Every person who violates someone's natural rights shall:
1. immediately cease violating them;

2. return the goods thereby alienated;

3. compensate the victim for damage inflicted and profits foregone;

4. pay fines to the victim for willful infringement of his rights.

IV (fines)

If the parties concerned fail to agree on the nature or extent of the fine, it shall be determined by an independent and impartial court of law on the basis of the seriousness of the crime and the circumstances under which it was committed.

V (sanction)

Every person who refuses to remedy the rights he violated loses, to the benefit of his victim and to the extent required for remedy, his right to dispose of his freedom and property, as long as he persists in his refusal.

VI (force)

Every person shall be free to defend his natural rights by using force against his attacker and to call upon police to restore them. In the absence of an impartial judiciary and police, every person shall be free, subject to his liability for his own violations, to use force himself to restore his violated rights.

VII (the police)

The police, including the military, shall not use force save when an independent and impartial court of law has verified that it is used:

1. at the request of a person whose rights have been violated;

2. against the person who violated them;

3. for the sole purpose of remedying such violation;

4. with the least violent means available; and

5. after the violator has refused to comply voluntarily.

VIII (the judiciary)

Every person shall be free to exercise the profession of judge. Judges shall judge only on the basis of facts as presented, not on a person's opinions, achievements, or bodily characteristics. Judges shall only authorise the imposition of obligations that are derived from natural rights.

Rights

From these legal principles, the following rights are derived. First, a set of rights that apply to adults. Then the rights pertaining to children and one special right pertaining to women. Rights not listed shall be upheld only if they are consistent with the principles set forth above.

Every person shall be free:

1. to live according to his own, peaceful beliefs;
2. to express, in his own language and manner, his thoughts and opinions;
3. to reside in any country, and to move in and out of it along with his possessions, provided he poses no physical danger;
4. to enjoy the privacy of his home, business, papers, and effects, including his mail and telecommunications;
5. to found a family and to raise and educate his children according to his own insights, if he finds a willing mate;
6. to assemble with any others and to join and resign from any voluntary association;
7. to offer his services to people of his choice;
8. to break any employment contract as long as he honours its performance bond;
9. to undertake any economic activity, including the adjudication or enforcement of natural rights, and to keep its profits;
10. to sell, buy, lease, rent, lend, borrow, retain, or give away property by mutual agreement;
11. to exploit his land and waters, and any material in them;
12. to repossess the land, buildings, and other property taken

from him in violation of natural rights;

13. to prevent others from spoiling his property by polluting it;

14. to criticise or petition any government institution and avail himself of any services it offers; [Of course "government," as we currently know it, won't exist.]

15. to keep and bear arms, excluding weapons of mass destruction; [Actually, persons and companies (composed of persons) retain the right to use whatever devices they deem necessary to defend themselves from attackers, or to deter them, such as aggressive Statist militaries.]

16. to use force himself when his rights are in clear and present danger;

17. to dissolve any government institution which systematically violates natural rights.

Children shall enjoy the same freedom as adults except for restrictions imposed by their parents in the interest of their safety, health, and development. Children become adults when they behave as adults. Children are entitled to receive from their parents: food, clothing, shelter, health care, and education. Parents shall not be liable for the activities of their children unless they could have prevented them. Contracts concluded by a child may be dissolved by a court of justice at the request of the child or any of its parents. When parents are unable or unwilling to care for their child, the child or others acting on its behalf may appeal to a court to appoint a legal guardian who will assume the parental rights and responsibilities.

Women shall be free to abort their pregnancies, at their own discretion and expense.

Rules of Procedure in criminal matters

The following rules shall guide the actions of those who provide judicial or police services.

1. Every person accused of having violated a natural right shall be presumed innocent until proven guilty by an impartial court of justice. Until then, he shall be entitled:

1.1 to agree with the plaintiff on initiating, interrupting, and terminating any litigation before a judge of their choice;

1.2 to refuse to submit to a judge who is forced upon him as long as the judge's impartiality is not assured and his request, if any, for a jury has not been granted; [A jury of supposedly one's peers in America currently consists of people summoned by the State for "jury duty," which means (typically registered voters) being plucked out of the community, then subjected to a screening process by lawyers of the defense and prosecution, then informed (and uninformed and misinformed) by judges about specific codes of conduct, and finally to leave their jobs for as long as the non-speedy trial takes—that is, if they can't find a way out of this coercive, costly, and cumbersome process. Any jury in a free system, however, would consist of paid professionals (or perhaps volunteers serving on a rotation basis). They would be versed in the objective procedures and laws of liberty and allowed to pursue rational methods of fact-finding and due process, unlike today. Yet in all likelihood, juries wouldn't be necessary because their main purpose is to protect citizens from statist tyranny.]

1.3 to be informed, in writing and in a language which he understands, of the nature and cause of the charges against him;

1.4 to try to refute those charges (but no plea of ignorance of natural law shall be accepted);

1.5 to be assisted and represented by counsel of his choice and to keep his communications with that counsel confidential;

1.6 to be allowed adequate time for the presentation of his defence;

1.7 to resist interrogation, to decline to supply evidence against himself or his organisation, and to refuse confession;

1.8 to inspect the evidence brought against him and to cross-examine his accusers and their witnesses;

1.9 to bring in his own witnesses to testify under the same conditions as the witnesses against him;

1.10 to be given a prompt trial, without undue delays, and to receive a copy of its proceedings;

1.11 to reject procedural and evidentiary rules which infringe upon the principle of presumed innocence;

1.12 to decide whether to permit friends, family, the press, and others to attend his trial.

1.13 to present his defense in writing and to elucidate his defense orally at his trial.

2. Every person arrested shall:

2.1 be informed immediately of the reasons for his arrest, his right to remain silent, and the consequences of making statements;

2.2 be given proper food, clothing, shelter, and accommodation as well as instant communication with legal advisors and those who could assist with posting bail;

2.3 be spared torture, assault, mutilation, sterilisation, and other cruel or inhumane treatment; [Of course, if such methods are actually being entertained, let alone perpetrated, we likely have many other problems to deal with—as we do today with unaccountable governments scoffing at fair treatment and due process.]

2.4 be brought without undue delay before a grand jury or impartial court of justice, failing which he shall be entitled to instant release;

2.5 be instructed, in writing and in a language which he understands, of the reason and nature of the charges against him;

2.6 be released from detention when the court finds the charges lacking in credibility or when sufficient guaranty has been given to insure that he will appear at the trial and obey the judgement, and his release would not frustrate the investigation;

2.7 be permitted to receive mail and visitors.

3. Every person convicted of having violated a natural right shall be entitled:

3.1 to be informed, in writing, and in a language which he understands, of the reasons for his conviction;

3.2 to appeal once against his verdict and to have its interpretation of rights reviewed by a separate court;

3.3 to avoid forcible execution of his verdict by complying voluntarily.

4. No person finally convicted or acquitted shall be put in jeopardy again, by the same or by another court, for the same activity.

5. Every person falsely arrested, unduly detained, or mistakenly convicted shall be compensated by the responsible parties.

6. Every person in clear and present danger shall be entitled to use force himself in order to:

6.1 defend his rights against immediate attack;

6.2 stop an attack in progress;

6.3 arrest his attacker caught red-handed;

6.4 seize his attacker's assets for remedying the rights he infringed whenever these assets risk disappearing before a police or judicial agency can secure them;

6.5 conserve proof or evidence; provided that an impartial court of justice certifies, either before or immediately afterwards that: (1) the proof or evidence is or was at risk of being lost and (2) the least violent means available will be, or were, used.

7. Every person whose natural rights have been violated shall be entitled:

7.1 to initiate proceedings against the violator;

7.2 to halt such proceedings and to suspend or stop the execution of any verdict in his favour;

7.3 to ignore any verdict of acquittal which does not state the reasons for the defendant's acquittal;

7.4 to appeal from the verdict in appeal when it overturns the original verdict;

7.5 to have a court's interpretation of rights reviewed by a separate court;

7.6 to have these rights exercised by his heirs if he died or by his agent if he is unable otherwise to exercise them himself.

8. Every parent whose child's natural rights have been violated shall be entitled to seek justice on the child's behalf. If the violator is one of its parents or legal guardians, the child's nearest relatives are entitled to bring suit. [Theoretically, not only the child's nearest relatives, but also any rational adult has the right to seek justice on the child's behalf in a court of law.]

9. Unless other arrangements are agreed to beforehand by the parties involved, the costs incurred by the courts for dispensing justice, as well as any legal costs of the litigants, shall be borne by the defendant if he is convicted, and by the plaintiff if the defendant is acquitted.

All these rules outlined by Michael van Notten essentially reflect a principled, common sense form of law—that is, customary law. There's no convoluted legalese formulated by workers of the State to contend with. Thus, adjudication functions efficiently. Insurance companies or any other types of justice agencies that deviate from these principles can't last long. People will find justice elsewhere.

Criminality, as it exists in our present society, is mainly the result of a legalized monopoly in the realm of supposed rights-protection. The Bill of Law will make sure that criminals, namely, those who violate rights—including governmental officials—bear full responsibility for their actions; clearly, our current system flagrantly mocks this idea. When law enforcement is left to the free market, people tempted by criminality will have many disincentives to do wrong and many incentives to be responsible, productive individuals.

It's vital to remember that State-run schools will no longer exist. These schools do more than unapologetically squelch learners' intrinsic motivation and try to replace it with extrinsic motivators, such as teachers' orders, praise, and punishments. They also foster socially acceptable criminality, because so-called public education funds its operations (and mandates attendance) via the coercive methods of statism. This system may arguably be the biggest creator of criminal mindsets in human history, be they in schoolyard bully garb or later in pressed uniforms donning shiny badges. All disrespectful types seem welcome, as long as they employ socially acceptable disrespect, that is, the unquestioned policies of politics. We also shouldn't forget that the "business" of the corrections system depends on governmental diktats to churn out an ample supply of law-breakers (drug laws being one blatant example). Essentially, the State and criminality were made for each other, sewn from the same rights-smothering cloth.

In a free market, the people themselves are the first line of defense regarding their rights. The citizens construct a system in which the ideas, rules, and procedures of the Bill of Law are common knowledge. Hardly any legal precept is as easy to understand as "Respect the rights and property of others and trade with them voluntarily." The rest just fills in the details, if any problems occur.

Making Sense Of Foreign Policy Nonsense

Regarding a military, only a couple more things need to be clarified. An offensive force is not necessary in a free society. People who engage in trade have no time or inclination to destroy their economic and social relationships with people abroad. Those in other countries (though not necessarily their governments) by and large appreciate this and don't desire to inflict injuries on a peaceful and friendly populace elsewhere. These free market factors, by the way, are the *only* antidote to terrorism. A police State, or any less extreme domestic or foreign policy, is assuredly not. Even the tiny, tightly controlled nation of Israel, which is supported heavily by the United States' money and weaponry, can't secure its borders and ensure safety from terrorist attacks. A police State is more effective at wreaking havoc on its own citizenry than perhaps any other form of government. A quick study of Gestapo tactics in Hitler's Germany will provide a horrific view of what happens in such an environment.

Perhaps the biggest falsehood promoted after the 9/11 attacks has been the notion that "They hate us (that is, want to kill us) because of our freedoms." Even granting the unjustified notion of "our freedoms," all the evidence, including repeated statements by jihadist Osama bin Ladin himself, point to the contrary. The evidence shows that suicide bombers arise mainly on account of foreign occupation of their perceived territory and oppression of certain domestic populations. Virtually every case of terrorism, regardless of the religion of the perpetrators (or their type of fundamentalism), yields such a pattern of political grievance and subsequent horrific tactics. Since terrorists can't utilize statist military power, they resort to killing civilians in an attempt to induce political change.

Terrorists want to alter political policies of their own country or of the occupying forces, or both. Though their actions are abominable, terrorists do have a definite rationale. Unfortunately, one of the last things that the leaders of occupying forces want to do when confronted by fanatical resistance is leave. That, among other things, would mean losing face and conceding to the enemy. Instead, they continue to slap the hornets' nest of dissent and blame all the despicable results on the hornets, caring little about the loss of innocent lives. Collective punishment of entire populations by military forces soon becomes the order of the day. American military destruction of Iraq, its people and infrastructure, and Israeli military destruction of Lebanon, its people and infrastructure (as well as continued oppression of people in the occupied territories of Palestine) are prime examples of this process. More hegemonic foreign policy measures will only encourage still more terrorism blowback, especially in statist areas immersed in such theocratic and revengeful tribal ideologies as the Middle East.

History has shown that terrorists can only be effectively neutralized by those who live among them. Without the support or tacit approval of sizable segments of the local population, the angry hornets have no places to nest. Therefore—and this is psychology 101—the primary way to end terrorism is to end military interventions and statist foreign policies that promote ill will in countries of people who are keen on noticing political double standards, lies and hypocrisy, alliances with despotic puppet regimes, and State-sanctioned mass murder. Ending the United States' egregious rights-violations, stopping its foreign occupations, and ceasing support for any and all governments in the Middle East, will go a long way to foster goodwill in the vast majority of people there. This naturally coincides with peaceful relations and free trade. Those who embrace a nonviolent form of Islam (or any other faith, for that matter) seek a more prosperous future for themselves and their children, just like the rest of the world.

A voluntarily funded military, to the extent that it's needed, will be used only for defensive purposes. Any large companies or people that might need protection from aggression in far-away places (or close to home) must pay for it out of their own pockets. The various people they do business with also have a vested interest in preventing any attacks on their trading routes.

But what about other governments that might attempt to take over and control a free society? Well, they would realize that they have everything to lose and nothing to gain from unprovoked aggression. Even in recent history, few power-hungry warfare States have desired to target countries that haven't provoked them (or their declared allies), either through military actions or economic sanctions. (Switzerland, by the way, remains a case study in defensive neutrality.) State rulers get very anxious about anything that threatens their power structure, control, and authority. So, their first concern is to maintain stability and security for themselves, to preserve their own hides within their own countries. Police State regimes of fear serve this purpose well, as does massive statist indoctrination. Just as we Americans were brought up to pay homage to Old Glory, say the Pledge, obey the law, and pay our taxes, children in other countries are taught similarly, but sometimes with more intensity and frequency. Statist control of the media further emphasizes that the State and its rulers must be esteemed above all else.

If aggressive rulers have nothing to fuel their propaganda machines, they can't convince their people that going to war makes any sense. With no hint of truth or context to their prewar slogans, rulers would appear plainly as madmen to soldiers and civilians alike. Hence, certain slogans are necessary to win the first battle—the one for the hearts and minds of the citizenry: "Look at how they've treated us!" "They want to kill us all!" "They pose a grave danger to our society!" "They want to see us all suffer and starve!" "Look at how they've dealt with others!"

"Fight them for what they've done to your brothers and sisters, mothers and fathers, aunts and uncles!" "They believe that they're better than you; just look at their tactics!" "See how evil they are!" "We must strike them before they strike us!" Clearly, such statements can come from the mouths of leaders of democratic and totalitarian regimes alike.

If, for some odd reason, another country's government *did* target a free society without the support or sympathies of its populace, it would face quick and overwhelming retaliation from numerous decentralized and distributed forces. Retaliation would be directed specifically at the leaders giving the orders—that is, assassination of the despots would be the primary method of attack, along with destruction of immediate offensive threats. This would assuredly cause aggressive leaders to think twice before making a false move. Most would definitely question the perceived wisdom in attacking a highly innovative and advanced free market system, in which individuals are willing to defend their highly valued freedoms. Since swift victory is primarily about strategic information and technological superiority, the market of complete liberty will beat any State-controlled market, hands down.

Because a free market provides a brilliant example to others throughout the world of life's great possibilities, the political grip of various statist regimes will be steadily pried loose. After all, a free country offers no symbols of the collective, such as government or State "leaders," for other rulers to blame and target. A free country therefore invites no governmental or military aggression; it provokes no retaliatory measures either. Consequently, statist regimes will be left without an enemy, except the one within their own borders—the people. They will face internal collapse, like the U.S.S.R. did, and like China's regime eventually will, barring any foolish gamesmanship on the part of the U.S. government.

America has really come to a fork in the road, and only one direction leads to our safety and security. Liberty can spread quickly. It works as a universal solvent for bad ideas and policies. Of course, some statist rulers are more aware than others of the threat this poses to their power and control structures. Some may try desperately to protect their positions by withdrawing from the world marketplace and hence further oppressing their own people. Statist interference with international trade is of course morally and economically damaging. It creates a downward spiral of great losses for everyone involved. In extreme cases, it can kill millions.

For example, perhaps the only reason that North Korea (DPRK, fittingly the Democratic People's Republic of Korea) hasn't hit rock bottom and disintegrated is because of foreign aid and foreign coercive measures. The governments of the U.S., China, and others have, among other sordid things in coordination with U.N. organizations, been feeding the DPRK military for years. Dictatorial rulers tend to distribute foreign assistance to those who are most valuable to their regime, on down the influential pecking order. Leaders of States everywhere know this; it's the same situation in African countries.

Many U.S. and Chinese officials believe that if the North Korean regime were to collapse, a refugee crisis of epic proportions would ensue, causing unpredictable political problems. So, they actually believe it's better to forcibly keep an utterly impoverished and tortured people within their own State's borders than to really do something to help their plight. The Chinese State doesn't even allow North Korean refugees safe passage to Mongolia, which is willing to accept them. Much like the psychotic plot of a horror film, people are treated as creatures to control and slay: better to send refugees back to their national slaughterhouse, than to allow them freedom to travel to places of less oppression. Totalitarian regimes such as the People's Republic of China keep short leashes on people, especially ones who dare to break the State's laws.

The former Union of Soviet Socialist Republics would have probably hit rock bottom decades beforehand too had it not been for the financial and moral help of the various Western powers. American statesmen and their financial cronies were most helpful to Stalin after WWII. Obviously, when political leaders share the same statist premises, we can expect the terrible aftermath.

So, back to our pursuits of happinesses. The above talk about war and statism is just a bad dream in a voluntary society. Given the incalculable benefits of such a society—and the incalculable drawbacks of present political systems—you might wonder why the status quo remains so. Why is it so difficult for so many people to accept the idea of complete liberty, let alone work diligently to implement it?

IX

IF IT'S NATURAL TO BE FREE, WHAT'S STOPPING US?

Anti-Social Political Behaviors: Lying, Cheating, And Stealing

By now, it's probably apparent that complete liberty is more than just a political and economic system. It's also an ethical one. It outlines a new way for people to deal with each other, not simply in their personal interactions, daily affairs, and business relations, but in the way they interpret their form of government and therefore how it interacts with and affects everyone. It's easy to let government go on being itself —big, plodding, intrusive, even dangerous and deadly, doing things that hardly any of us appreciate on a personal level. But the State is composed of particular persons doing particular jobs, and that's the real issue.

Lying, cheating, and stealing are not admirable behaviors. Forcing people to do things against their will is not a way to gain respect. Yet, these behaviors are given more acceptable names in politics in order to disguise their essentially coercive quality. Those in the mainstream press are accomplices in this game of doublespeak. The political news is often a verbatim press release from governmental officials. Even the information dispensed by political opinion givers is something reminiscent of the discourse in George Orwell's *1984*. Interviews with politicians and bureaucrats never touch on the reality of what individuals in government are doing to us. After all, if reporters raised awareness of this reality, they would likely be banned from political access. But being banned from access is just what reporters *need* in order to shake them out of their misguided practices and encourage honesty with the American public. John Stossel is about the only person in the establishment who exposes the absurd nature of governmental processes. His peers look like statist lapdogs in comparison.

Fortunately, people in America still appreciate good challengers of authority. This no doubt explains the uplifting individualistic themes, justice-oriented plots, and heroic characters of many Hollywood films. Also, the high ratings of Comedy Central's *The Daily Show* and *The Colbert Report* reveal that many Americans enjoy a bold and satirical look at politics-as-usual and a witty skewering of those in positions of power. On some level, most Americans sense that there's something really wrong with politics. So at the very least, we should mock it; we should laugh at it.

But, of course, we can do more than poke fun at aspects of the coercive system and at those who spend their time and energy trying to run it (and report on it). We've seen that in order to strike at the root of the vices of politics, to see them for what they actually are, we need to understand the nature of self-ownership and voluntarism. Such an understanding allows us to sharpen a principled ax that we can use to cut down the entire rotten tree of taxation and destroy its expansive root system of regulation.

The ominous taxation tree towers over our entire country, and over all the benevolent potential market trees and flowers. Its many branches of government reach over all of us, letting in scant sunlight. This particular tree also provides ample room for all sorts of political and legal creatures to call home. The problem is, political animals aren't keen on coming down from a tree by ordinary pleas that they become less meddlesome, or that they should mistreat us less. After all, from their various perches, what need do *they* have of more sunlight? They seem to be getting plenty from the skies above, and the market below is just a necessary place where ordinary people toil for the common good of the rotten tree.

Though oftentimes it may be more difficult to reason with people involved in government, we all have the same basic needs. All of us are best nourished when we find wholesome, moral places to work. The market will assuredly accommodate everyone now working in government in ways they're presently unable to envision. Indeed, leaving their positions will create a vastly more promising and much richer economic environment for everyone.

From our shaded standpoint in the fertile soil of the market, one might think that convincing the rest of the grounded folks of the merits of chopping down the entire tree wouldn't be too difficult. It's choking off our sunlight, after all, depriving us of a much better, more dynamic, and hope-filled future, both personally and as a society.

Part of the problem is that the inhabitants of the taxation tree think that they're involved in something really important, and they continually try to convince us of this by instituting all kinds and degrees of symbiosis and parasitism in the economy. They also try to convince us of how unimportant our individual rights are. We've been taught that we *need* government and that we should *want* government.

Government, in fact, needs *us* to sanction its immoral and unjust actions, because it clearly doesn't have enough resources and prisons (or will) to subdue a rationally disobedient populace. Without most people's conformity and support, the whole coercive system will disintegrate. In other words, the State can't sustain itself by brute force alone; it relies on obedient people losing sight that they vastly outnumber the State's enforcers.

Thus, to muster support and curry our favor, government provides us schooling, grants, tax incentives, subsidies, import tariffs and quotas, privileges, assistance, programs, vast public/private partnerships, etc.— all to make it seem as if we're part of the tree too. Government thus encourages us to sit in the tree, take in the sunlight, and heartily consume its magical fruit with blissful moral ignorance (definitely *not* the tree of knowledge of good and evil).

Reliance on government is part and parcel of its determination to rule over and "take care of" all aspects of our lives. As the late Harry Browne used to say (who was twice the Libertarian Party's U.S. Presidential candidate), government is good mainly at one thing: breaking your legs, handing you a set of crutches, and then saying, "See, if it weren't for us, you wouldn't be able to walk!" Because of the State's encroachment on virtually every aspect of the economy, all of us are now hobbling around on government-issued crutches.

Some pretend that their crutches are kind gifts from unquestionable authorities. To bolster this view, they assert "But government is doing many useful things!" Indeed, some people in government are involved in activities that are trying to be helpful to many people. But the key question always confronts them: What are the *means* by which your organization is trying to help?

Of course, apologists of statism are quick to dismiss this inquiry. It doesn't have legitimacy to them, because "the people" have supposedly spoken in elections, and they think the taxation tree, while in need of some pruning, is indispensable to their lives and well-being. The end therefore justifies the means, they say. We wouldn't want a market to be lit by radiant sunlight, now would we? It might start thinking that it doesn't need us!

Unfortunately, many of us tend to believe that our crutches don't bother us all that much. Many of us think that if we just follow the rules and obey the laws (as if we could possibly know them all and thus do so) then our lives will somehow be fulfilling. Yet, whatever sort of fulfillment can be had by such an approach, it's a far cry from living optimal lives, that is, lives proper to independently thinking, choosing, and acting human beings. Lysander Spooner described the nature of this regrettable situation in *No Treason: The Constitution of No Authority*:

> The fact is that the government, like a highwayman, says to a man: "Your money, or your life." And many, if not most, taxes are paid under the compulsion of that threat.
>
> The government does not, indeed, waylay a man in a lonely place, spring upon him from the roadside, and, holding a pistol to his head, proceed to rifle his pockets. But the robbery is none the less a robbery on that account; and it is far more dastardly and shameful.
>
> The highwayman takes solely upon himself the responsibility, danger, and crime of his own act. He does not pretend that he has any rightful claim to your money, or that he intends to use it for your own benefit. He does not pretend to be anything but a robber. He has not acquired impudence enough to profess to be merely a "protector," and that he takes men's money against their will, merely to enable him to "protect" those infatuated travelers, who feel perfectly able to protect themselves, or

do not appreciate his peculiar system of protection. He is too sensible a man to make such professions as these. Furthermore, having taken your money, he leaves you, as you wish him to do. He does not persist in following you on the road, against your will; assuming to be your rightful "sovereign," on account of the "protection" he affords you. He does not keep "protecting" you, by commanding you to bow down and serve him; by requiring you to do this, and forbidding you to do that; by robbing you of more money as often as he finds it for his interest or pleasure to do so; and by branding you as a rebel, a traitor, and an enemy to your country, and shooting you down without mercy, if you dispute his authority, or resist his demands. He is too much of a gentleman to be guilty of such impostures, and insults, and villainies as these. In short, he does not, in addition to robbing you, attempt to make you either his dupe or his slave.

Spooner has here eloquently portrayed the psychology of enslavement of Americans. The State is the substitute highwayman in our lives. A real highwayman would be much easier to deal with; there's no chance of being permanently duped and enslaved by him. From birth to grave government tries to deny us self-ownership and stifle our rationality. Unlike the highwayman, we seem to naturally become accustomed to capitulating to its constant demands, just as a child must capitulate to the demands of an authoritarian parent. But, of course, we aren't children anymore. Yet are we, in a profound way, still locked into a survival mode that resembles a suffering child?

One thing's for certain regarding this issue: It's *impossible* to correct the immoral and unjust behavior of State employees by obeying them and acting as if we aren't being victimized. Such a practice, the practice of thanking our leg breakers for the crutches they've provided us, or complaining that the crutches don't fit properly, or at most wishing that we didn't have to wear crutches, is indicative of the Stockholm syndrome. The name comes from a 1973 bank hostage crisis in Stockholm, Sweden, in which the hostages became quite sympathetic to their captors. The formal definition is as follows: an emotional attachment to a captor formed by a hostage as a result of continuous stress, dependence, and a need to cooperate for survival. Thus, the victim identifies and aligns with—essentially, excuses the actions of—his or her oppressors. The phenomenon is probably as old as humankind itself. Untold generations of children have had to cope with authoritarian parenting methods, as opposed to ones that fully respect and nurture their reasoning abilities. (In contrast, lenient parenting methods, which are without coherent structure, consistent guidance, and understandable education are arguably not much of an improvement over authoritarian parenting methods.)

America is faced with a hostage crisis of epic proportions. Even though the ransom has been paid by the victims over and over again, the captors are never satisfied. Nearly everyone is afflicted with varying degrees of the Stockholm syndrome—even though, as noted, we can at any time collectively disarm our captors. The more we trick ourselves into believing that placating our captors will keep them from destroying our lives, the more our lives (and society) become mere shadows of what they could be.

Obeying unjust laws and regulations and allowing our wealth to be taken from us is also similar to paying bribes in order to survive. Regardless of whether ransom or bribes is the most accurate depiction, such behavior will never restore our lives, our dignity, and our freedoms. Nor will it ensure our Lives, our Fortunes, and our sacred Honor, to speak in the Founders' terms. Remember, the dastardly and shameful practices of the State's employees can't be appeased. Further appeasement will only beget more of such practices—more of the game wherein the State's employees pretend to be our protectors and providers, and we pretend not to be their dupes and slaves. Therefore, we must strip the State *itself* of its power, by exposing it for what it truly is.

Noticing The Obvious, And Judging It Properly

While evidence for the biggest crime imaginable is in plain sight, there are those who don't want to stand up against immorality and injustice. Even though they may not be directly involved in govern-

174

ment, they certainly tow the party line. For instance, you may wonder, as I have, why independent media tend to lean in the Marxist direction. They seem to be as blind to the coercive essence of the State as those in government—or, they're just as aware of it, and they don't care. Most of them probably think that if only *they* had the governmental tools at their disposal, then they could shape the world to their own liking. The environment would be saved, no one would be poor, there would be no more wars, everyone would have equality, the market would play fairly, and so on. What they fail to acknowledge, of course, is that the good can't be achieved by irrational means. You can't make people more rational by foisting irrationality upon them.

Individual rights and property are more fundamental concepts to the creation of a good world than anything else. Society is only as good as the persons residing in it, and how they treat each other. The less individuals and their property are respected and dealt with through reason, the less good can be accomplished.

The way to a better world must start with complete repudiation of a moral code that holds the sacrifice of individuals and their property as proper for the common good. By that inverted ethical standard, there can be no end to the sacrifices; soon, they consume an entire civilization, because each person who abides by this code has his or her own values to force on everyone else. Under this code, people's values are transformed by government into endless needs, to be satisfied by those most able (as well as those less able).

From Communism to Democracy, to a constitutional Republic, the premise is the same: The able, who can be anyone for any reason, must be sacrificed to the needy, who can be anyone for any reason. This obviously creates ongoing turf wars of special interests, each vying for their day in the sun, their governmental branch to perch on—for the "good" of the few, at the expense of the many.

One may wonder when the news media will become objective about the full nature of these abominations. Clearly it's within the average person's capacity to report and judge events based on logical thought and evidence. One doesn't have to drop the context in which things occur. Chasing metaphorical and literal ambulances may get people's attention, but it also loses sight of why so many accidents are happening.

Ayn Rand wrote about the need to distinguish between "the metaphysical and the man-made." Things don't just "happen," without causes. People make choices, and they take actions that may or may not have been necessary or preventable. In particular, when it comes to actions of governments and their abettors, and the ensuing negative repercussions in the world, nothing is more important than discovering how they could've been prevented, or at least mitigated. In other words, we need to distinguish not only what's caused by nature versus what's caused by human choice. We also must distinguish between human choices stemming from the unfettered use of reason versus those from coercion.

Rather than reporting events out of context, journalists and investigators need to follow the logical bouncing ball. They need to go to the causal source of any issue. That way, they can ground themselves in reality and facts, and ask essential questions that point the way to a dramatically better world for all of us.

It's too common today for us to be exposed to only two aspects of any political or economic issue, which are merely two sides of the same fraudulent coin. Conservatives desire to have government *their* way, and liberals desire to have government *their* way. Neither of which is the correct way. Some are enamored with the idea that Republicans will take them to the promised land of low taxes, Constitutionally constrained and accountable government, law and order, and traditional values. Others are enamored with the idea that Democrats will take them to the promised land of effective and benevolent government, tolerance, equality, and progressive values. Still others are enamored with the idea that an independent man on a white horse will ride to election victory and rescue them from big, inefficient, and corrupt government —and replace it with a small government of, by, and for the People.

Few of these ideas are without some good intentions, of course. In the minds of most people, they all reflect a certain desire to make the world a better place. The folly is in their contradictory nature, in the notion that sacrificing rational values is both good and proper. On some level, most people sense this. This may be why, at base, they don't quite trust the words that come out of the mouths of politicians and bureaucrats. Most feel that there's something really slimy and slithery about politics, and anyone who pays the slightest bit of attention will see that it wreaks of ulterior motives. But many are unable or unwilling to pinpoint exactly why. Nonetheless, the constant antisocial activities of lying, cheating, and stealing continue to render politics guilty as charged. Our proxy highwayman is in plain sight.

Prohibiting voluntary contracts, voluntary trade, voluntary ownership, and voluntary use of property can never lead to any sort of promised land. Instead, it always leads to variations of hell on Earth. Anyone who believes that force is preferable to persuasion among human beings, or that theft is preferable to trade, should realize that one can't logically exclude oneself from the effects.

Liberty-Oriented Values and Virtues

As stressed earlier, if you want complete liberty, you must advocate both freedom for yourself and freedom for others. Liberty must be put into proper context. So, in addition to formulating a new understanding of the nature of government, we need to formulate a new understanding of what freedom means for all humans. We need to promote beneficial values and virtues in relation to others. Values such as reason and self-esteem and virtues such as self-reliance, integrity, honesty, and self-responsibility must be incorporated into our ways of living—and demonstrated to our children.

Reason is our essential method of interacting with the world and with others. The fist, club, gun, fine, or jail cell are its opposites. Coercion is the antithesis of rationality. You can't force yourself or someone else to think or feel differently. That's not how the brain works. Human beings require evidence, facts, and logical identification and integration of ideas in order to make sense of things.

Disappointingly, some people believe that we ought to be coerced into *doing* various things, such as paying taxes; if we don't, we should be forced to live in a jail cell. If we resist at any point, we should be restrained or even killed. Rather than appealing to reason, these self-contradictory beliefs and practices appeal to insanity, the loss of rational functioning. When employees of the State force others (who've violated no one's rights) to do various things, the end result in society is the law of the jungle—a code of morality fit for unthinking primates. Those who enforce jungle law are much more suited to commanding troops of baboons than telling fellow humans what to do.

The fact that some people think that forcing others is the answer to their financial woes, be they social or political in nature, tells us that they don't fully believe in the effectiveness of their own reasoning capacities. In other words, they reason that their faculty of reason is impotent, and therefore people must be forced. This necessarily diminishes their level of self-esteem.

Self-esteem involves a firm belief in the efficacy of one's mind and one's worthiness for happiness. The first component enables us to cope with life's challenges, while the second provides the feeling that we're fit for existence, that we're "good enough." Developing confidence in your own mind's ability to function as nature intended—that is, rationally—and appreciating your own sense of worth as a unique human being with great potential for happiness are keys to generating and maintaining genuine self-esteem.

Integrity is tied to this, of course. If we do things that we know are wrong or don't make rational sense, our self-esteem suffers. We are being dishonest with ourselves if we believe that what we profess and what we do shouldn't be logically connected. We then betray our deeper understanding. If we've adopted values from the culture without consideration of whether they're good for us and good for others, then we become mostly dependent on traditions and institutions for our code of morality. Like the bad political memes that infect society, bad ethical memes promote inconsistent values and virtues, which diminish our practice of integrity.

Honesty and intellectual self-reliance become doubly critical when the culture offers us ideas that contradict our ability to be rational and accept facts. Honesty entails the willingness to honor *reality*, to always acknowledge what's happening (and what's happened) rather than to ignore or distort it, or just make something up. It relies on our inherent ability to identify and integrate information, that is, to reason.

Self-reliance reflects the belief that no one can do our thinking or feeling or deciding for us. This is as it should be. No one has your particular perspective, knowledge, opinions, and capabilities. Therefore, you are in the best position of taking charge of your life, as you see fit. Others may be helpful and comforting, or they may want you to uncritically accept their pronouncements and judgments. But you are the prime mover of your life. To take charge of your thoughts, feelings, and actions means that you accept the fact that you're a responsible person. Other people are responsible persons too. None of us is a piece of putty in the hands of others, to be molded as they desire. Even conformity to unjust edicts of authorities is a personal choice, and the more we decide to conform, the more we look like putty.

Self-responsibility reflects the belief that each of us is the ultimate decision maker in our lives. You are the architect of your actions, because you are the thinker of your thoughts. This, too, is as it should be. You wouldn't want others to be in charge of your character and reputation, would you? That would deny others their own responsibility to themselves. Each of us is thus accountable for what we believe and what we do.

Notice that government, through taxation, regulation, and monopolization attempts to rob us of these vital values and virtues. In an utter erosion of honesty, it tells us that all is as it should be, that there's nothing of great concern to be aware of. It discourages us from taking responsibility by trying to counteract our own will and reason, by trying to usurp our crucial decision-making ability. In an unequivocal act of incivility and dishonor, the State coerces us into taking care of others and coerces others into taking care of us. Primarily, though, we are coerced into taking care of the State. By imposing their services upon us, employees of the State leave us little choice in crucial matters of our security and the security of our communities.

Government basically destroys the opportunities for shaping our lives in the ways we truly want. It further pretends that we can't rely on ourselves. Instead, we must rely on authorities (other selves) to tell us what to do and what not to do—and submit to them regardless of whether we disagree with their irrational pronouncements. Government diminishes our growth in self-esteem and integrity by fostering credulity in coercion and dependence on nonsense ideas. Finally, it hands us a twisted code of morality, which tells us that we aren't sovereign and that we don't fully own ourselves and our property.

The psychological shock waves all these things send throughout the country truly suppress the American spirit of independence and individuality. Thus, our entire population ends up with a split personality, in which people relate to others personally in one fashion (respectfully) and to others politically in another fashion (disrespectfully).

Another ethical consequence concerns the decline of social virtues that Thomas Paine knew were necessary for good communities to sustain themselves. In addition to reasonableness and honesty, they involve such things as generosity, goodwill, kindness, and helpfulness. Though Americans are still supremely generous, and give enormous sums of money and assistance to those in need around the world, the State's system of taxation and regulation steals and wastes much of our wealth. It leaves us with a small fraction of what would otherwise be available to give to others less fortunate, or better yet, to invest in ways to help them help themselves.

Additionally, as mentioned earlier, bad money tends to drive out good money, meaning that helpful people are either prevented from helping others in need or are forced into the government's official way of doing things. The aftermath of the levy breach in New Orleans, for instance, not only exposed the destructive policies of the Army Corps of Engineers, but also proved once again that the Federal Emergency Management Agency is hazardous to our health. The sooner Americans can divest themselves of these life-threatening organizations, the better. We will then swap the anchors thrown to us by government for marketplace life preservers.

Since accountability isn't connected to the consumption of tax revenues, few take responsibility for how and where the money is spent and the quality of the services that are (and are not) provided. The unintended consequences of this have become case studies in mismanagement of resources and creation of unhealthy dependencies. For instance, the "War on Poverty," like all statist wars, is mainly a war on taxpayers, using the recipients as fodder for further boondoggles. Observe the results: more misery; more corruption; and, more failure.

A rational vision of the future entails realizing the futility in promoting contradictory political ideals. If we desire a fantastically better world for ourselves and others, the only way to achieve it is to rid ourselves of subhuman ways of dealing with one another. We must look upward instead of downward when it comes to morality. Upward is the evolutionary destiny that we must decide to fulfill. With that in mind, let's finish with an analysis of concrete ways to evolve in the short term, so that we might achieve complete liberty in *our* lifetime, not merely in smart discourse with friends at a coffee shop, or in our pleasant dreams, or in some future time unreachable to us.

X

LIVE FREELY AND NOT DIE!

In Search Of The Governed's Consent

Article 3
That government is, or ought to be, instituted for the common benefit, protection, and security of the people, nation or community; of all the various modes and forms of government that is best, which is capable of producing the greatest degree of happiness and safety and is most effectually secured against the danger of maladministration; and that, whenever any government shall be found inadequate or contrary to these purposes, a majority of the community hath an indubitable, unalienable, and indefeasible right to reform, alter or abolish it, in such manner as shall be judged most conducive to the public weal.

Article 14
That the people have a right to uniform government; and therefore, that no government separate from, or independent of, the government of Virginia, ought to be erected or established within the limits thereof.

George Mason   *Virginia Declaration of Rights*

Article 3 above probably reminds you of Jefferson's words in the *Declaration of Independence*. Indeed, Thomas saw no need to reinvent the political wheel in these matters. Both his and Mason's idea was to emphasize that government should be designed to serve the interests of the people, rather than the people existing to serve the interests of government. Clearly, it didn't take long for this idea to become reversed.

Each man was well aware of this possibility, which explains why they were quick to mention that if government turns into some kind of monster, the people have an indubitable, unalienable, and indefeasible right to reform, alter or abolish it, according to the welfare of the community.

Now, we've seen how the idea of monopolistic government leads directly to lack of choices and coercive control of the citizenry. In Article 14 above, Mason falsely assumed that a legalized monopoly of government is the way for law to be uniform and equitable. Maybe he believed that such a coercive monopoly would be easier to control and more servile than independent or separate "governments."

Yet, to authorize an organization to have sole power over the affairs of a group of people immediately ignores those who would rather be left alone or organize their own methods of governance. Centralized, collectivistic governance in fact lacks legal authority, because it defies the nature of agency and voluntary contracts. Remember, government isn't the end; people's security is. Individuals and their decision-making capacities precede any notions of government.

Only an ideology based on collectivism views people as a herd and disregards individuals. Collectivism seeks to corral people into a system of governance not of their choosing. This, of course, exposes the basic misunderstanding of how government actually works. Notions such as "common benefit" and "public weal" create a sense of universality or mutual bond, but in reality they belie the nature of how persons in communities (be they towns, cities, states, or nations) interact.

Individuals, by the hundreds, thousands, and millions make countless choices in the marketplace of products, services, values, ideas, and relationships. To speak of their general welfare really means to speak of the total sum of each person's needs and context—something that no coercive, monopolistic government can ever hope to ascertain. Only when unanimity exists, based on sound principles, can one speak in broad, community-wide terms. The idea that safety and security for people can or should be provided by a single organization called government, even if funded voluntarily, is analogous to mandating a single provider of food, water, and shelter for everyone. Imagine the chaos and chronic shortages resulting from *that* scenario. The grim history of

Communism saves us the trouble of imagining it.

Obviously, every sane person wants safety and security for themselves and their loved ones. That's incontrovertible. So, the main question is this: How do we enable the satisfaction of each person's safety and security? This is the question that the Framers faltered on (and, obviously, most people today continue to falter on). Essentially, they assumed the conclusion—that government exists; therefore, we must have government—and they constructed a political system around that faulty conclusion, paying no attention to its negation of individual rights.

We certainly know that *individuals* exist, so it's most wise to begin a political system with that assumption. Embracing this simple fact leads us directly to the conclusion that individuals must be free to construct any political system of their choosing—so long as it doesn't violate individual rights. As we discovered, the *only* system capable of respecting individual rights is *a market-based one*. This conclusion follows from the nature of voluntary contracts. Again, each of us is free to contract with whomever we like and trust. Just as importantly, each of us is free not to contract with whomever we don't like and don't trust.

Rather than leading to criminality, chaos, confusion, and shortages —rather than leading to a disintegration of community standards and a proliferation of vices—enterprising individuals in the marketplace work to ensure that people get what they want and remain satisfied, so they become repeat customers. When given the choice, people tend to gravitate to those goods and services that they most value. They pay for only what they want, and they get only what they pay for—a la carte ordering writ large. Most people take these economic rights to trade for granted, at least where the State hasn't coerced them to do otherwise. All we have to do is apply this same principle to politics.

Instead of a one-size-fits-all approach to government that maintains itself by initiatory force and prevention of choices, the marketplace can provide myriad ways to ensure your safety and security—all without any extra costs or unwanted aspects, which are *always unavoidable* with the State.

Given the current nature of politics in America (not to mention the rest of the world), how likely is it that most people will become more aware and work to change things dramatically for the better? How likely is it that the people will discard entrenched power structures and stagnant institutions and replace them with rights-respecting, market-place providers of formerly governmental services?

Well, the answers to these questions depend primarily on how many people are exposed to these new political ideas and new ways of thinking about themselves and their rights (that is, new to *them*; the ideas have been around for quite awhile). Yet, being exposed to these ideas is one thing. Acting on them is another, which again raises the issue of integrity.

Most people still abide by a political morality that allows for, or rather mandates, the initiation of force, instead of retaliatory force. Of course, morality is intimately tied to psychological processes, to feelings and subconscious thoughts. Any change in point of view, then, requires moving the rest of the psychological mountain. Most people feel that they have only a shovel with which to work, rather than heavy earth-moving equipment. Such a feeling can trick them into thinking that the status quo is easier and preferable to revolutionary change.

A change in point of view can indeed seem daunting. It may require that we restructure not just our belief system, but also our friendships, family relationships, jobs, work relations, voting habits (specifically the habit of voting itself), and so on. But it's basically a problem of psychological and moral inertia—which must be acted upon by something sufficiently provocative, such as better ideas and self-generated behaviors, as well as inspiring actions of others. If left unchallenged, our present political opinions shaped by the State might continue for many more centuries, just like humanity has plodded along politically since time immemorial.

We must come to realize that government is a detrimental burden, not the benefactor of the community, state, and nation. It doesn't create law and order; it creates a seemingly permanent, insidious form of societal chaos. All of us are slowly dying from government, failing to actualize our full potential as members of an advanced civilization on a marvelous biosphere. Government continues to make a mockery of our self-actualization abilities, as individuals, as adults, and as a society.

This takes us back to remedies. Each of us can disseminate our knowledge as widely as possible, in any particular style deemed most effective, that free trade applies to *all* forms of peaceable human interaction. Governmental services should be no exception to the rule of voluntarism. To make such an exception is to create a colossally inconsistent form of morality, which is only possible by abandoning rationality when it's most needed—when it pertains to how we treat each other politically.

In addition to spreading the good words of freedom and rationality, we can also direct our efforts at strategic projects. Persons who really value liberty can't accept the status quo; the possible future civilization(and their lives in it) is much too glorious. No matter how many stand against them, or how many sit on the sidelines, individuals will continue to attempt to subdue or restrain the elements of statism they believe are most harmful to our lives and well-being.

In America today there are numerous libertarian organizations and "think tanks" that focus on specific political and economic issues, which exist on both the state and federal levels. They address such things as ending drug prohibition, separating education from the State (privatizing it), rectifying property rights-violations by the State, repealing taxes and regulations, and holding Congress more accountable for the bills they pass but seldom read. DownsizeDC.org makes the last their signature issue with their proposed "Read the Bills Act." Each voting season, many groups pressure politicians, get petitions signed for candidates, propose bills and ballot measures or propositions, and request referendums. Some research is usually required to determine the viability and effectiveness of each cause. In the end, however, most of these activities still entail playing the game of politics.

Democracy abides by the unfair and convoluted rules of statism, not the simple principles of liberty. This partially explains why so many millions of Americans aren't interested and motivated to support such campaigns. Public choice theory demonstrates why it's so difficult to change a Democracy into a system of liberty by playing politics. The individual cost of fighting a particular special interest issue is often much higher than the potential individual rewards concerning a favorable outcome on that issue. The modus operandi of special interests (and governmental services in general) is to disperse the costs and concentrate the benefits. That way, few persons who incur part of the dispersed costs will make much fuss, and the people who directly benefit will get their way. Additionally, entrenched, influential, and vocal countervailing groups are adept at running campaigns of dishonesty, misinformation, disinformation, and other types of unseemly propaganda, which can frustrate even the best of libertarian causes. Public choice theory also notes that politicians are motivated by self-interest as much as the average person. Therefore, we should harbor no collectivistic delusions about the nature of the political game.

Needless to say, those with vested interests in the use of coercion fool themselves and others about the effects of their victories. They destroy widespread opportunities for everyone, while establishing narrow benefits for few. And, eventually, even those benefits will disappear.

Instead of playing the game of politics and trying to do damage control, we must stop giving the State our sanction. There's no substitute for a populace informed about the true nature of government and the vital alternatives of self-ownership, reason, and choice. Without such political wisdom, at best we'll continue to take one step forward and then be pushed two or three steps backward.

Statism will continue to be the dominant theme in America until more people begin to realize the immense importance of their individual lives. Pundits will continually rehash typical topics regarding the next president and dominant party in Congress, the nature of Supreme Court members and their past and future rulings, the policies of the new Federal Reserve Board Chairman, Ben Bernanke, and so on. On this last issue, it's a safe bet that he'll continue Alan Greenspan's dangerous monetary policies and drive our governmentally constructed Titanic toward even worse icebergs in the years ahead. But my goodness, what nice deck chair arrangements! On the federal level, we face sizable problems indeed. However, each state has its own particular set of serious snafus.

How much does all this matter in the grand scheme of things, in regard to the ideas of liberty? Not a whole lot. Better ideas, because they're grounded in reason and reality, will ultimately win. Thanks to the Internet, there's just too much access to good information at this stage for bad ideas and actions to overwhelm us. With any luck, the complete liberty memes will spread quickly enough to soften the various blows that the State is known to deliver to economies, both national and local. Liberty-oriented radio shows and podcasts such as Free Talk Live can definitely help matters (www.freetalklive.com). Introducing people to truthful alternatives to politics-as-usual will certainly speed up our social evolution.

First, Free A State

But is there a way to greatly accelerate the spread and implementation of liberty memes? There definitely is: by concentrating them in a specific geographical region. Fortunately, a project to do this is already underway—The New Hampshire Free State Project.

Indeed I've saved the best for last. Just when you think that you'll have to wait an interminable amount of time before we can ever begin to uproot the tree of governmental coercion and step into the life-giving sunlight of a new age, along comes a quicker way:

> I hereby state my solemn intent to move to the state of New Hampshire. Once there, I will exert the fullest practical effort toward the creation of a society in which the maximum role of civil government is the protection of life, liberty, and property.

Statement of Intent   Free State Project
    (www.freestateproject.org)

Granted, after reading this far, the idea of "civil government" protecting us probably rings a bit hollow. Nonetheless, this idea follows from the Founding Fathers' classical liberal notions, which are arguably better than the notions of most of their descendants. Whether or not a so-called civil government is a significant step towards a liberty-oriented society, any government that taxes, regulates, and enforces monopolies truly demonstrates its highly uncivil nature. Such a criminal organization is unfit for a free people.

And, you might ask, "Isn't a 'free state' an oxymoron?" Indeed, it is. Any State, by definition, is antithetical to the principle of individual sovereignty and human choice. Nonetheless, just as groups of people historically have seceded from overarching nation-States, secession of the individual from aggressive federal, state, and local governments is part of the process of attaining complete liberty. Given the vast expanse of the United States, the seeds of freedom must be planted somewhere. New Hampshire's ground is arguably more fertile than most, for it remains one of the least oppressive states in America, if not *the* least (and, for what it's worth, it's one of the original thirteen colonies). Most importantly, the region within its borders, like anywhere else in the union, can become privately owned, thereby dissolving its borders into simply the jurisdiction of property owners, both commercial and private. Additionally, its many state "services" can be replaced with voluntary ones.

Because Free State Project members (and potential members) represent a whole ideological range of liberty lovers, full agreement at the outset about the real nature of government would prove difficult. For example, some members who advocate "limited" government seem to be comforted by the thought of having a smaller form of tyranny, a reduced malignant tumor, if you will—even though the State's assumed control of roads and general infrastructure always reveals its metastasized nature. In turn, many believe that playing politics can yield good results. Such beliefs and behaviors may be the central reason why the Libertarian Party (on both national and state levels) hasn't gained much cultural ground over the last thirty-plus years, since the party's inception.

Principles are powerful things, especially when individuals stick to them. Thus, it behooves every libertarian to fully understand the principles of liberty and apply them consistently. There's no need to compromise in these matters. Compromise only begets more of the same.

We can't get rid of the insuperable problems of politics by playing more politics, that is, by obeying unjust laws and following inane rules. No liberty-minded person can satisfy the demands of governmental workers who systematically commit unjust acts and promote immoral ideas. Moreover, it's impossible to vote for rulers who aren't authorized to rule over us. Simply put, we can't live freely as rights-respecting, autonomous adults by respecting the traditions and policies of disrespectful organizations.

By and large, voters see the control of other people's lives and property as *worthwhile*. They believe in taxation, regulation, welfare, and war in their various forms, based on a whole host of misguided premises, as well as fears. Voters and candidates alike accept the nature of the political process—coercion—and think (or feel) that it can bestow good things upon them. To expect them to begin voting with a libertarian mindset contradicts the very reason for voting in the first place. "Swing voters" are often the focus of campaigns, which follows from the notion that you can appeal to people's better judgment through sound bites and big names on street corner signs. I'm pretty sure it doesn't get much more nonsensical than this.

Is it possible to liberate ourselves from the pernicious effects of voting by engaging in the same process? Is it wise to follow inane political rules in the hope of getting rid of them?

Furthermore, can we expect non-voters to begin voting for principled libertarians who are set on abolishing the very institution in which they're seeking office? People who don't vote either want nothing to do with politics or they're too busy trying to live their lives to pay attention to how politics is oppressing them. Either way, they rightly see voting as pointless. They always lose, and politics always wins; statist wolves will never turn down fine meals of individual sheep.

Lastly, since limited-government (or small-government) libertarians apparently don't want to dispense with fantasies of benevolent or benign statism, their compromised arguments will always succumb to the more consistent arguments of their statist competitors. Simply put, liberty and the State don't mix.

What we need is not watered-down statism, but rather, fully-drowned statism. Let it sink to the bottom of the corrupt pond of politics and be covered with the darker notes of history. When people realize the State's true nature, voting is no longer "necessary." Politicians and voting are then seen for what they are: ways to infringe on individual rights and personal sovereignty.

Nevertheless, whether they desire to dive right into the clear and refreshing pool of freedom, or to ease in from the shallow end, most Free State Project members agree that no one has the right to forestall the progression toward a society of liberty. The faster it can be implemented, the faster people can begin living according to reason rather than force.

Americans need not be fearful of major political changes for the better. As our semi-Fascist, semi-Communist State continues to confront us, as well as our loved ones, our friends, our acquaintances, our coworkers, our associates, and our fellow traders, we ought not continue to comply. Terrible police State history need not repeat itself. Remember, we far outnumber those who seek to oppress us; and so, they need our sanction in order to continue perpetrating their acts of coercion.

Granted, nearly all of us have been inculcated by State-run schools in a culture of self-sacrifice and blind obedience to authority, so we tend to easily accept a very diluted formulation of liberty. It's definitely way past time to reassess our education and behavior in these matters.

Eventually, everyone will reflect on the nature of their political and moral education, because we still have residual elements of the Enlightenment in America, perhaps more so than any other place on the planet. These elements will enable everybody to embrace complete liberty ideas at some point in their future.

The Free State Project simply aims to gather and unite persons who already understand libertarianism and, hence, want some semblance of liberty as soon as possible. It thus becomes a potent catalyst for change. The greater the concentration of highly motivated freedom-oriented activists in a single state, especially a state as small as New Hampshire, the faster the principles of liberty can be promoted and adopted. Remember, liberty, like smiling, is contagious.

Now, certainly there are various people in New Hampshire who harbor unwarranted fears about the principles of liberty and those who seek to enact them, just like the rest of America. Some journalists and politicians and even residents have expressed at most luke-warm acceptance, and at worst outright disapproval, of New Hampshire being chosen as the Free State in 2003. Evidently they don't take the state's motto, "Live Free or Die," as seriously as the man who penned it in 1809, General John Stark.

Upon moving here in the spring of 2006, I spent some time at the state capital, in Concord, to observe the "sausage" being made there. All my suspicions were confirmed. Essentially, much like other states, representatives and officials (city and town governments too) create reams of legislation and legal minutia that they translate into decisions about what to do with *other people's property* as well as about management of state and local governments. As usual, individuals are sacrificed to the collective, for the "good of the people." Such an experience definitely exposes the inconsistency between New Hampshire's bold motto and its mind-numbing bureaucratic system. (In case you're wondering, the state senate passed and amended a whole host of new bills. One of them created a commission to "study" whether state representatives should be lackeys to D.C.'s mandate to implement a national ID card, or "Real ID," essentially an internal passport system, which remains a favorite of police States everywhere—to keep us all safe from terrorists, of course. Visit www.freestateblogs.net and www.nhliberty.org for assorted sausage-making updates.)

Naturally, some who are concerned about how libertarian ideas will alter the current state of affairs might ask, "Why us? Who do these people think they are, seeking to change the state of New Hampshire?" Greek mythology may provide a poetic answer for them. The Free State Project is symbolic of Hercules releasing Prometheus from his bondage by Zeus. Once freed, Prometheus can again bring great talents and achievements to humankind. This time, he brings us ideas that will put *all* of Pandora's evils back in their box. In so doing, a totally free market will be a godsend for every person fortunate enough to experience it.

Aside from various New Hampshire residents who may be reticent to welcome complete liberty, there are countless others who are, and will be, greatly inspired. All those who are disenchanted with politics can join the campaign to institute personal freedom and total respect for property—as a lifestyle. Interestingly, even the architects of the New

Hampshire State Constitution proposed a way out of an unacceptable predicament:

> Article 10. [Right of Revolution.]
> Government being instituted for the common benefit, protection, and security, of the whole community, and not for the private interest or emolument of any one man, family, or class of men; therefore, whenever the ends of government are perverted, and public liberty manifestly endangered, and all other means of redress are ineffectual, the people may, and of right ought to reform the old, or establish a new government. The doctrine of nonresistance against arbitrary power, and oppression, is absurd, slavish, and destructive of the good and happiness of mankind.

June 2, 1784   *New Hampshire State Constitution*

The last sentence clearly summarizes the idea that government is created to serve the people, and when the people are instead forced to serve government (via special interest legislation, regulation, and taxation), it's incumbent upon the oppressed to do something about it. But taking political action, whether through redress, reform, or reconstruction, must be grounded in sound principles that respect individual rights. By that standard, then, various words and phrases in Article 10 provoke some rigorous analysis.

Who exactly instituted the government, and what are its specified ends? What are the means and methods by which "common benefit, protection, and security," are bestowed on the "whole community"? What does "public liberty" really mean, and when exactly is it endangered? Furthermore, what are the people's values and virtues, and what is the nature of their consent?

Such questions focus on the inherent contradiction in government trying to be all things to all persons. Few, if any, persons who accept the State can ever agree on just where to draw the line concerning the public good and the desired ends of government. Nevertheless, they normally agree on how government operates and acquires its resources:

Article 12. [Protection and Taxation Reciprocal.]
Every member of the community has a right to be protected by it, in the enjoyment of his life, liberty, and property; he is therefore bound to contribute his share in the expense of such protection, and to yield his personal service when necessary. But no part of a man's property shall be taken from him, or applied to public uses, without his own consent, or that of the representative body of the people. Nor are the inhabitants of this state controllable by any other laws than those to which they, or their representative body, have given their consent.

June 2, 1784 *New Hampshire State Constitution*

Certainly, each person living in a community has the right to be left alone by others—others who may even desire to infringe on the enjoyment of one's life, liberty, and property. This follows from your right to self-defense, which reflects self-ownership and hence your freedom to stop others from initiating force against you. Naturally, it follows that each person must bear the expense in preventing and dealing with such rights-violations, though the aggressor must pay in the end. No one possesses a right to governmental services at taxpayers' expense. As mentioned earlier, purchasing insurance policies through a reputable agent will be a good way to deal with these kinds of potential expenses.

It definitely doesn't follow that the process of rights-protection should be monopolized, and that persons in the community should be forced ("bound") to contribute money and even labor ("personal service when necessary"). That would be in violation of their right to contract. Each person retains the right to contract, or not, with any particular form of protection from rights-violators. Apparently, that's why the framers of the New Hampshire Constitution inserted the invaluable statement, "no part of a man's property shall be taken from him, or applied to public uses, without his own consent." An individual's property can be taken and "applied to public uses" *only* when that person consents.

Unfortunately, these framers didn't stop there. They allowed for consent also to be given, supposedly on behalf of the individual, by "the representative body of the people." As is the case in *any* constitutional Republic, such representatives are definitely not chosen legal agents, acting in a voluntary fashion. The individual hasn't authorized them to act on his or her behalf. Rather, representatives usurp individual rights and property from people in the name of the public good, which often means satisfying a variety of agendas of the powerful, influential, and vocal. It's back to special interests once again.

No collectivistic project on Earth is so important that it requires stealing the property of individuals in order to further itself. Without consent, there can be no willing trade. Without voluntary exchange, there can be no rational interaction. These are the basic facts that politically minded people throughout history have tried to ignore, and even ridicule—at the cost of their self-respect and humanity.

We know that democratic votes or townhall meetings don't equal consent, for there will usually be at least one individual who disagrees. (Curiously, only under dictatorships is "unanimity" achieved.) When it comes to acquiring and utilizing another's property, there's no logical or moral substitute for consent and voluntary trade. This is the case regardless of the size of the geographical area or the population. Towns aren't exempt from these observations merely because government may be more accessible or "closer to the people."

Collectivistic (political) theft of someone's property is no different in principle than individual theft. Typically, as Lysander Spooner noted for us, the only distinction is that the individual thief doesn't attempt to deny that his action *is* theft—and he doesn't try to justify his theft through references to the common good, general welfare, public interest, community, and the well-being of children.

If you've ever witnessed the goings-on of local politics, you're no doubt familiar with the amount of deception (of self and others) and context-dropping that's exercised. Mayoral elections, city council and school board meetings, zoning and planning commissions, legislative proceedings, etc., all demonstrate what happens when people have access to a community chest of tax dollars and regulatory powers. They zealously rule over others to deal with the "needs of the people." Of course, the very last need on the list (in truth, it's not even on the list) is to respect the rights of the individual, the smallest, most persecuted minority in the world.

The only way to reverse this perverse situation is for enough people to consider it worth reversing, band together, and get to work on changing politics-as-usual. That's why the Free State Project holds such promise, why "Liberty in our lifetime" will become more than its marketing slogan; it will be made real. Focused effort by liberty-minded activists in New Hampshire is much better than scattered effort across a whole nation.

How many people are necessary? Judging by what I've seen, heard, and discussed with others, as well as the progress of the few hundred already in the state, a thousand more will probably make a sizable impact—hence, the Free State Project's "First 1000 pledge" (http://freestateproject.org/first1000), whose signers have pledged to move to New Hampshire before 2009. A group that's devoted strictly to liberty agendas and laissez-faire policies can be a major motivator and inspiration for everybody. Unlike special interests, this resonates with the "silent majority" who are disgusted with politics and politicians. If the over 7,500 current FSP members (as of 1/07) were to move to New Hampshire as soon as possible, rather than wait for the membership to hit 20,000, that would be something to behold. It could seriously weaken the walls of the statist house of cards.

We must keep in mind that reason and reality are on the side of freedom. And so is morality. The state government is winning, more or less, by default. Similar to other states in America and in D.C., anti-liberty lobbyists influence politicians and governmental officials on a daily basis. It's "business" as usual, following from public choice theory. Similar to other states, too, most of the nonvoting as well as many of the voting public aren't very informed about what's actually happening on the floors of the legislature. Given its mind-numbing quality, it's hard to blame them.

Some people vote for their slate of Democrats or Republicans as if they were opposing sports teams, but ones that aggress against innocent bystanders. The "lesser of two evils" mentality also runs rampant. Most base their choices on age-old notions of what constitutes "good government," which reflects the "necessary evil" premise of the State (the same one Thomas Paine unfortunately extolled). The press, as usual, is composed predominantly of statist intellectuals. So, what little information the public gets is definitely not the whole story. The Keene Free Press (www.keenefreepress.com), however, is a new and very refreshing exception.

In New Hampshire each town has relative autonomy in many governmental aspects. Counties are not as politically significant as in other states, which has its libertarian benefits. Some free staters will work on freeing various towns and cities first and then the entire state. A multi-pronged approach will probably prove most effective. Whether it's the work of the first 1,000 members or the first 20,000 members, to say that the project will change the political and economic landscape for the better would be an understatement. There are no losers in the creation of liberty, because it's the only way to an environment in which everyone's person and property—and rationality—are fully respected.

Free staters and their supporters can tackle any number of essential issues. Privatizing education and other public service monopolies will restore quality service and help end state ownership and control of one's property via the taxes imposed on it. Dispensing with health care regulations and licensure, as in any other industry, will dramatically reduce both entrepreneurial costs and consumer prices, as well as significantly increase quality and quantity of services. Ending federal and state agencies' violations of personal freedoms like drug use will foster self-responsibility and greatly reduce crime, police violence and corruption, and health hazards. Implementing a plan, for instance based on homesteading, to privatize state-owned and managed land, water, and airspace will ensure legal accountability, efficient use of resources, admirable stewardship, and enforcement of a cleaner environment—as well as generate vast economic opportunities, noticeably benefiting everyone. Instituting a money-backed currency, for instance of gold or silver, will expose federal reserve notes as the humongous sham they are; a sound, free market medium of exchange will bestow mighty financial blessings on the populace.

Clearly, this just covers some of the high points. Free Staters, with the help of an invigorated grass roots' movement of like-minded people, can address many other pertinent issues. Of course as mentioned, some people will resist these agendas. The mindless collective turns out to be the same no matter where one lives. It ignores individuals and sees only the needs and behavior of groups (and the misbehavior of individuals who defy it). It only sees others who can be molded into its image and likeness—a dependent, faceless mass of humanity that conforms to the "public will," that is, those in control of State power.

People involved in politics at the state, county, city, or town levels are typically not friendly to independent thought and actions. They don't like things that challenge their ideas and authority. They're fearful of change, and so they don't like people rocking their boat (the boat of the mindless collective) and asserting all their natural rights. Instead, they mainly seek to control governmental resources and maintain governmental influence regarding the lives and property of everyone else.

Many in politics are busybodies or so-called do-gooders, people who relish involving themselves in any issue that hints of "community standards" or "public health" or "the needs of our children," and so on. Obviously, people in the private sector who are involved in these issues demonstrate much better ways to achieve similar goals, to the extent that they do in today's statist environment. Most political officials are champions of a particular pet cause that further diminishes individual rights. Nearly all are wholeheartedly opposed to changing the way politics works, let alone getting rid of it entirely. They simply don't envision better alternatives. They see paychecks and short-term goals, which means dropping the context in which they're working—a coercive, unjust monopoly funded with stolen wealth. People who champion the cause of freedom and voluntarism continually remind them of this context.

As noted, given the vested interests that maintain the status quo, to play the political and legal game by its absurd rules can't result in respect for individuals and a free market. After all, running for elected office as a saboteur, or trying to get a bill passed to repeal State power and restore various rights, or making a solid case in court to a judge about why the State has no jurisdiction, not to mention can't provide a fair trial and isn't a complaining party (assuming he'll let you present such a case), or informing a jury of their right (even obligation) to nullify bad laws—all have been frustrating, if not futile, activities for most libertarians in states throughout America. Even though the last activity (jury nullification) seems most promising, especially for the Free State Project, each of these activities is a bit like trying to explain a global positioning system to those who resolutely want to believe that the Earth is flat. We not only speak a different language; we also don't share the same premises.

So, we must discover ways to build bridges across this premise gap. The challenge is to motivate people, via the court of public opinion, to accept the idea of complete liberty and its implications for politics. This is why strength in numbers is key, why concentration of individual efforts is the best hope. The quest for complete liberty essentially begins and ends in the minds of enlightened individuals. The majority of people in a particular region must be informed of, and shown, a better way to live. We must teach the language of liberty to young, inquisitive, and resilient minds, regardless of their actual ages. We must introduce sound premises and principles to persons who are suspicious of, and have chosen not to involve themselves in, "politics-as-usual." This is the primary way to alter the political theater.

Nonetheless, the sky's the limit as to how to effectively discontinue federal, state, and local interference in the marketplace. Each FSP member is left to his or her own ingenuity and innovativeness to effect changes. Being decentralized and non-hierarchical, the Free State Project represents the best in the American entrepreneurial spirit of independence and resourcefulness. The virtues of self-initiative, self-responsibility, self-reliance, honesty, and self-trust, all reflect a fundamental trust in others to live similarly (as well as a distrust in the mindless collective).

Dissolution of the state's government will happen when it's no longer granted legitimacy by most people—and when viable free market alternatives are offered. To this end, like-minded free staters and others will develop specific strategies to facilitate market solutions as well as expose the illegitimacy of the State. They'll basically inform their communities about the merits of voluntarism and the demerits of coercion.

Aggression typically only begets more aggression in politics. Especially in today's cultural climate, any retaliation against the force initiated by State officials tends to legitimize and increase their violent actions (even though self-defense against a potentially lethal attack remains a fundamental right). For better or worse, long gone are the days of tarring and feathering tax collectors and their assorted comrades. Therefore, strictly non-violent activism will directly promote the goal of complete liberty. Reasonable people best recognize unjust laws and their immoral enforcement when officials harass and arrest those who've harmed no one and violated no one's property rights. Peaceful protests and demonstrations, civil disobedience, non-conformity and non-compliance in relation to taxes, unjust laws, and regulations are all powerful forms of activism. In addition, by combining activism with explanations of free market alternatives and voluntary solutions, we can open new avenues for understanding and change in communities.

Currently, the particular free staters who are most inclined to agree with these ideas, that is, who see no valid reason to play politics, live in the Keene area, which is in southwestern New Hampshire. Keene is a city of over twenty thousand people and is the home of Keene State College, the state's largest liberal arts university, which serves approximately five thousand students. Being a city instead of a town, it's more legally tied to state government; therein lies one of its challenges. Visit the forum on www.nhfree.com for further information and details about all the liberty lovers there and their admirable activism.

Another approach to activism, though certainly down the road a few years, is to build a complete liberty town from scratch. Imagine what a tourist attraction that would be: the first-ever town in the United States with an advanced community of trade and commerce that respects the freedoms of its residents! Instead of being located in some distant part of the third world, with the accompanying economic and geopolitical drawbacks, such a town would be in a main birthplace of liberty. For those who've read Ayn Rand's magnum opus, *Atlas Shrugged*, envision a Galt's Gulch for all to see and visit, and emulate. After all, what's achieved in New Hampshire will be a great example for the rest of America, and the world.

In order to have complete liberty in our lifetime, we must commit ourselves to the idea that nothing else is proper for us—beings who own ourselves and flourish by means of reason.

Let's now end with the eloquent words of a man who died long ago but who knew how powerful an idea can be, especially one whose time has come:

> THESE are the times that try men's souls. The summer soldier and the sunshine patriot will, in this crisis, shrink from the service of their country; but he that stands by it now, deserves the love and thanks of man and woman. Tyranny, like hell, is not easily conquered; yet we have this consolation with us, that the harder the conflict, the more glorious the triumph. What we obtain too cheap, we esteem too lightly: it is dearness only that gives every thing its value. Heaven knows how to put a proper price upon its goods; and it would be strange indeed if so celestial an article as FREEDOM should not be highly rated.

December 23, 1776   Thomas Paine   *The Crisis*

ADDENDUM

Important IAQ (infrequently asked questions)

Is it necessary to move to New Hampshire in order to achieve complete liberty? What if I can't move, or simply don't want to, for a variety of personal reasons?

This pertains to the issue of "herding libertarian cats," does it not? Some say that most libertarians are too independent to pick up and move across the country in order to join a movement that involves taking a stand against oppressive government. Given that the Free State Project only has just over a third of the signers needed to initiate their relocation to New Hampshire, this may well be true. So, if you really enjoy living where you are, then by all means don't sacrifice that enjoyment. Instead, start a movement where you reside presently! Ideally, each of us should pick a place in America where we would most like to experience complete liberty, and then get to work on achieving it there.

This book has been about the demise of the State (on all levels) and the rise of voluntary America, not just voluntary New Hampshire. All will not be lost if you don't move; you won't be enveloped in unstoppable tyranny outside the statist borders of New Hampshire. As mentioned in Chapter 10, although this state is relatively freer in some aspects, it's currently fraught with the same governmental ills as the rest of the Union. We can't escape the culture, after all, with its assorted themes of authoritarianism, sacrifice, and collectivism. Of course, we could all just move to a deserted island in the South Pacific and have "complete liberty" there, but honing our survival skills isn't what we're trying to achieve.

When I wrote that "Focused effort by liberty-minded activists in New Hampshire is much better than scattered effort across a whole nation," I did so from the standpoint of what's been happening—or rather, not been happening—in the various states, instead of from the standpoint of future possibilities. Things tend to change over time. For example, the Free State Wyoming Project is now underway (www.freestatewyoming.org). Just as each state has its own advantages and disadvantages, each project will too. There are no large cities in New Hampshire (or in Wyoming), which might make it easier to change things for the better. On the other hand, a free town in a rural area will offer fewer noticeable economic benefits than a free large city in a cosmopolitan area. Ultimately, it's probably best to choose a place that reflects your preferences for lifestyle, job opportunities, cultural activities, and so on.

How many libertarians throughout America actually believe in complete liberty?

I've seen no good surveys about this. In my own experience, I would guess somewhere between 10 and 30 percent, though it could be higher. Throughout my time in New Hampshire over the past year, it appears that free staters are similarly constituted. Given that complete liberty is based on correct premises about human nature and economics, as well as about the nature of government, the percentages can indeed change. In addition to gaining knowledge about complete liberty, it's crucial that individuals address their particular fears about dispensing with statism. The negative psychological dynamics operating in our culture, and on our emotions, can hinder full clarity in these matters. This leads to the next, all-important question.

Will most free staters in New Hampshire eventually direct their focus to achieving complete liberty instead of minimal government?

The answer to this depends on how many free staters determine that playing politics isn't a viable strategy for upholding our rights. This question certainly touches on the FSP's "Statement of Intent," which says nothing about getting rid of government entirely, but rather that civil government's maximum role is to protect life, liberty, and property. As previously noted in Chapter 10, "civil government" is as contradictory as a "free state." The classical liberal idea that "small government is beautiful," tends to contribute to our predicament—for it concedes the premise of statism to the enemies of freedom. As a direct consequence, the vital and essential message of self-ownership becomes deemphasized or ignored altogether.

The actions of some free staters who believe in complete liberty have been criticized mostly by those who believe in representative, albeit Constitutionally limited, government and/or by those who simply believe that everyone should abide by the State's rules for changing itself. Some believe that "the law" must be obeyed, regardless of its infringement on individual rights, typically because they feel that the personal or societal consequences for disobeying it are too dire. We are back to our fears, once again.

Unlike the heroic characters in *Atlas Shrugged*, we have no magnificent place designed especially for us by a man named John Galt. Who is John Galt? In essence, he's a man who couldn't tolerate living in a defective and disrespectful society, so he went on strike; he withdrew his productive mind from that society, convinced others to do likewise, and created a place that would function respectfully in accordance with the rights of individuals. Galt's Gulch was a place of honor that showed reverence for the human spirit, the American spirit.

You too may be somewhat "on strike," like I have been most of my adult life, searching for a particular lever with which to move the world in a more enlightened direction—or at least trying to avoid the worst forms of our highly regulated and taxed, mixed economy. Of course, the longer we remain on strike, the more pressing the need for cultural change becomes; our precious lives may start to feel like they're slipping by. On the other hand, many of you may not see the point in going on strike, and I understand that. But I also understand that neither you nor I can fully escape the web of statist intervention and status quo institutions that restrict our capacities and impede our achievements on a daily basis. None of us truly desires to live a life of quiet desperation, like Dagny Taggart and Hank Rearden would've done, had it not been for the persuasive influence of Galt as well as Francisco d'Anconia.

The key thing to remember, and to remind others, is that *we all could be living so much better lives*—more fulfilling, enriching, and opportunity-filled lives—if we had compete liberty. Therefore, there's no substitute for explicitly promoting it to everyone. Our fellow Americans can handle the truth in these matters, especially when it's presented appropriately to their specific contexts. After all, if our neighbors don't recognize their own freedoms to be autonomous decision-makers, they'll continue to play politics and/or apathetically watch the State's law-enforcers inflict pain and suffering on innocent people. In many respects, it's more than the institutions of the State that we're up against; it's the viewpoints of everyone around us. Thus, the next question.

Isn't wanting to change the present system and people's ideas about government putting the political trailer in front of the philosophical truck? In other words, aren't people unprepared for such major social, political, and economic changes, given their present philosophical ideas and accompanying fears?

There are many factors involved in this question, to be sure. Typically, big "O" Objectivists immediately answer "yes" to it, which is in line with their general disdain for promoting political ideas outside their proper ethical, epistemological, and metaphysical context. Yet, such principles as self-ownership and property rights don't necessarily require a course in objective philosophy. Most intellectuals don't have to become Objectivists in order for radical political change to occur. In fact Objectivism's political branch essentially favors the structure of the State over complete liberty, thus opposing radical change.

So long as government runs the educational system, ideas counterproductive to liberty will continue to be mainstream, and better ideas will be lost to all but a minority of curious minds. However, paradigm shifts don't happen because people wait around for them to happen—that is, wait around for *other* people to change their minds and behaviors. Motivated people seek ways to make things happen.

John Galt's job was easier than ours, by the way. He just had to convince other productive individuals to withdraw their sanction by moving to a place free of any tyranny. We, however, can't just leave our troubled world behind, to fend for itself, while we live in total freedom. We must find ways to change this unfree world. I invite you to join the forum at www.completeliberty.com, which will be dedicated strictly to brainstorming ways to do this—to achieve complete liberty as quickly as humanly possible.

And drum roll, please...Do you think that the process of achieving complete liberty entails preparing oneself to do jail time?

Most libertarians, for a variety of good reasons, believe this to be the scariest proposition. Consequently, throughout America, millions of libertarians continue to live reasonably good, law abiding lives—just like those who agree (more or less) with the political status quo, as well as those who actively promote it. But must a reasonably good life come at the cost of submitting to governmental employees' demands that you sacrifice your choices, actions, and property? Is living among people who will unleash egregious rights violations upon you if you don't follow their irrational orders any way to live? Is there any reasonable aspect to this living environment? For that matter, is it a proper place in which rear children?

Obedience to unjust authority should never be the price that any rights-respecting person has to pay in order to live outside a jail cell. This bears on Ayn Rand's discussion of "sanction of the victim." Essentially, we allow governmental officials to threaten us and coerce us, while we try to peacefully live among them and pursue our own goals. As I've outlined, such conformity only begets more of the same, more of the game wherein governmental officials pretend to be our protectors, and we pretend not to be their dupes and slaves. Spooner's words are indeed accurate. No rational person in a free market who assumed the responsibility of being your protector would even so much as think about gunning you down without mercy if you tried to defend yourself and your property.

Of course, the more we engage in pleasurable activities, the more we can evade this issue. In many ways, the American way of life tends to ignore the eternal problems of politics and the pervasive obedience to authority arising from it—or giving rise to it; the causation is indeed reciprocal. Oftentimes, there are just too many cool places to go, great people to see, and fun things to do to really motivate us to focus on the nature of our political plight. But huge problems remain, irrespective of how carefully we follow the State's rules: "Tax time"; victimless "crimes"; police harassment; regulatory nightmares in business and personal life; horrendous effects of fiat currency; death and suffering in semi-socialized health care; and so on. These are not things to be overlooked by people who genuinely believe in the pursuit of happiness.

I've had many discussions about this issue with my friend Russell Kanning of the Keene Free Press, who once again is in a small jail cell as I type these words, basically on account of choosing not to obtain the state-required official documents in order to drive his car on the monopolized roads of government. Once again, he's harmed no one and violated no one's property rights. Thus, there's no tort, no complaining party, and the government has no standing, in addition to no legitimacy. Exposing the government's violent racket by not conforming to it's edicts is Russell's way of leading people to see the essential truth in these matters. Russell is a libertarian doer; he walks the talk. To the extent that we continue to conform to the government's irrational, immoral, and unjust demands, we are only "libertarian talkers," as Russell has good-naturedly remarked on various occasions. Yet millions of libertarian talkers could dramatically alter the course of human history by becoming libertarian doers as well, especially at the same time and in an orchestrated fashion.

We have two choices, as I see it: Either comply and enable further oppressive acts, or start demanding that our rights be respected. The State's coercive behavior will come to an abrupt end when more and more people decide not to tolerate a shred of subjugation. This is how an undignified civilization can transform itself into a dignified one.

Ultimately, each of us must decide when it's necessary and feasible to stop enabling our oppressors. Most of us have lifestyles in which being put in a cage for an extended length of time would result in a lot of personal turmoil and financial losses. This partially explains how our oppressors get away with their despicable actions—through creating fear of losing the rest of our freedoms. So, each of us must pick our particular issues and protest and disobey in the way that minimizes as much as possible the negative impact on our own lives and families.

Many libertarians are in cages throughout America for no valid reason, alongside hundreds of thousands who are also victims of unjust laws and their contemptible enforcement. It's time to start encouraging our fellow Americans to help us put a stop to these abominations. In doing so, we should look to and depend on each other (the free market), rather than the corrupt tools of government, to bring about wholesome changes. Whether this will eventually entail flooding the statist jail cells, one can only speculate. In this day and age, there's no greater deed than exposing the violent nature of the organization known as government, which means showing people "the gun in the room," as Stephan Molyneux has put it (www.freedomainradio.com). Of course, the gun remains in its holster when we comply. In contrast, the tax case of the brave Plainfield, New Hampshire couple Ed and Elaine Brown has amply exposed the guns of the IRS, Federal District Court, and U.S. Marshals. Staunch resistance to their demands directly threatens their perverse way of life.

Ultimately, the most important thing is to introduce people to the principles of complete liberty in a fashion that you believe is best in your context. And the sooner we can create a voluntary America, the sooner we can pursue our happiness, unfettered by the ills of the State.

BIBLIOGRAPHY

Note: I've categorized the following hundreds of titles according to primary topic covered; however, some conceptual overlap with other topics is to be expected. Also, if any of the Web links have become defunct, just google the title and author to find the new URL. Since many of the links are quite long and thus unwieldy, I've replaced them with shorter ones from tinyURL.com, which simply redirects to the original links.

BOOKS

Culture

America (The Book): A Citizen's Guide To Democracy Inaction
by the writers of The Daily Show and Jon Stewart
http://tinyurl.com/huvx8

Everyday Irrationality: How Pseudo-Scientists, Lunatics, And The Rest Of Us Systematically Fail To Think Rationally
by Robyn M. Dawes
http://tinyurl.com/zup85

For Your Own Good: Hidden Cruelty In Child-Rearing And The Roots Of Violence
by Alice Miller, Hildegarde Hannum (Translator), Hunter Hannum (Translator)
http://tinyurl.com/kex3h

Free Culture: How Big Media Uses Technology And The Law To Lock Down Culture And Control Creativity
by Lawrence Lessig
http://www.free-culture.cc/

How To Be A Successful Tyrant
by Larken Rose
http://www.tyrantbook.com/index.html

Irrationality: Why We Don't Think Straight
by Stuart Sutherland
http://tinyurl.com/hz5om

Meltdown: The Predictable Distortion Of Global Warming By Scientists, Politicians, And The Media
by Patrick J. Michaels
http://tinyurl.com/fx9ff

Natural Capitalism: Creating The Next Industrial Revolution
by Paul Hawken, Amory Lovins and L. Hunter Lovins
http://tinyurl.com/zjc4y

Punished By Rewards: The Trouble With Gold Stars, Incentive Plans, A's, Praise, And Other Bribes
by Alfie Kohn
http://tinyurl.com/szgz4

The World Is Flat: A Brief History Of The Twenty-first Century
by Thomas L. Friedman
http://tinyurl.com/g8pzj

Unconditional Parenting: Moving From Rewards And Punishments To Love And Reason
by Alfie Kohn
http://www.alfiekohn.org/up/index.html

Economics

Against The Dead Hand: The Uncertain Struggle For Global Capitalism
by Brink Lindsey
http://tinyurl.com/hpxdv

An Army Of Davids: How Markets And Technology Empower Ordinary People To Beat Big Media, Big Government, And Other Goliaths
by Glenn Reynolds
http://tinyurl.com/fpbv4

Classical Economics: An Austrian Perspective On The History Of Economic Thought
by Murray N. Rothbard
http://tinyurl.com/nd8u8

Defending The Undefendable: The Pimp, Prostitute, Scab, Slumlord, Libeler, Moneylender, And Other Scapegoats In The Rogue's Gallery Of American Society
by Walter Block
http://tinyurl.com/gp66y

Economic Freedom Of The World 2005
by James Gwartney and Roberty A. Lawson, with Erik Garzke
http://tinyurl.com/f2zmt

Economic Science And The Austrian Method
by Hans-Hermann Hoppe
http://tinyurl.com/kr7dj

Economics For Real People: An Introduction To The Austrian School
by Gene Callahan
http://tinyurl.com/zcwg8

Freakonomics: A Rogue Economist Explores The Hidden Side Of Everything
by Steven D. Levitt and Stephen J. Dubner
http://tinyurl.com/fs37y

Man, Economy, And State & Power And Market
by Murray Rothbard
http://www.mises.org/rothbard/mes/chap15d.asp

Markets Don't Fail!
by Brian P. Simpson
http://tinyurl.com/f4csr

Money, Bank Credit, And Economic Cycles
by Jesús Huerta de Soto
http://tinyurl.com/e8ofr

Private Means, Public Ends: Voluntarism vs. Coercion
by J. Wilson Mixon (ed)
http://tinyurl.com/g4tmf

The Bottomless Well: The Twilight Of Fuel, The Virtue Of Waste, And Why We Will Never Run Out Of Energy
by Peter W. Huber and Mark P. Mills
http://tinyurl.com/zs8gg

The Fortune At The Bottom Of The Pyramid: Eradicating Poverty Through Profits
by C. K. Prahalad
http://tinyurl.com/j66j4

The Hyperinflation Survival Guide: Strategies For American Businesses
by Dr. Gerald Swanson
http://www.hyperinflation.net

The Power Of Productivity: Wealth, Poverty, And The Threat To Global Stability
by William W. Lewis
http://tinyurl.com/fk3uz

The Race To The Top: The Real Story Of Globalization
by Tomas Larsson
http://tinyurl.com/ev7p9

The Ultimate Resource 2
by Julian Lincoln Simon
http://tinyurl.com/kdpj9

The Voluntary City: Choice, Community, And Civil Society
by David T. Beito, Peter Gordon, and Alexander Tabarrok (eds)
http://tinyurl.com/4veav

The World Economy: A Millennial Perspective
by Angus Maddison, Donald Johnston, Organisation for Economic Co-Operation and Development
http://tinyurl.com/khdv5

Law and Property

Adventures In Legal Land
by Marc Stevens
http://www.adventuresinlegalland.com

An Unreasonable Woman: A True Story Of Shrimpers, Politicos, Polluters, And The Fight For Seadrift, Texas
by Diane Wilson
http://tinyurl.com/kggs6

Economics And Ethics Of Private Property
by Hans-Hermann Hoppe
http://tinyurl.com/dn5h5

Free Market Environmentalism
by Terry L. Anderson and Donald R. Leal
http://tinyurl.com/jo4w7

Hooked: Pirates, Poaching, And The Perfect Fish
by G. Bruce Knecht
http://tinyurl.com/qsyhn

Law's Order: What Economics Has To Do With Law And Why It Matters
by David D. Friedman
http://tinyurl.com/epxpm

Street Smart: Competition, Entrepreneurship, And The Future Of Roads
by Gabriel Roth (ed) edited by Gabriel Roth
http://tinyurl.com/ez4a8

The Enterprise Of Law: Justice Without The State
by Bruce L. Benson
http://tinyurl.com/y8nn6b

The Future Of Ideas: The Fate Of The Commons In A Connected World
by Lawrence Lessig
http://tinyurl.com/h75pw

The Law Of The Somalis: A Stable Foundation For Economic Development In The Horn of Africa
by Michael van Notten, Spencer Heath MacCallum (ed)
http://home.arcor.de/danneskjoeld/X/Som/index.html

The Structure Of Liberty: Justice And The Rule Of Law
by Randy E. Barnett
http://tinyurl.com/y3qd5o

Water For Sale: How Business And The Market Can Resolve The World's Water Crisis
by Fredrik Segerfeldt
http://tinyurl.com/e78xp

Governmental Domestic Policy

Bad Trip: How The War Against Drugs Is Destroying America
by Joel Miller
http://tinyurl.com/kuqtd

Disabling America: The Unintended Consequences Of The Government's Protection Of The Handicapped
by Greg Perry
http://tinyurl.com/eqkec

Healthy Competition: What's Holding Back Health Care And How To Free It
by Michael F. Cannon
http://tinyurl.com/f8z58

Medicare's Midlife Crisis
by Sue A. Blevins
http://tinyurl.com/ktzh2

More Guns, Less Crime: Understanding Crime And Gun-Control Laws
by John R. Lott Jr.
http://tinyurl.com/elg5u

Mugged By The State: Outrageous Government Assaults On Ordinary People And Their Property
by Randall Fitzgerald
http://tinyurl.com/facb6

Noble Vision
by Gen LaGreca
http://tinyurl.com/zoege

The Cure: How Capitalism Can Save American Health Care
by David Gratzer
http://tinyurl.com/y5f2pk

Governmental Foreign Policy

Blowback: The Costs And Consequences Of American Empire
by Chalmers Johnson
http://tinyurl.com/zvo76

Dying To Win: The Strategic Logic Of Suicide Terrorism
by Robert Pape
http://tinyurl.com/grh9h

Eastward To Tartary: Travels In The Balkans, The Middle East, And The Caucasus
by Robert D. Kaplan
http://tinyurl.com/f9f87

Faith At War
by Yaroslav Trofimov
http://www.faithatwar.com

Generation Kill: Devil Dogs, Iceman, Captain America, And The New Face Of American War
by Evan Wright
http://tinyurl.com/ggj6t

Inside The Wire: A Military Intelligence Soldier's Eyewitness Account Of Life At Guantanamo
by Erik Saar and Viveca Novak
http://tinyurl.com/jcdzo

Resurrecting Empire: Western Footprints And America's Perilous Path In The Middle East
by Rashid Khalidi
http://tinyurl.com/j39my

Shake Hands With The Devil: The Failure Of Humanity In Rwanda
by Roméo Dallaire and Samantha Power
http://tinyurl.com/ebf68

The Costs Of War: America's Pyrrhic Victories
by John Denson (ed)
http://tinyurl.com/hej8s

The Empire Has No Clothes: U.S. Foreign Policy Exposed
by Ivan Eland
http://tinyurl.com/ds2yv

The Experience Of World War I
by J.M. Winter
http://tinyurl.com/je7om

The Illusion Of Victory: America In World War I
by Thomas Fleming
http://tinyurl.com/g8rel

The New Nuclear Danger: George W. Bush's Military-Industrial Complex
by Helen Caldicott
http://tinyurl.com/hp2ax

The Sorrows Of Empire: Militarism, Secrecy, And The End Of The Republic
by Chalmers Johnson
http://tinyurl.com/farcm

War Is A Force That Gives Us Meaning
by Chris Hedges
http://tinyurl.com/hsnlt

Governmental Ills

Beyond Politics: Markets, Welfare And The Failure Of Bureaucracy
by William C. Mitchell and Randy T. Simmons
http://tinyurl.com/kko3j

Breach Of Trust: How Washington Turns Outsiders Into Insiders
by Tom A. Coburn and John Hart
http://tinyurl.com/raqym

Death By Government
by R. Rummel
http://tinyurl.com/rusyx

Downsizing The Federal government
by Chris Edwards
http://tinyurl.com/oke71

Drug Crazy: How We Got Into This Mess And How We Can Get Out
by Mike Gray
http://tinyurl.com/moe3n

Drug War Crimes: The Consequences Of Prohibition
by Jeffrey A. Miron
http://tinyurl.com/6l9fo

Empire of Debt: The Rise Of An Epic Financial Crisis
by William Bonner, Addison Wiggin
http://tinyurl.com/o3zzn

End Of Money And The Struggle For Financial Privacy
by Richard W. Rahn
http://tinyurl.com/lpwx8

I Am Not A Number: Freeing America From The ID State
by Claire Wolfe
http://tinyurl.com/rouen

Tethered Citizens: Time To Repeal The Welfare State
by Sheldon Richman
http://tinyurl.com/mkanb

The Creature From Jekyll Island: A Second Look At The Federal Reserve
by G. Edward Griffin
http://tinyurl.com/o5col

The Gulag Archipelago: 1918-1956
by Aleksandr I. Solzhenitsyn
http://tinyurl.com/syybd

Towards A Liberal Utopia
by Philip Booth (ed)
http://tinyurl.com/rsfyf

Why Government Doesn't Work
by Harry Browne
http://tinyurl.com/s8b25

Philosophy and Psychology

Atlas Shrugged
by Ayn Rand
http://tinyurl.com/mc3tk

Objectivism: The Philosophy Of Ayn Rand
by Leonard Peikoff
http://tinyurl.com/n4ldp

Sic Itur Ad Astra: The Theory Of Volition (Volume 1)
by Andrew J. Galambos
http://tinyurl.com/q5vae

Six Pillars Of Self-Esteem
by Nathaniel Branden
http://tinyurl.com/okt94

The Age Of Rand: Imagining An Objectivist Future World
by Frederick Cookinham
http://tinyurl.com/oh7u8

The Ayn Rand Lexicon: Objectivism From A To Z
by Ayn Rand, Harry Binswanger (ed)
http://tinyurl.com/s9854

The Psychology Of Self-Esteem
by Nathaniel Branden
http://tinyurl.com/mz9x5

Political History

American Dynasty: Aristocracy, Fortune, And The Politics Of Deceit In The House Of Bush
by Kevin Phillips
http://tinyurl.com/ppyel

Democracy In America
by Alexis de Tocqueville
http://tinyurl.com/l9asz

Democracy: The God That Failed: The Economics And Politics Of Monarchy, Democracy, And Natural Order
by Hans-Hermann Hoppe
http://tinyurl.com/lv7xr

From Mutual Aid To The Welfare State: Fraternal Societies And Social Services, 1890-1967
by David T. Beito
http://tinyurl.com/oygsh

Good To Be King: The Foundation Of Our Constitutional Freedom
by Michael Badnarik
http://tinyurl.com/mvy8o

Gulag: A History
by Anne Applebaum
http://tinyurl.com/pxexf

How Capitalism Saved America: The Untold History Of Our Country, From The Pilgrims To The Present
by Thomas Dilorenzo
http://tinyurl.com/njxby

How The Scots Invented The Modern World: The True Story Of How Western Europe's Poorest Nation Created Our World And Everything In It
by Arthur Herman
http://tinyurl.com/la7vh

Liberty For Latin America: How To Undo Five Hundred Years Of State Oppression
by Alvaro Vargas Llosa
http://tinyurl.com/eutzr

Perilous Times: Free Speech In Wartime: From The Sedition Act Of 1798 To The War On Terrorism
by Geoffrey R. Stone
http://tinyurl.com/lw43q

Pol Pot: Anatomy Of A Nightmare
by Philip Short
http://tinyurl.com/o2dvg

Stealing God's Thunder: Benjamin Franklin's Lightning Rod And The Invention Of America
by Philip Dray
http://tinyurl.com/nxag5

The "Uncle Eric" Books
by Richard J. Maybury
http://www.chaostan.com/eric.html

The Challenge Of Liberty: Classical Liberalism Today
by Carl P. Close and Robert Higgs (eds)
http://tinyurl.com/q2dnm

The Encyclopedia Of Revolutions And Revolutionaries: From Anarchism To Zhou Enlai
by Martin L. Van Creveld (ed)
http://tinyurl.com/mmcdh

The Escape From Hunger And Premature Death, 1700-2100: Europe, America, And The Third World
by Robert William Fogel, Richard Smith (ed), Jan De Vries (ed), Paul Johnson (ed), and Keith Wrightson (ed)
http://tinyurl.com/razhe

The Myth Of National Defense: Essays On The Theory And History Of Security Production
by Hans-Hermann Hoppe (ed)
http://tinyurl.com/ryeko

The Politically Incorrect Guide To American History
by Thomas E. Woods Jr.
http://tinyurl.com/rjme4

The Real Lincoln: A New Look At Abraham Lincoln, His Agenda, And An Unnecessary War
by Thomas Dilorenzo
http://tinyurl.com/mgtsn

The War Between The States: America's Uncivil War
by John J. Dwyer (Intro), John Paul Strain (Illus), George Grant, J. Steven Wilkins, Douglas Wilson, Tom Spencer, and John J. Dwyer (ed)
http://tinyurl.com/oqjb6

They Made America: From The Steam Engine To The Search Engine: Two Centuries of Innovators
by Gail Buckland, David Lefer, and Harold Evans
http://tinyurl.com/r7r8h

Voices Of A People's History Of The United States
by Howard Zinn and Anthony Arnove (eds)
http://tinyurl.com/njfch

Wilson's War: How Woodrow Wilson's Great Blunder Led To Hitler, Lenin, Stalin, And World War II
by Jim Powell
http://tinyurl.com/nc5lp

The Political Economy Of Stalinism
by Paul Gregory
http://tinyurl.com/rkfow

Political Philosophy

Against Politics: On Government, Anarchy, And Order
by Anthony de Jasay
http://tinyurl.com/lwuel

Anything That's Peaceful: The Case For The Free Market
by Leonard Edward Read
http://tinyurl.com/mcmn7

Anarcho-Capitalism: An Annotated Bibliography
by Hans-Hermann Hoppe
http://www.lewrockwell.com/hoppe/hoppe5.html

For A New Liberty
by Murray Rothbard
http://www.mises.org/rothbard/newlibertywhole.asp

Government Without Taxes: Operating For-profit And Paying Dividends To Its Owners:
The Constitution For Capitalism
by Donald Kirchinger
http://www.atlantisgovernment.com/press.html

Healing Our World
by Dr. Mary J. Ruwart
http://www.ruwart.com/Pages/Healing

I Must Speak Out: The Best Of The Voluntaryist 1982-1999
by Carl Watner
http://tinyurl.com/n577c

Market For Liberty
by Morris Tannehill and Linda Tannehill
http://www.mises.org/store/Market-for-Liberty-P302C0.aspx

Molon Labe!
by Boston T. Party
http://www.javelinpress.com/molon_labe.html

No Treason. No. VI, The Constitution Of No Authority
by Lysander Spooner
http://www.lysanderspooner.org/bib_new.htm

Philosophers Of Capitalism: Menger, Mises, Rand, And Beyond
by Edward W. Younkins (ed)
http://tinyurl.com/rbqtp

The Capitalist Manifesto : The Historic, Economic And Philosophic Case For Laissez-Faire
by Andrew Bernstein
http://tinyurl.com/qwvo5

The Case Against The Democratic State
by Gordon Graham
http://tinyurl.com/pgnsq

The Ethics Of Liberty
by Murray N. Rothbard, Hans-Hermann Hoppe (ed)
http://www.mises.org/rothbard/ethics/hoppeintro.asp

The Incredible Bread Machine: A Study Of Capitalism, Freedom, & The State
by R. W. Grant
http://tinyurl.com/rpg8a

ONLINE ARTICLES

Culture

All human life is indexed on the web: Search engines are changing the face of business forever
by Tony Glover
http://tinyurl.com/7mbqs

American Democracy Indicted
by Anthony Gregory
http://www.lewrockwell.com/gregory/gregory114.html

Are Conservatives Naïve or Just Plain Stupid?
by Laurence M. Vance
http://www.lewrockwell.com/vance/vance39.html

Wikipedia survives research test
http://news.bbc.co.uk/1/hi/technology/4530930.stm

Beyond Patriarchy: A Libertarian Model of the Family
by Roderick T. Long
http://libertariannation.org/a/f43l2.html

Conservative Nonsense in the War on Drugs
by Jacob G. Hornberger
http://www.lewrockwell.com/hornberger/hornberger75.html

For the War and Against the Troops
by Anthony Gregory
http://www.lewrockwell.com/gregory/gregory110.html

Hands Off Google!
by Justin Raimondo
http://antiwar.com/justin/?articleid=8467

Health Care Crisis? How About a Recreation Crisis?
by John Merline
http://www.tcsdaily.com/article.aspx?id=013006D

Intelligence in the Internet age
by Stefanie Olsen
http://tinyurl.com/gqzdd

Interesting Findings from fMRI Scans of Political Brains
reviewed by Dr. Priya Saxena
http://www.rxpgnews.com/specialtopics/article_3287.shtml

Judging Google
by Glenn Harlan Reynolds
http://www.tcsdaily.com/article.aspx?id=013106D

LEAP: Law Enforcement Against Prohibition
http://www.leap.cc/

Marxists' Apartment A Microcosm Of Why Marxism Doesn't Work
by The Onion - America's Finest News Source
http://www.theonion.com/content/node/38517

Retirement? Not in this lifetime
by Dave Barry
http://www.jsonline.com/story/index.aspx?id=413188

Surfing and Site Guide - Internet World Stats
http://www.internetworldstats.com/surfing.htm

The Abstract Concept of Human Liberty
by Robert LeFevre
http://www.fee.org/publications/the-freeman/article.asp?aid=852

The Ground Zero Grassy Knoll - A New Generation of Conspiracy Theorists are at Work on the Secret History of 9/11
by Mark Jacobson
http://newyorkmetro.com/news/features/16464/index.html

The Hazards of Truth-Telling
by Thomas Szasz
http://www.fee.org/publications/the-freeman/article.asp?aid=4859

The Man Behind the Mask
by Joshua Katz
http://www.lewrockwell.com/orig7/katz-j3.html

The Meaning of Freedom
by Frank Chodorov
http://www.lewrockwell.com/chodorov/chodorov6.html

The Moses Complex
by Arnold Kling
http://www.tcsdaily.com/article.aspx?id=022806E

The Power Of Us - Mass collaboration on the Internet is shaking up business
BusinessWeek online
http://www.businessweek.com/magazine/content/05_25/b3938601.htm

The Sociology of Taxation
by Hans-Hermann Hoppe
http://www.mises.org/story/2068

The Translucent Generation
by Alex Krupp
http://www.alexkrupp.com/translucent.html

Toward an Educational Renaissance
by Chris Cardiff
http://www.fee.org/publications/the-freeman/article.asp?aid=3070

University Implicated In Checks-For-Degrees Scheme
by The Onion - America's Finest News Source
http://www.theonion.com/content/node/30632

Wal-Mart You Don't Know
by Charles Fishman
http://www.fastcompany.com/magazine/77/walmart.html

What's Become of Americans?
by Paul Craig Roberts
http://www.lewrockwell.com/roberts/roberts158.html

Wikipedia alternative aims to be 'PBS of the Web'
by Daniel Terdiman
http://tinyurl.com/9zbbc

Will the University Survive?
by Tim Swanson
http://www.mises.org/story/2013

Economics

California's Man-Made Drought
by Dirk Yandell and Michael C. Paganelli
http://www.fee.org/publications/the-freeman/article.asp?aid=1000

Canada's Private Clinics Surge as Public System Falters
by Clifford Krauss
http://tinyurl.com/ls6bk

Combine the Power of the Internet and the Gold Standard
by Wayne Dawson
http://libertariannation.org/a/f73d1.html

Corporations and the Public Interest
by Jonathan Rowe
http://www.context.org/ICLIB/IC41/Rowe.htm

Discretion is the New Rule
by Thorsten Polleit
http://www.mises.org/story/2084

Does the widening US trade deficit pose a threat to the economy?
by Frank Shostak
http://www.mises.org/story/2029

E-prescribing project improves generic medication use
by Caroline Broder
http://www.healthcareitnews.com/story.cms?id=4543

Economics for the Citizen
by Walter E. Williams
http://www.lewrockwell.com/orig2/w-williams2.html

For Society To Thrive, The Rich Must Be Left Alone
by George Reisman
http://mises.org/story/2073

Government in Business
by Murray N. Rothbard
http://www.fee.org/publications/the-freeman/article.asp?aid=252

Home of the Slave?
by Michael Bradshaw
http://www.ncc-1776.org/tle2006/tle362-20060409-08.html

How Powerful Is Productivity?
by Nick Schulz
http://www.techcentralstation.com/061705A.html

Money in a Free Nation
by Joanna Parker
http://libertariannation.org/a/f73p1.html

NPR : For Workers, 'The World Is Flat' Thomas Friedman on Fresh Air
http://www.npr.org/templates/story/story.php?storyId=4600258

Pharmaceutical Business -Fighting the Clock
by Karen J. Watkins
http://pubs.acs.org/cen/coverstory/8004/8004pharmaceuticals.html

Reclaiming Medicine for Patients and Physicians
by Gilbert Ross M.D
http://www.tcsdaily.com/article.aspx?id=021406D

The Absence of History
by Bill Bonner
http://www.lewrockwell.com/bonner/bonner222.html

The Economics of Taxation
by Hans-Hermann Hoppe
http://www.mises.org/story/2061

The Forgotten Private Banker
by Richard Sylla
http://www.fee.org/publications/the-freeman/article.asp?aid=3241

The Third Industrial Revolution
by Hans F. Sennholz
http://www.mises.org/story/2105

Toward a Reconstruction of Utility and Welfare Economics
by Murray N. Rothbard
http://www.mises.org/story/2205

Uncertainty and Its Exigencies: The Critical Role of Insurance in the Free Market
by Hans-Hermann Hoppe
http://www.mises.org/story/2021

Voluntary and Coercive Cartels: The Case of Oil
By David Osterfeld
http://www.fee.org/publications/the-freeman/article.asp?aid=2333

Wal-Marts of An Earlier Age
by Clifford F. Thies
http://www.mises.org/story/2087

What Economics Is Not
by Llewellyn H. Rockwell, Jr.
http://www.lewrockwell.com/rockwell/economics-not.html

What Is Society?
by Ludwig von Mises
http://mises.org/story/2072

Why Medicine Is Slowly Dying in America
by Michael J. Hurd
http://www.fee.org/publications/the-freeman/article.asp?aid=1657

Ethics

Government Is Not Compassion, Part 1
by Glen Allport
http://www.strike-the-root.com/columns/allport/allport1.html

Government Is Not Compassion, Part 2
by Glen Allport
http://www.strike-the-root.com/columns/allport/allport2.html

In Defense of Moral Agents
by Roy Halliday
http://libertariannation.org/a/f73h2.html

Who's the Scrooge: Libertarians and Compassion
by Roderick T. Long
http://libertariannation.org/a/f12l1.html

Governmental Domestic Policy

Annual Privatization Report 2004
by Geoffrey F. Segal (ed)
http://www.rppi.org/apr2004/anpr2004.shtml

Beware the Alchemists
by Ludwig von Mises
http://mises.org/story/2030

Coercion: It's What's for Dinner in Postconstitutional America
by Sheldon Richman
http://www.fff.org/freedom/fd0508b.asp

Drug Policy Issues and Statistics
http://www.newsbatch.com/drugpolicy.htm

Drug War Facts
http://www.drugwarfacts.org

Ending Corporate Welfare as We Know It
by Lawrence W. Reed
http://www.fee.org/publications/the-freeman/article.asp?aid=4281

Fannie Mae Distorts Markets
by Robert Blumen
http://www.mises.org/story/986

How Government Solved the Health Care Crisis: Medical Insurance that Worked—Until Government "Fixed" It
by Roderick T. Long
http://libertariannation.org/a/f12l3.html

How the FBI Let 9/11 Happen: Never mind Moussaoui, the smoldering gun was right there all the time
by Jeff A. Taylor
http://www.reason.com/links/links033006.shtml

Ironic Triangle
by Sheldon Richman
http://www.fee.org/publications/the-freeman/article.asp?aid=4452

John Hughes Was Right
by Mark Storer
http://www.tcsdaily.com/article.aspx?id=030206C

Look! Up in the Sky! It's An Inflation-Fighting Fed!
by Cyd Malone
http://mises.org/story/2237

So Many Missed Opportunities
by Veronique de Rugy
http://www.techcentralstation.com/062205B.html

Speech to the Philadelphia Society: Immigration, Economic Growth, and the Welfare State
by Benjamin Powell
http://www.independent.org/issues/article.asp?id=1505

Stupid in America
by John Stossel
http://abcnews.go.com/2020/Stossel/story?id=1500338

The Biggest Medicare Fraud Ever
by James Bovard
http://www.fff.org/freedom/fd0505c.asp

The Spend of Our Union Is Strong
by Veronique de Rugy
http://www.tcsdaily.com/article.aspx?id=020106F

Uncle Sam's Iron Curtain of Secrecy
by James Bovard
http://www.fff.org/freedom/fd0504c.asp

What Do Farmers Want from Me?
by Russell Roberts
http://www.fee.org/publications/the-freeman/article.asp?aid=4375

What Hunger Insurance Could Teach Us about Health Insurance
by Joseph Bast
http://www.fee.org/publications/the-freeman/article.asp?aid=2114

Where's the Revolution?
by Duane D. Freese
http://www.tcsdaily.com/article.aspx?id=020606A

Governmental Foreign Policy

Abolish the CIA!
by Chalmers Johnson and Tom Engelhardt
http://www.antiwar.com/engelhardt/?articleid=3927

America's war on the web
by Neil Mackay
http://www.sundayherald.com/54975

Hobbes, Locke and the Bush Doctrine
by Nathan Smith
http://www.techcentralstation.com/062105C.html

Interview with Thomas P.M. Barnett
by Max Borders
http://www.tcsdaily.com/article.aspx?id=012406D

Iraq and the Democratic Empire
by Llewellyn H. Rockwell, Jr.
http://www.lewrockwell.com/rockwell/iraq-democraticempire.html

Our History with Iraq
by Chip Gagnon
http://www.ithaca.edu/politics/gagnon/talks/us-iraq.htm

Quotes on War
http://antiwar.com/quotes.php

Salvation by Starvation
by Aaron Singleton
http://www.lewrockwell.com/orig7/singleton-a2.html

Some Common, Bad Arguments for the Recent U.S. Policy Towards Iraq
by Gene Callahan
http://www.lewrockwell.com/callahan/callahan152.html

The Justice and Prudence of War: Toward A Libertarian Analysis
by Roderick Long
http://www.mises.org/story/2310

The U.S. Global Empire
by Laurence M. Vance
http://www.lewrockwell.com/vance/vance8.html

The Way Out of Iraq: Policy Reports
by Ivan Eland
http://tinyurl.com/ohl2m

Tracing the Trail of Torture
by Tom Engelhardt and Dahr Jamail
http://www.lewrockwell.com/engelhardt/engelhardt169.html

U.S. Money Aids World's Worst Dictators
by Benjamin Powell and Matt Ryan
http://www.independent.org/newsroom/article.asp?id=1671

Why All the Foreign Bases?
by Sam Baker
http://www.lewrockwell.com/orig7/baker1.html

With Friends Like These, U.S. Enemies Don't Seem As Bad
by Ivan Eland
http://www.independent.org/tii/news/040107Eland.html

Governmental Ills

A Picture of Dorian Government
by Michael Tennant
http://www.lewrockwell.com/orig6/tennant8.html

Anarchy, Violence and the State
by Stefan Molyneux
http://www.lewrockwell.com/molyneux/molyneux15.html

Crippling Competition, Part 1
by Scott McPherson
http://www.fff.org/freedom/fd0512d.asp

Crippling Competition, Part 2
by Scott McPherson
http://www.fff.org/freedom/fd0601d.asp

Death and Taxes: ...~mibi
http://www.deviantart.com/deviation/9410862/

Disarming the Law-Abiding
by John R. Lott, Jr.
http://www.lewrockwell.com/lott/lott48.html

Does Government Always Have to Grow?
by Stephen Davies
http://www.fee.org/publications/the-freeman/article.asp?aid=4372

Happy Birthday Federal Register!
by Alastair J. Walling
http://www.tcsdaily.com/article.aspx?id=031506G

Historical Per-Person Share of the National Debt
by Daylan Darby
http://www.lewrockwell.com/orig7/darby1.html

How Big Is Bush's Big Government?
by Mark Brandly
http://mises.org/story/2116

Intervention
by Ludwig von Mises
http://www.fee.org/publications/the-freeman/article.asp?aid=519

On Being Anti-State, Anti-War, and Anti-Bush
by Anthony Gregory
http://www.lewrockwell.com/gregory/gregory109.html

Perverse Incentives
by Brad Edmonds
http://www.lewrockwell.com/edmonds/edmonds274.html

Six Questions on the American "Gulag" for Historian Kate Bro
http://www.harpers.org/sb-six-questions-kate-brown-1158926209.html

Socialized Medicine: The Canadian Experience
by Pierre Lemieux
http://www.fee.org/publications/the-freeman/article.asp?aid=2638

The Awesome Powers of Government
by Murray Weidenbaum
http://www.fee.org/publications/the-freeman/article.asp?aid=4696

The Human Rights Deception
by Richard W. Stevens
http://www.fee.org/publications/the-freeman/article.asp?aid=3777

The Line-Item Veto Won't Work
by Cecil E. Bohanon and T. Norman Van Cott
http://www.fee.org/publications/the-freeman/article.asp?aid=1568

The Moral Consequences of Paternalism
by Daniel B. Klein
http://www.fee.org/publications/the-freeman/article.asp?aid=2552

The State and Its Five Rationales
by Llewellyn H. Rockwell, Jr.
http://www.lewrockwell.com/rockwell/five-rationales.html

Translating the Emperor's Speech
by Anthony Gregory
http://www.lewrockwell.com/gregory/gregory107.html

U.S. Senate: Reference Constitution of the United States
http://www.senate.gov/civics/constitution_item/constitution.htm

United States Electoral College - Wikipedia, the free encyclopedia
http://en.wikipedia.org/wiki/U.S._Electoral_College

Who Captures Whom? The Case of Regulation
By Michael Rozeff
http://www.mises.org/story/2320

The Word Thieves
by Stephanie R. Murphy
http://www.lewrockwell.com/orig6/murphy-s5.html

Law

Against Politics: Polycentric Law
http://www.againstpolitics.com/polycentric_law/index.html

A Legal System for a Free Society
by Bertel M. Sparks
http://www.fee.org/publications/the-freeman/article.asp?aid=877

Bill of Law
by Michael van Notten
http://libertariannation.org/a/f54v1.html

Breach of contract - Wikipedia, the free encyclopedia
http://en.wikipedia.org/wiki/Breach_of_contract

Common law - Wikipedia, the free encyclopedia
http://en.wikipedia.org/wiki/Common_Law

Consideration - Wikipedia, the free encyclopedia
http://en.wikipedia.org/wiki/Consideration

Contract - Wikipedia, the free encyclopedia
http://en.wikipedia.org/wiki/Contracts

Contract theory - Wikipedia, the free encyclopedia
http://en.wikipedia.org/wiki/Contract_theory

Declaratory judgment - Wikipedia, the free encyclopedia
http://en.wikipedia.org/wiki/Declaratory_judgment

Equity - Wikipedia, the free encyclopedia
http://en.wikipedia.org/wiki/Equity

Free-Market Justice Is in the Cards
by J.H. Huebert
http://www.lewrockwell.com/orig3/huebert8.html

Gateway to an Altered Landscape: Law in a Free Nation
by Richard O. Hammer
http://libertariannation.org/a/f61h2.html

Injunction - Wikipedia, the free encyclopedia
http://en.wikipedia.org/wiki/Injunction

Justice System Is 'Broken,' Lawyers Say
by Henry Weinstein
http://www.truthout.org/cgi-bin/artman/exec/view.cgi/4/4989

Law and Order
by Arnold Kling
http://www.tcsdaily.com/article.aspx?id=041406C

Law and Violence
by Roy Halliday
http://libertariannation.org/a/f61h4.html

Law as Property in a Free Nation
by Philip E. Jacobson
http://libertariannation.org/a/f61j1.html

Law by Country - United States Substantive Law - Constitution of the United States
http://www.law.emory.edu/FEDERAL/usconst.html

Law, Property Rights, and Air Pollution
by Murray N. Rothbard
http://www.mises.org/story/2120

Laws by Source: Uniform Laws Legal Information Institute, Cornell Law School
http://www.law.cornell.edu/uniform/vol7.html

Maxims of equity - Wikipedia, the free encyclopedia
http://en.wikipedia.org/wiki/Maxims_of_equity

Replevin - Wikipedia, the free encyclopedia
http://en.wikipedia.org/wiki/Replevin

Review by Roy Halliday: To Serve and Protect by Bruce L Benson
http://libertariannation.org/a/n029h1.html

Review by Sean O. Haugh: Justice Without Law by Jerold S. Auerbach
http://libertariannation.org/a/f33h2.html

Society in Jail
by Jeffrey Tucker
http://www.mises.org/story/2107

Somali Customary Law
by Spencer Heath MacCallum (ed)
http://home.arcor.de/danneskjoeld/X/Som/Editorial.html

Specific performance - Wikipedia, the free encyclopedia
http://en.wikipedia.org/wiki/Specific_performance

Standard form contract - Adhesion contract Wikipedia, the free encyclopedia
http://en.wikipedia.org/wiki/Adhesion_contract

The Anticrime Industry in a Free Nation
by Roy Halliday
http://libertariannation.org/a/f41h1.html

The Idea of a Private Law Society
by Hans-Hermann Hoppe
http://www.mises.org/story/2265

The Nature of Law, Parts I-IV
by Roderick T. Long
http://libertariannation.org/a/f13l2.html

Toward Voluntary Courts and Enforcement
by Richard O. Hammer
http://libertariannation.org/a/f32h1.html

Unconscionability - Wikipedia, the free encyclopedia
http://en.wikipedia.org/wiki/Unconscionability

Unjust enrichment - Wikipedia, the free encyclopedia
http://en.wikipedia.org/wiki/Unjust_enrichment

Would You Like Fries With Your Arbitration?
by Manuel Lora
http://www.lewrockwell.com/lora/m.lora16.html

Political History

100 Years of Medical Robbery
by Dale Steinreich
http://www.mises.org/story/1547

A Brief Tax History of America
by Charles Adams
http://www.lewrockwell.com/orig2/adams7.html

Anti-Federalism - Wikipedia, the free encyclopedia
http://en.wikipedia.org/wiki/Anti-federalists

Bill of Rights - History of the Constitution
http://www.billofrights.com/HistoryoftheConstitution.htm

Democracies Do Not Make War on One Another...or Do They?
by Matthew White
http://users.erols.com/mwhite28/demowar.htm

Democracy, or Who Made You King?
by Dmitry Chernikov
http://www.lewrockwell.com/orig3/chernikov1.html

DiLorenzo and His Critics on the Lincoln Myth
by James Ostrowski
http://www.mises.org/etexts/ostrowski.asp

Drifting In and Out of Socialism: The Case of Ireland
by James L. Payne
http://www.fee.org/publications/the-freeman/article.asp?aid=1772

Economy of the Soviet Union - Wikipedia, the free encyclopedia
http://en.wikipedia.org/wiki/Economy_of_the_Soviet_Union

First Twelve Articles of Amendment - The U.S. Constitution Online
http://www.usconstitution.net/first12.html

Friedrich Engels
http://www.spartacus.schoolnet.co.uk/TUengels.htm

History of the United States dollar
http://www.answers.com/topic/history-of-the-united-states-dollar

How Medical Boards Nationalized Health Care
by Henry Jones
http://www.mises.org/story/1749

It all began, as usual, with the Greeks
by Murray N. Rothbard
http://www.mises.org/story/2054

Ivan's War
by Bill Bonner
http://www.lewrockwell.com/bonner/bonner196.html

Just War
by Murray N. Rothbard
http://www.lewrockwell.com/rothbard/rothbard20.html

Learning From Experience
by Ivan Pongracic
http://www.fee.org/publications/the-freeman/article.asp?aid=2395

Life, Liberty, and ...
by Albert Jay Nock
http://mises.org/story/2412

Lincoln's legacy of corruption
by Ilana Mercer
http://www.worldnetdaily.com/news/article.asp?ARTICLE_ID=26440

Lysander Spooner
by Wendy McElroy
http://www.lewrockwell.com/mcelroy/mcelroy107.html

Madison's Introduction of the Bill of Rights - The U.S. Constitution Online
http://www.usconstitution.net/madisonbor.html

Manifesto of the Communist Party
by Karl Marx and Frederick Engels
http://www.anu.edu.au/polsci/marx/classics/manifesto.html

Massachusetts Compromise - Wikipedia, the free encyclopedia
http://en.wikipedia.org/wiki/Massachusetts_compromise

Mercantilism
by Laura LaHaye: The Concise Encyclopedia of Economics
http://www.econlib.org/library/Enc/Mercantilism.html

North America's First Experience with Paper Money: Card Money in New France
by Martin Masse
http://www.mises.org/story/2091

Rainbow $10 Bill and Hamilton Versus Jackson
by Morgan Reynolds
http://www.lewrockwell.com/reynolds/reynolds15.html

Review by David Gordon: The Costs of War: America's Pyrrhic Victories by John
V. Denson (ed)
http://tinyurl.com/rkn7q

Rothbard's "Left and Right": Forty Years Later
by Roderick T. Long
http://mises.org/story/2099

The Antifederalists Were Right
by Gary Galles
http://www.mises.org/story/2335

The Forgotten Essentials of Jefferson's Philosophy
by David Mayer
http://tinyurl.com/gzcpo

The Latest Defamation of Jefferson
by Thomas DiLorenzo
http://www.lewrockwell.com/dilorenzo/dilorenzo100.html

The Most Successful Fraud in American History
by Gary North
http://www.lewrockwell.com/north/north445.html

The Origin of Religious Tolerance
by Wendy McElroy
http://www.fee.org/publications/the-freeman/article.asp?aid=3394

The Origins of Individualist Anarchism in the US
by Murray N. Rothbard
http://www.mises.org/story/2014

The Rocky Road of American Taxation
by Charles Adams
http://www.mises.org/story/2110

The Santa Clara Blues: Corporate Personhood versus Democracy
by William Meyers
http://www.iiipublishing.com/afd/santaclara.html

The Trouble With Socialist Anarchism
by Per Bylund
http://www.mises.org/story/2096

The Utopia of Liberty: A Letter to Socialists (1848)
by Gustave de Molinari
http://www.mises.org/story/2089

Thomas Paine
http://www.ushistory.org/paine/

Virginia Declaration of Rights - Wikisource
http://en.wikisource.org/wiki/Virginia_Declaration_of_Rights

War Collectivism in World War I
by Murray N. Rothbard
http://www.lewrockwell.com/rothbard/rothbard91.html

What Came To Be
by Per Bylund
http://www.lewrockwell.com/orig6/bylund4.html

Political Philosophy

A Model Lease For Orbis
by Spencer Heath MacCallum
http://libertariannation.org/a/f33m1.html

A Paper Tiger for a Free Nation
by Roy Halliday
http://libertariannation.org/a/f51h4.html

A Peaceful Ferment In Somalia
by Spencer Heath MacCallum
http://rkba.org/libertarian/maccallum/MacCallum-Somalia98.html

A Senate for the Free Nation Foundation, and for a Free Nation As Well
by Phil Jacobson
http://libertariannation.org/a/f64j1.html

A Single-Owner Proprietary Nation: Advantages, Problems, and Solutions
by Roy Halliday
http://libertariannation.org/a/f62h2.html

Anarchy, State, and Mixture, Part I: Six Possibilities
by Roderick T. Long
http://libertariannation.org/a/f84l1.html

Archive of Libertarian Nation Foundation papers
http://libertariannation.org/a/

Basic Questions About a Free Nation
by Roy Halliday, Spencer MacCallum, and Philip Jacobson
http://libertariannation.org/a/f64h6.html

Beyond the Boss: Protection from Business in a Free Nation
by Roderick T. Long
http://libertariannation.org/a/f41l2.html

Bourgeois Families in a Free Nation
by Roy Halliday
http://libertariannation.org/a/f43h1.html

Business in a Free Nation
by Richard O. Hammer
http://libertariannation.org/a/f41h3.html

Can We Escape the Ruling Class?
by Roderick T. Long
http://libertariannation.org/a/f21l2.html

Defending a Free Nation
by Roderick T. Long
http://libertariannation.org/a/f22l3.html

Defense Through Free-Market Sport
by Douglas Nusbaum
http://libertariannation.org/a/f64n1.html

Dismantling Leviathan from Within, Part I: Can We? Should We?
by Roderick T. Long
http://libertariannation.org/a/f24l3.html

Dismantling Leviathan From Within: Part II: The Process of Reform
by Roderick T. Long Part II: The Process of Reform
http://libertariannation.org/a/f31l3.html

Dismantling Leviathan From Within Part III: Is Libertarian Political Action Self-Defeating?
by Roderick T. Long
http://libertariannation.org/a/f32l1.html

Dismantling Leviathan From Within, Part IV: The Sons of Brutus
by Roderick T. Long
http://libertariannation.org/a/f33l3.html

Draft Constitution for a Reviving or New Nation
by Michael Darby
http://libertariannation.org/a/f61d1.html

Economic Government
by Robert Klassen
http://libertariannation.org/a/f61k1.html

Forms for a Free Nation, Alternate Visions
by Philip Jacobson
http://libertariannation.org/a/f71j1.html

From Nation-State To Stateless Nation: The Somali Experience
by Michael van Notten
http://www.liberalia.com/htm/mvn_stateless_somalis.htm

Funding Public Goods: Six Solutions
by Roderick T. Long
http://libertariannation.org/a/f21l4.html

How States Fall and Liberty Triumphs
by Llewellyn H. Rockwell, Jr.
http://www.lewrockwell.com/rockwell/states-fall.html

Is Somalia a Model?
by Alan Bock
http://www.antiwar.com/bock/b042903.html

ISIL Animated Introduction to the Philosophy of Liberty
http://www.isil.org/resources/introduction.html

Journal of Libertarian Studies
http://www.mises.org/jlsdisplay.asp

Let's Discuss the Amount of Coercion Needed in a Free Nation
by Roy Halliday
http://libertariannation.org/a/f64h7.html

Libertarian Community of Utopia: One Country, Three Systems
by Adrian C. Hinton
http://libertariannation.org/a/f72h3.html

Libertarian Responses to Terrorism
by Roy Halliday
http://libertariannation.org/a/n030h1.html

Market Anarchism, the Solution to the Dilemma of Taiwan Independence
by Bevin Chu
http://www.lewrockwell.com/chu/chu13.html

Nonviolent Civilian Defense
by Robert Mihaly
http://libertariannation.org/a/n030m1.html

One Nation, Two Systems: The Doughnut Model
by Roderick T. Long
http://libertariannation.org/a/f34l1.html

Panarchy
by P. E. de Puydt
http://libertariannation.org/a/f72d1.html

Planning a New Nation
by Michael van Notten
http://libertariannation.org/a/f71v1.html

Politics Versus Proprietorship: Remarks Prefatory to Discussion of the Orbis Constitution
for Proprietary Communities
by Spencer Heath MacCallum
http://libertariannation.org/a/f34m1.html

Review by Bobby Matherne: Towards Social Renewal: Rethinking the Basis of Society
by Rudolf Steiner
http://www.doyletics.com/arj/towardss.htm

Selecting a Site for a Free Nation in an Unfree World
by Roy Halliday
http://libertariannation.org/a/f71h2.html

Slavery Contracts and Inalienable Rights: A Formulation
by Roderick Long A Formulation
http://libertariannation.org/a/f22l1.html

Society without a State
by Murray N. Rothbard
http://mises.org/story/2429

The Basics of Constitutions
by Richard O. Hammer
http://libertariannation.org/a/pph1.html

The On Line Freedom Academy
by Jim Davies
http://tolfa.us/

The Origins of States
by Roy Halliday
http://libertariannation.org/a/f84h1.html

The Perils of Positive Rights
by Tibor R. Machan
http://www.fee.org/publications/the-freeman/article.asp?aid=2993

The Production of Security
by Gustave de Molinari
http://mises.org/story/2088

The REAL Limón Project
by Rigoberto Stewart
http://libertariannation.org/a/f54s1.html

The State is a Form of Life, a Legitimate Peer in the Family of Organizations
by Richard O. Hammer
http://libertariannation.org/a/f63h4.html

Utopia Watch: From Upstate New York to the Horn of Africa
by Spencer MacCallum
http://libertyunbound.com/archive/2005_05/maccallum-utopia.html

Property Issues

A New Form of Intellectual Property Protection
by Bobby Yates Emory
http://libertariannation.org/a/f61e3.html

A Plea for Public Property
by Roderick T. Long
http://libertariannation.org/a/f53l1.html

A Theory of Property Rights for a Free Nation
by Roy Halliday
http://libertariannation.org/a/f52h2.html

Baseline rights and restrictions in all licenses Creative Commons
http://creativecommons.org/about/licenses/fullrights

Categories of Free and Non-Free Software Free Software Foundation
http://www.fsf.org/licensing/essays/categories.html

Choose a License Creative Commons
http://creativecommons.org/license/

Copy Fighting
by Tom W. Bell
http://techcentralstation.com/080502B.html

Copyleft - Wikipedia, the free encyclopedia
http://en.wikipedia.org/wiki/Copyleft

Creative Commons Legal Code
http://creativecommons.org/licenses/by-sa/2.5/legalcode

Fashion Has No Owner
by Albert Esplugas and Manuel Lora
http://www.lewrockwell.com/lora/m.lora29.html

File Sharing: It's Music to Our Ears: Making P2P Pay Artists
http://www.eff.org/share/compensation.php

Government and Microsoft: a Libertarian View on Monopolies
by François-René Rideau
http://fare.tunes.org/liberty/microsoft_monopoly.html

Homesteading for Fun and Survival
by Manuel Lora and Jeffrey Tucker
http://www.mises.org/story/2106

Homesteading: the Creation of Property
by Bill Walker
http://www.lewrockwell.com/walker/walker18.html

IBM says it won't assert patents against Linux kernel
by Ed Scannell
http://www.infoworld.com/article/04/08/04/HNdonofirokeynote_1.html

Ideas As Property
by Roy Halliday
http://libertariannation.org/a/f44h2.html

Identity theft - Wikipedia, the free encyclopedia
http://en.wikipedia.org/wiki/Identity_theft

Intellectual property - Wikipedia, the free encyclopedia
http://en.wikipedia.org/wiki/Intellectual_property_rights

Intellectual Property Information
by Stephan Kinsella
http://www.stephankinsella.com/ip/index.php

Intellectual Property Rights Viewed As Contracts
by Richard O. Hammer
http://libertariannation.org/a/f32h3.html

Land Policy and the Open Community: The Anarchist Case for Land-Leasing versus Sub-division
by Spencer H. MacCallum
http://libertariannation.org/a/n029m1.html

Mises Economics Blog: Intellectual Property
http://blog.mises.org/blog/archives/001771.asp

Nineteen Propositions About Property
by Richard O. Hammer
http://libertariannation.org/a/f53h1.html

On Andrew J Galambos and His Primary Property Ideas
by Alvin Lowi, Jr.
http://www.above-the-garage.com/rblts/primary_property_lowi_1.htm

Patents Are An Economic Absurdity
by François-René Rideau
http://fare.tunes.org/articles/patents.html

Real property rights vs. fiat property rights
by Tracy Saboe
http://www.geocities.com/tracysaboe/fiatproperty.html

Selling Free Software -Free Software Foundation
http://www.fsf.org/licensing/essays/selling.html

Street Performer Protocol - Wikipedia, the free encyclopedia
http://en.wikipedia.org/wiki/Street_Performer_Protocol

Tall Grass, Parked Cars, and Other So-Called Offenses
by Scott McPherson
http://www.fee.org/publications/the-freeman/article.asp?aid=3925

The Definition of "Property" and "Property Rights" in a Free Nation
by Gordon Neal Diem, D.A.
http://libertariannation.org/a/f53d3.html

The Economic Theory Concerning Patents for Inventions
by Arnold Plant
http://www.compilerpress.atfreeweb.com/Anno%20Plant%20Patent.htm

The Intellectual Property Debate
by George Winborne
http://libertariannation.org/a/f33w2.html

The Libertarian Case Against Intellectual Property Rights
by Roderick T. Long
http://libertariannation.org/a/f31l1.html

The Spectrum Should Be Private Property: The Economics, History, and Future of Wireless Technology
by B.K. Marcus
http://www.mises.org/story/1662

The Uneasy Case for Copyright - Wikipedia, the free encyclopedia
http://en.wikipedia.org/wiki/The_Uneasy_Case_for_Copyright

Things to think about before you apply a Creative Commons license to your work
http://creativecommons.org/about/think

Who Owns the Internet?
by Tim Swanson
http://www.mises.org/story/2139

Why "Free Software" is better than "Open Source" -Free Software Foundation
http://www.fsf.org/licensing/essays/free-software-for-freedom.html

You Treat Me Like Property
by Vedran Vuk
http://www.mises.org/story/2058

Zoning is Theft
by Jim Fedako
http://www.mises.org/story/2077

INDEX

www.ingramcontent.com/pod-product-compliance
Lightning Source LLC
Chambersburg PA
CBHW082130290526
45794CB00008B/2986